D1298417

Mothering
THE MIND

Mothering
THE
MIND

Twelve Studies of Writers and Their Silent Partners

EDITED BY

Ruth Perry and
Martine Watson Brownley

HOLMES & MEIER
NEW YORK   LONDON

PR
106
.M64
1984

First published in the United States of America 1984 by
Holmes & Meier Publishers, Inc.
30 Irving Place
New York, N.Y. 10003

Great Britain:
Holmes & Meier Publishers, Ltd.
131 Trafalgar Road
Greenwich, London SE10 9TX

Book design by Stephanie Barton

Library of Congress Cataloging in Publication Data
Main entry under title:

Mothering the mind: twelve studies of writers and their silent partners.

    1. Authors, English—Psychology—Addresses, essays,
lectures. 2. Authors, American—Psychology—Addresses,
essays, lectures. 3. Authors—Family relationships—
Addresses, essays, lectures. 4. Creation (Literary,
artistic, etc.)—Addresses, essays, lectures.
5. Influence (Literary, artistic, etc.)—Addresses,
essays, lectures. 6. Psychology and literature—
Addresses, essays, lectures. 7. Love, Maternal—
Addresses, essays, lectures. I. Perry, Ruth, 1943–
II. Brownley, Martine Watson, 1947–.
PR106.M64 1984   820'.9'353   83-10849
ISBN 0-8419-0892-3
ISBN 0-8419-0893-1 (pbk.)

Manufactured in the United States of America

To our mothers,
Charlotte Sagoff and Martine Watson Brownley

Contents

Mothering
THE MIND

Introduction
$\smile$ Ruth Perry

$\smile$The usual point of literary biography has been to explain
the extraordinary achievement of special individuals—to uncover the
forces behind the impulse to write and to bring to light the particulars of
their lives transmuted into art. Absent from this picture is any recognition of the ways in which other persons have helped to create the work
by virtue of their relationship to the artist and the way they fill out his or
her psychic universe. I want to call attention to a particular function that
other persons can and do serve in fostering creativity. I call it "mothering the mind," recognizing always that mothers' responses to their children are fashioned from mothers' care, their work, their necessities, and
their power. How does one person help to create the conditions for
another's creativity? What is the combination of response, encourage-

3

ment, expectation, and utter detachment that helps to catalyze creative work? This volume is the occasion for a group of scholars to reflect together on this problem and to describe the enormous influence that certain central figures—lovers, sisters, patrons, mothers, aunts, friends, husbands—have had on the lives and work of fourteen writers.

For millennia women have woven and spun, pounded, stirred, and hoed—with their children on their laps, in their arms, on their backs, and playing at their feet. The mother's presence has made it possible for these children to slip back and forth from fantasy to reality, construct-ing, demolishing, and reconstructing their worlds—in short, playing—in the space sheltered by the mother's eyes, hands, and voice.

Through playing, children heal and test, shape and experiment, accommodate and get used to things. Play is the compensatory blessing that comes with the curse of consciousness; it develops concurrently with the individual's sense of an independent inner reality not always syn-chronized with external circumstances. It is a way of trying on solutions in the mind, of experimenting with what is and what ought to be. Freud, for instance, theorized that the compulsive repetitive elements of play helped children "to work over in the mind some overpowering experi-ence so as to make oneself master of it."[1] But because it has to be free and curious, and completely experimental, play must be guarded from ex-ternal threat and even protected from its own consequences. Play, then, is a duet with reality, patterned in the sheltered space first established by the mother or primary caretaker for the child, its terrain covering ever-shifting proportions of self and world.

The notion that adult creativity grows out of such early childhood experiences with play, first adumbrated by Freud, has been explored by D. W. Winnicott, who remarks:

> . . . No human being is free from the strain of relating inner and outer reality. There is relief from this strain in an intermediate area of experi-ence which is not challenged (arts, religion) which is in direct continuity with the play area of a small child who is completely lost, absorbed, in play.[2]

The idea for this collection of essays sprang from the possibility of a relationship analogous to that of children playing in the presence of their mothers, in that of writers and those people with whom they had long-term relationships which in one way or another facilitated their work. I do not want even to imply that by "mothering the mind" I mean a smothering, self-sacrificing, one-way devotion on the part of one per-son for another—the enslavement of one person to another's purposes. As the ego psychologists seem to understand, "good enough" mothers have other things on their minds and do not focus their attention exclusively on their children. Present but not necessarily attentive, a mother can also function as a background for her children's foreground activity, a sheltering canopy upon which they can project fantasies, desires, and thoughts.[3]

In using this analogy of children playing in the presence of their mothers, I do not want to suggest, either, that art is simply grown-up play. Art has too much craft and will in it for this to be simply true. But both children's play and grown-ups' art have a special relation to the rest of life. Each takes place in a transitional psychic area halfway between inner and outer reality, between dreaming and "real life," a special psychological space that is set aside from ongoing duties and daily requirements. This extraordinary spatial and temporal status is often literalized in the conditions of artistic work and in children's play: Children can become so absorbed in play that they forget to go home for dinner or even to go to the toilet; art too is worked out in protected space set apart from the rest of life, be it an atelier, a dance studio, or a writer's study. To some extent the conventional materials of art—paint, clay, words— help to constitute this separation from the ongoing events of daily life. And finally, both play and art are natural functions, engaged in for pleasure of an unusual, intellectually elaborated sort.

The twelve studies in this volume experiment with the idea that certain writers depended upon particular other persons to help create the conditions, the inspiration, the atmosphere for their work. Thinking about Samuel Johnson with Hester Thrale or John Locke with Damaris Masham—the way these men relied physically and emotionally upon these women for support, and even for homes in which to work—we felt it to be true that a great many artists had benefited from the energy, intelligence, and understanding of some other person in their lives, male or female, friend or relative, younger or older. George Eliot relied this way upon George Henry Lewes, and Gertrude Stein upon Alice B. Toklas. These necessary others have never been credited properly for the role they played except in the way of informal gossip, and yet to a greater or lesser extent the artistic achievements were shaped by their presences.[4]

When we began to investigate the subject, in our first conversation about individual cases, it became clear that there was no one formula for "mothering the mind," for aiding and abetting another's creation. Each relationship between a writer and his or her "mothering" figure had its own properties, configurations determined to some unknowable extent by the childhood experiences and psychological needs of the writers and the subjects they undertook to explore in their writing. The functions of the "mothering" figures included intercepting the world, conferring unconditional approval, regulating the environment, supplying missing psychic elements, and mirroring certain aspects of the self of the artist. Each seems to have been an appreciative audience for the writer whose work he or she enabled, a living embodiment of the "ideal reader" whom literary critics used to posit, the perfect audience often projected by the text itself. Each provided not only admiration—although that too—but also a hearing, external verification, that nod that confirms a writer's hold on his or her subject as well as on sanity itself.

The implication of this collection is that such relationships are more central to the creative process than we had hitherto imagined. One of the corollary issues raised by these studies is the nature of the mutual creativity implicit in the activity of the Other. For often there have been not one but two creators, not of the written language but of the order of the fictive world whose presence speaks with a single voice and which we know as a single text. The intellectual space created by the words of a Mary Moody Emerson, a Dorothy Wordsworth, a Leonard Woolf—as well as the meaning of their gestures and acts—undoubtedly constitutes a wide range of creative behavior, which is seldom seen as such because it was symbiotic, responsive, and intended only for its unique audience of one.

It is not a misnomer but rather a kind of shorthand to speak of "mothering the mind." It is a process that begins very early, with the beginnings of the self. An infant first experiences itself in the presence of—and in relation to—the mother or primary caretaker who holds it, feeds it, cleans it, and so on. This regular intervention permits the infant the experience of going-on-being, of a "self with a past, present and future," and protects that experience from being too much impinged upon by the outer world of stimulation or the inner world of biological need.[5] This caretaking protects the space available to play and exploration and subsequently permits a creative interaction with the world. The repeated satisfaction of primitive needs also builds up in the infant trust in a benign environment and gives it the experience of a world that fosters being, comfort, and health—a world in which it is safe to have any thought or feeling. Apparently the mind cannot perceive the world as fluid, cannot play or creatively fantasize, unless this primary trust has been experienced, however briefly.[6] Infant gratification has also been imagined by adult psychologists as involving the illusion of magical mental control, omnipotence of thought, a state in which the mind can make things come true in reality simply by thinking them. This, of course, is the repeated temptation of art.

In addition to clearing space for experiences of the self, the mother or primary caretaker also provides the child with its first external verification of inner feeling by reflecting back to the infant its own behaviors and sensations. When a baby cries, its mother often shows concern; when a baby coos and gurgles, its mother smiles and talks to it. These mirroring responses give the infant its first "objective" access to its inner world, help it to explore that new terrain, as it were. The mother's face is the first way an infant sees itself. (Winnicott says in a quite literal-minded way that seeing one's reflection in an actual mirror later in life only replicates this primary experience.)[7] If there is no responsiveness to the infant's expressions of feeling, if the infant looks and does not see itself feeling what it feels, its creative capacity begins to atrophy. Perceiving oneself as others do is important to psychic health. Schizophrenics, for instance, cannot get well without such experiences.[8]

Mothers also provide the first social reactions the child encounters to its demonstrations of feeling, a foretaste of how it will be received by the world. They enact the earliest human consequences of the child's activities and help the infant construct a sense of its own agency and its own history.

Paradoxically, then, the capacity to be alone (as D. W. Winnicott so appealingly calls it), the capacity to think, to muse, to commune with one's deepest feelings—surely the primary capacity of any artist—can develop only in the presence of another (who reflects the self back to one); it thus grows along with a complicated contrapuntal recognition of what is Other and external to the self.[9] It follows that the most propitious conditions for writing, for playing with versions of reality, might include the presence of another—someone who bears a complicated relationship to that initial presence in which the self came into being. Writing is a solitary activity, but like all art it is done for a potential audience (one has to be able to imagine an audience to write at all), and its materials come from interaction between the self and the outside world. Just as an infant needs company—not even necessarily protection or support—to relax into itself, it may be that the adult human being is freed up to play, to interact flexibly with the environment, by the presence of another person. One may feel that the Other establishes one's right to exist, or domesticates the space, or puts a human stamp on the moment. Another mind, especially if it has its own activities, takes away the strain of isolation and releases energy for inner exploration.[10] As D. W. Winnicott states it:

> It is only when alone (that is to say, in the presence of someone) that the infant can discover his own personal life. The pathological alternative is a false life built on reactions to external stimuli. When alone in the sense I am using the term, and only when alone, the infant is able to do the equivalent of what in an adult would be called relaxing. The infant is able

to become unintegrated, to flounder, to be in a state in which there is no orientation, to be able to exist for a time without being either a reactor to an external impingement or an active person with a direction or interest or movement. The stage is set for an id experience. In the course of time there arrives a sensation or an impulse. In this setting the sensation or impulse will feel real and be truly a personal experience.[11]

What is called here an "id experience" or an "impulse" is no different in kind from the imaginative flash that is cherished by a writer or painter, that moment of inspiration which comes when all is prepared and passively standing in readiness. There are other names for this "state in which there is no orientation," this ability "to exist for a time without being either a reactor to an external impingement or an active person with a direction or interest or movement"—we sometimes have called it courting the muse or praying for grace.[12] What we hope for, when we wait for it, is that moment of integration which seems simultaneously to come from within and from without and which lights up a moment, a story, a picture, or a poem and gives it meaning.

In classical child-development terms, the necessary Other—she whose presence makes possible the consciousness of self—has been a mother. But it does not have to be. Children grow up with many different people in their environment who reflect them back to themselves: siblings who are receptive to their jokes and stories, uncles and neighbors who appreciate their pictures and encourage their own expressive behaviors. As these essays show, the "mothering" figures for the writers included here were sometimes women and sometimes men: husbands, wives, friends, aunts, sisters, lovers—and mothers. Virginia Woolf, herself the recipient of much "unconditional love" from her husband Leonard, perhaps depicted it best in those remarkable scenes in *To the Lighthouse* in which Mr. Ramsey turns to his wife for "sympathy" and Mrs. Ramsey gathers her force and sends streaming into the air a fountain of energy to quench Mr. Ramsey's need and sustain him in his temporary failure of nerve. This scene defines the concept, inasmuch as "mothering the mind" is what the reader understands the father and son each to be vying for: James in his infantile way wants his mother to provide a soothing background to his activity on the floor with scissors and catalogues, while Mr. Ramsey wants more active encouragement and reassurance. (Although she herself had a whole string of "mother figures" in her life, Virginia Woolf was really allergic to such demands on herself to do "mothering," as Jane Marcus's essay in this volume explains.) Mr. Ramsey's behavior may be continuous with that of a child who plays for hours and hours at games of his own devising, but who needs to touch home base from time to time with the mother or primary caretaker to be reassured between excursions into the world. The psychologist Margaret Mahler calls this kind of behavior in children "emotional refuelling," and connects it with the "practicing" stage in the development of play.[13]

There are related intellectual/spiritual phenomena that help define the kind of nurture I am interested in here. We can learn only from certain people, for instance; their least observation finds a comfortable corner in the mind and settles in to stay, whereas others, no matter how perspicacious or gifted, simply do not register with us in the same way. Some writers speak to us, and others leave us cold. We all recognize what it feels like to be within the magic circle of good friends, among whom we feel more real, more unique, more vivid, more ourselves. With such friends we always discover the words to say what we mean; their receptivity helps us find a suitable voice; they seem to meet us on our own ground.

Something about our friends, our lovers, our favorite teachers, the authors who speak to us, recalls and activates the experience of the ontologically secure self—or of painful deprivation if that comes closer to the bone. For we should not forget the large part that deprivation plays in symbol formation, that need motivates art as it engenders human relationships, and that both are attempts to make the world give us what we want. Artists in particular are under some kind of compulsion to create what would otherwise not exist in the world, whether they are adding to the stock of something that is in short supply, or integrating certain elements, or reproducing a particular configuration for psychic reasons of their own. A remarkable number of creative artists lost one or both parents when very young, or suffered deeply from social shame or lonely alienation. They turned to art to restore their losses and to create what they never had and always longed for, rather than to reimagine something actually experienced.

Proust felt that all art was an effort to recover a lost past, whether it had ever existed in reality or not. A writer was always looking backward, he felt, past the memory of a particular Romanesque church or the scent of a madeleine cake dipped in tea, to a partly invented edenic time when all desire was fulfilled, a golden age of symbiotic closeness with the mother. This is not to say that the writers represented here did or did not have satisfactory childhoods, did or did not experience the integration that their art strives for. The "Freudian" explanation of attachment to a "mothering" or nurturing figure (an anaclitic love object)[14] as compensatory, whether an extension or revival of early libidinal attachment, is inappropriate; the need for "mothering" is a universal and ongoing need of the self, which everyone must find some means of satisfying. In this introduction I am interested in the mothering of infants only as an informative analogy for mothering the mind, and venture no further in analyzing the configuration of artists' needs, relationships, or psychological histories.

Probably the most important function of "mothering" the mind of an adult, as of an infant, is to ease the movement between inner and outer reality so as to create more usable space between the two in which to work.[15] The "mother's" simple accord about basic values and assumptions extends the area in which inner and outer reality overlap and, by sharing the space, protects it from threat from without. Her nonjudgmental consent and appreciation encourage more private thought and fantasy forms. Adrienne Rich, in "Conditions for Work: The Common World of Women," reminds us that H.D. turned to her friend Bryher for support and assurance when "reading" the hieroglyphs on the wall in Corfu with her "crystal-gazing stare." "Shall I go on?" she asked, and Bryher replied without hesitation, "Go on." "We were 'seeing' it together," remarks H.D. of her inner vision, "for without her, admittedly, I could not have gone on."[16]

A shared interest in a particular dimension of human experience might encourage conversation and thought about that dimension. Or the "mother" might make a less conscious contribution to the medium in which private thoughts and fancies grow. She might, for instance, call forth certain qualities that are central to the work, qualities that seem to press for externalization in the texts—or she might embody them. In some of the cases that follow, we can see how the "mothering" figures fit the authors' fictions in special ways, as if they could have been found in them, or as if the works half created them. Thus, Jonathan Swift's need for a big/little mother, for a Glumdalclitch, created Stella; and George Eliot's need for an approving male relative, one who combined the allure of a Tom Tulliver with the steadiness and loyalty of a Caleb Garth, created George Henry Lewes.

Virginia Woolf seemed to have in mind nurturing relations of the sort this book is concerned with, when she pointed to the beneficient female influence in the lives of various great writers:

> And I looked at the bookcase again. There were the biographies: Johnson and Goethe and Carlyle and Sterne and Cowper and Shelley and Voltaire and Browning and many others. And I began thinking of all those great men who have for one reason or another admired, sought out, lived with, confided in, made love to, written of, trusted in, and shown what can only be described as some need of and dependence upon certain persons of the opposite sex. That all these relationships were absolutely Platonic I would not affirm, and Sir William Joynson Hicks would probably deny. But we should wrong these illustrious men very greatly if we insisted that they got nothing from these alliances but comfort, flattery and the pleasures of the body. What they got, it is obvious, was something that their

own sex was unable to supply; and it would not be rash, perhaps, to define it further, without quoting the doubtless rhapsodical words of the poets, as some stimulus, some renewal of creative power which is in the gift only of the opposite sex to bestow.

What she turns out to mean when you keep reading, however, is that the creative impulse, like any growing thing, needs to be cross-pollinated. She assumes that difference engenders; it is the logic of dialectic.

He would open the door of drawing-room or nursery, I thought, and find her among her children perhaps, or with a piece of embroidery on her knee—at any rate, the centre of some different order and system of life, and the contrast between this world and his own, which might be the law courts or the House of Commons, would at once refresh and invigorate; and there would follow, even in the simplest talk, such a natural difference of opinion that the dried ideas in him would be fertilised anew; and the sight of her creating in a different medium from his own would so quicken his creative power that insensibly his sterile mind would begin to plot again, and he would find the phrase or the scene which was lacking when he put on his hat to visit her. Every Johnson has his Thrale, and holds fast to her for some such reasons as these, and when the Thrale marries her Italian music master Johnson goes half mad with rage and disgust, not merely that he will miss his pleasant evenings at Streatham, but that the light of his life will be "as if gone out."[17]

Woolf is wrong to suppose that only women can provide for the creative impulse in men, or that women are valuable to the process largely because they represent the Other, and thus can fertilize the arid sameness. For one thing, as the following essays show, men also can mother. For another, this relation is primary to the experience of the self and to creativity, and therefore is crucial to any artist, of whatever gender, class, or sexual persuasion. That is why, when a feminist friend objected to the tenor of this book, and wrote that "we can only be liberated when we rid ourselves of mothering in metaphor as well as in fact," my instinctive response—equally feminist, I think—was that the world needed more nurturers, not fewer, and that the way to solve the problem of women's overdeveloped sense of responsibility for others was not to abolish the role of mothers but to extend it as an available mode to men.[18]

In the essays that follow, the terms of the "mothering" differ, presumably because the cases differ as well as the interests of the essayists writing about them. Nevertheless, certain generalizations are possible. We can see that Samuel Johnson's Mrs. Thrale, Robert Browning's Elizabeth, and Jonathan Swift's Stella all granted permission to the figures they "mothered" to be infantile, but that they did so in different ways and for different reasons. Hester Thrale seems to have fulfilled for Samuel Johnson that infantile desire for an almost unconditional love (what neither his mother nor his wife managed so well) and provided him with a comfortable home as well. At his request, she also in certain ways played the parental authoritarian. Elizabeth Barrett permitted Robert Browning to play the role of his own mother and to take care of her as of a second self. She let him safely feel by proxy the helplessness of a dependent child, and at the same time minister to that dependence and care for that externalized helplessness. Although Browning adored his mother and grieved terribly for her when she died, he never returned to visit her after eloping with Elizabeth Barrett, as if he could not bear to have them both in the same room because he could not simultaneously manage both sides of the doubled relationship. And Stella, whom Jonathan Swift met at Moor Park when she was a little girl, was apparently able to switch back and forth with Swift between the twin pairs of father-and-daughter and mother-and-son, to play with him at his favorite game of reversing big and little, to give him the polymorphous pleasure of taking either role. In W. B. Carnochan's words, she let him "act his part as a vulgar-minded little boy"—she probably even enjoyed it—and she permitted him to imagine her in turn as either a scolding mother or a naughty girl.

Sometimes these relationships are more directly involved in the evolution of the art itself. Wordsworth and Emerson, for instance, each conceived of his artistic task as beginning at some point of contact with nature itself, and each at some stage implicated a female relative— Wordsworth his sister, and Emerson his aunt—in this contact. Wordsworth, more classically, wrote about his relationship with Dorothy as if she helped him get in touch with his own, original, preverbal self, based primarily on seeing and feeling, glorying in forms, as Vogler points out. He then drew upon these experiences on the edge of consciousness for his art, experiences that were fostered, shared, and even articulated by that artistic "mother," so that Dorothy ultimately became a stand-in for Mother Nature, an embodiment of the symbolic state of the universe. Emerson, on the other hand, for whom contact with nature, Barish believes, was itself a mediatory, not a final stage, saw his aunt not as a natural force but as a force *in* nature, a gifted seer of that light which she believed was best perceived where the woods were darkest. Characteristically, William Wordsworth saw Dorothy's relation to him—and, insistently, that of the natural world as well—as benign, sweet, and supportive; whereas Emerson pictured nature and his aunt as media, awesome and mysterious, through which God's presence shone to his own perceiving eye.

Not all these indispensable figures are cast in the role of the muse. Watts-Dunton (Dunton was his mother's name) and Leonard Woolf are depicted on these pages not as inspiring, not as aiding certain emotional flights, but as more routine caretakers whose job in part was to prevent Icarian adventures. They emerge as men who allowed creativity in their respective companions by taking charge of worldly irritations so as to leave their artist consorts free from domestic concerns and able to write. (It is worth noting that neither John Locke and Damaris Masham, nor the Brownings, nor Swift and Stella ever had to forage for a living, shop or cook or clean; each of these couples employed servants to do those caretaking functions.)

There is also an enormous category of behaviors that one learns from one's mother, internalizes, incorporates, and then reproduces in the world as part of recreating that mother in the self. Colette learned from Sido how to surround herself with a makeshift nature made up of cats and flowers and plants, the symbols of her mother's garden in the middle of noisy Paris. Paule Marshall learned from her mother to see the double-edged qualities, the ugly beauty of the lives around her, and how to use her language to exert control over the world. Alice Walker explicitly states that she learned to write in order to tell her mother's stories. In fact, Mary Helen Washington makes the case here that for black women writers (Paule Marshall, Alice Walker, Dorothy West), formal writing was a way to capture and validate an oral tradition transmitted through their mothers; writing fulfilled a promise to the generation before.

The creative thinkers studied in these essays are primarily writers, and there are any number of other literary figures with centrally important long-term relationships about whom these same questions could be asked with profit. There are also many other kinds of creativity that could be said to have blossomed as a result of supportive relationships such as these. Rosa Luxemburg's comrade and lover, Leo Jogiches, "mothered her mind"—encouraged her to write and speak, discussed with her ideas about socialism, recognized and applauded her genius.[19] Freud's dependent relationship with Wilhelm Fliess during the years that he was working out the theory of psychoanalysis made it possible for him to trace the patterns of his own unconscious, what Erik H. Erikson calls "the first transference in history to lead, through discovery of its own nature, to its own self-therapeutic liquidation."[21] While under the remarkable influence of his friendship with Fliess, Freud worked out his relation to his mother, developed his theory of the Oedipus complex, wrote *The Interpretation of Dreams,* and enunciated a new poetics of behavior.[21] And Theo Van Gogh protected and supported his older brother, Vincent, sent him money, rescued him from his interminable scrapes, marketed his pictures, and above all loved and prized him, listened to him, believed in him. There is some question as to whether Van Gogh would have survived physically or psychically to paint his pictures if it had not been for Theo. "O, Theo," he wrote, "if you suffer because you think you have no power of creative work, how much more should I be unhappy, for I can do nothing without your help. Smoke your pipe in peace, and do not torment yourself because we accomplish together and with less suffering, a work that neither of us could achieve alone."[22]

We have always known that literature has had its fathers. For one thing, the transmission of public culture has always been entrusted to men, and even when its materials have been borrowed from a female world, its terms have been male terms, reinscribing traditions that go back to the classical world. The caretakers of this tradition have been concerned with upholding canonical standards, wrestling with the influence of writers who have gone before, trying to master new forms, and dealing with themes such as immortality, honor, and duty, which examine the place of the individual in the public realm. If "mothering the mind" means providing the conditions, both space and support, for explorations that simultaneously take the artist inward and outward, "fathering the mind," as we have been using the locution, means a more insistent, judgmental, and directive exhortation. This more active role in a writer's life might mean actually shaping, editing, or directing the composition. It might mean setting the standards for the work, measuring it against the work of earlier practitioners, providing the context in a way that could be seen as claustrophobic or inspiring. To be a father is to confer a patrimony, to approve something and incorporate it into an existing tradition.

Gertrude Stein, somewhat humorously, wrote in 1937:

> There is too much fathering going on just now and there is no doubt about it fathers are depressing. Everybody nowadays is a father, there is father Mussolini and father Hitler and father Roosevelt and father Stalin and father Lewis and father Blum and father Franco is just commencing now and there are ever so many more ready to be one. Fathers are depressing. England is the only country now that has not got one and so they are more cheerful there than anywhere. It is a long time now that they have not had any fathering and so their cheerfulness is increasing.[23]

As she uses it, "fathering" has to do with exerting power over others, directing them according to one's will.

Virginia Woolf wrote that "poetry needs a mother as well as father,"[24] and this collection of essays is the beginning of an exploration into what that might mean. Whereas "fathering" has to do with keeping to the public standard, seeing to it that the rules of a culture are properly internalized, "mothering" probably operates in the early stages of creation, permitting and encouraging the more idiosyncratic tendencies of the art, those aspects done for personal therapeutic reasons, where the purpose is to heal and consolidate the self rather than to do homage to a public tradition. Both functions are necessary, of course: Tradition without private meaning is hollow; and individual expressiveness without a communal context, without an audience, is doomed to extinction.

Because there are as many kinds of "mothering" as there are configurations of need, circumstance, and experience, only an approach that preserves this multiplicity makes sense. Some essays in this collection will work better than others in illuminating what a particular reader sees as the most important dimension of "mothering the mind." For different readers, other selections will seem more helpful. But all readers, we hope, will find insight from the collection taken as a whole.

The organization of these essays is somewhat arbitrary, since the infinite variety of human relationships does not lend itself to easy classification. There are four clusters of essays. The first cluster looks at the way three very different women might be said to have played the role of muse in different ways to three important (male) thinkers of the English Enlightenment: John Locke (Damaris Masham), Jonathan Swift (Esther Johnson or "Stella"), Samuel Johnson (Hester Thrale). The second set of essays explores the dynamic of "mothering the mind" between people for whom that relationship was also sexual—as in Robert Browning's "mothering" of Elizabeth Barrett Browning, or George Henry Lewes's "mothering" of George Eliot, or Alice B. Toklas's "mothering" of Gertrude Stein. The third section, on "mothers real and imagined," contains essays about writers whose actual mothers (or more literal surrogate mothers) nurtured their creativity. The relationships considered in this section are between Paule Marshall and her mother, Alice Walker and her mother, Dorothy West and her mother, Colette and her mother, and Virginia Woolf and her mother and a string of surrogate mothers, most notably Dame Ethel Smyth. The last section of the book, on "friends as family and family as friends," contains an essay about Swinburne's friendship with Watts-Dunton, who, as John Jordan says, was "closer than a brother"; an essay about the extraordinary role that Emerson's aunt played in his life and the development of his thought; and finally, a piece about Dorothy and William Wordsworth, which extends the theory and applies the metaphor of mothering to the particulars of that case.

The set of relationships in the opening section are from a chronological period that is earlier than the historical settings of the other essays in this collection. It is no accident that the muse figures of this section are all women and the writers are all men, for the muse of inspiration in the seventeenth and eighteenth centuries was invariably conceived of as female. Furthermore, few women of that time could read or write well enough for anyone to imagine them playing the other part. Indeed, it is striking that the enabling women in this section were all educated far above what was common for women of their day. Both Hester Thrale and Damaris Masham were writers themselves—of diaries and letters, but also of published books. And Stella was educated by Swift himself, who saw to it that she was cultivated far above what was usual for her sex.

Damaris Masham, with whom John Locke lived the last thirteen years of his life, was the daughter of a philosopher, Ralph Cudworth, master of Christ's College, Cambridge. She was raised at the university and schooled in the doctrines of the so-called Cambridge Platonists, among whom her father was a leading thinker. According to O'Donnell, it was in challenging the tenets of the Platonist school in the person of Damaris Cudworth that Locke first began to work out the epistemological theories which later found their way into his *Essay Concerning Human Understanding*. And when Locke died, Leibniz wrote to Lady Masham to find out what he had thought about certain subjects, because no one was closer to Locke's thinking , and it was known that Locke often worked out his ideas in conversation with her. O'Donnell argues that Masham also mothered Locke's mind by creating the domestic world he observed and from which he thought through his examples. Lady Masham offered to this philosopher of the mundane the very humdrum details that she hoped to transcend by having as her daily companion one of Europe's foremost philosophers. O'Donnell shows us that Locke was interested in Lady Masham's recipes for marmalade and pudding and in what she knew about "the best Management of a Dairie." The two seem to play a game in which she disdains "women's subjects" (fashion, cookery) but threatens to write about them if he does not stop quizzing her about ideas that are over her head. The way their letters circle round the plain and practical facts of domestic life gives us a new appreciation of Locke's taste for commonsensical examples drawn from daily experience.

For Swift too, Stella provided the only family he ever had, although they never actually lived under the same roof. In fact, the image of the muse governing this section is not the distant, shimmering, hopelessly fickle muse of sometime inspiration, but rather a motherly, sympathetic figure for whom the artist performs and who repairs his ego. She is a confidante sufficiently intellectual to discuss the ideas and writing and to understand and appreciate what is valuable. Swift in effect created Stella, as Carnochan reminds us, to be "an extension of himself"; she came to have his opinions, his attitudes, and even to write a hand that looked like his. Created in his own image, she was the only other being entirely acceptable to him. The exclusiveness and secretiveness of their relationship can be seen as a measure of Swift's self-enclosure and selective misanthropy. The fluidity of Swift's writing, with its powerful ambivalences about human contact and the sense of unconscious energies flaring close to the surface, also informs his relationship with Stella. Like an unconscious wish-fulfillment, this friendship/marriage had everything in it—and nothing: sexuality and chastity, being-a-child and being-a-parent, intimacy and domesticity.

Samuel Johnson too was soothed and supported by the domestic life that revolved around Mrs. Thrale. He lived in the bosom of her family, as Locke had lived with the Mashams. In the household at Streatham, under the influence of Mrs. Thrale's ministrations, he surrendered the paternal stance he so easily assumed elsewhere. Certainly Boswell casts him as a Universal Parent, responding to Boswell's own puppyish enthusiasm with authoritative pronouncements upon men and events. And Johnson supported a strange assortment of dependents in his household on Gough Square, a blind old woman, a drunken doctor, a freed black servant—the peculiar offspring of his character and circumstances. Wanting to be taken care of himself, he looked after these people; desperate for moral firmness, praying to God and begging in his journal for strength and resolution, he provided it for others, and gave his advice freely. But he allowed Mrs. Thrale to take him under her wing—Mrs. Thrale, who bore twelve of her own children and raised them, cared for them, educated them, and buried them one by one, grieving deeply. She fussed over Johnson, listened to his disquisitions, nursed him when he was ill, invited his friends over, and even provided him with diverting and educational toys like the chemistry laboratory at Streatham.

Only three of the supportive, enabling relationships considered in this book are overtly sexual, and they are in the section on "lovers as nurturers." The Brownings' marriage was symmetrical from the point of view of who was the creator and who was the silent partner: they both wrote. The fact that Elizabeth was an invalid and that Robert Browning took care of her is more complicated than it seems at first, however, as Mermin explains. They both exaggerated Elizabeth Barrett's weakness because Robert Browning took better care of himself when he was playing caretaker to her: He arranged space for writing, addressed himself to real problems, and set himself to work. Mermin also describes the effects they had on one another's writing. He brought her out into the world physically, in which frame of mind she wrote the novel-length poem *Aurora Leigh,* which reflects on the society in which she found herself. Elizabeth Barrett, on the other hand, led Browning back into himself, and his later work is a series of remarkable dramatic monologues fraught with complicated self-relations.

In the case of George Eliot and George Henry Lewes, the sexual dimension of their relationship was highlighted by the fact that they "lived in sin" together for years in Victorian England, Lewes being unable to get a divorce from his legal wife. U. C. Knoepflmacher tells us that the first unbidden intimations of ideas for fiction came to Eliot in a half-waking, dreamy, post-coital state, when her mind relaxed its usual powerful focus and a less conscious part of her intelligence was given free rein. Lewes applauded this direction in her writing, and although their relationship was the cause of her painful rejection by her unsympathetic male relatives—whose approval was far too important to her—his presence also provided balm to the wound, because he encouraged this healing expression of her deepest feelings about love and sex and family life.

Stein and Toklas's life together was of course also notorious for its sexuality. And yet, as Catharine Stimpson reaffirms, their relationship was the most conventional of marriages. Toklas let Stein play the genius, while she played the appreciative helpmeet. She was, for Stein, the perfect "wife"—lover, inspiration, friend, mother, encourager, appreciative audience, editor, and typist. She gave Stein the support she needed to be an innovator in a hostile world. And Gertrude's language created a home—and a career—for both of them. Stimpson shows us how to understand Stein's innovative forms and experiments with language as a consequence of this lesbian marriage with Toklas, extending out into the world the experimental effects of her life in her poems and prose about women, about relationships, and about sex.

The argument of the third section is that for certain women writers it was their literal real-life mothers who "mothered their minds," whose presence or memory released their creative energies and freed them up to express themselves. Mary Helen Washington makes the point that for black women it was often the only source of support and encouragement for their artistic achievement. Furthermore, in black culture, with its oral tradition, a woman earns her place within the community—far more than is true of a white Western woman—by how she uses language: to defend herself, to create word pictures, to pray, to tease, and to tell the stories that have been passed down for generations. The anecdotes that Mary Helen Washington tells about Paule Marshall, Alice Walker, and

Dorothy West all reinforce the sense that for these writers their creative, writerly identities were bound up with images of their mothers talking—and with the strength, inventiveness, and relish of their mothers' language.

Colette's marriage to Willy, Lilienfeld tells us, had everything to do with her relationship to her mother, Sido. She needed him to get away from her mother (although Willy proved to be a kind of mother), and later she needed Sido to help her escape from Willy. Her writing was caught in the web of influences they wove between them—Willy forcing her to write what ended up as being repeated reinscriptions of her mother. Colette first began to write because Willy made her write. He dominated her as Sido had done before him, and it was this negative "mothering" that enabled the writing. Jane Lilienfeld's tableaux of Sido abducting her daughter before her first marriage (Demeter trying to outmaneuver Dis and save her Persephone) and of Willy locking her up in a room and forcing her to write (insisting that she turn her straw into gold) help one to name the passivity, the masochistic edge to Colette's voice—the helplessness of her honesty. Willy, like Sido before him, exercised great power over Colette. He commanded and enchanted her as her mother had done, and although the domination was not loving, as it had been with Sido, still these were the conditions that catalyzed the writing and enabled Colette to return to an earlier self.

Jane Marcus's essay about the relation of Virginia Woolf's mother to her art takes off from Woolf's own metaphor that being with her mother was "like being a violin and being played upon"; only her mother could bring forth the music of which she was capable. According to Marcus, Woolf divided the world into people who cared for the weak and ill (like her mother) and people who were cared for (like herself). Her mother spent her life serving others and died young; Virginia determined not to squander her years similarly. Even though she took her own life, Virginia Woolf lived longer than Julia Stephen had. As everyone knows, it was her husband, Leonard, who took care of her; his attention and care created the conditions for her work.

On the other hand, Marcus distinguishes between this kind of care—Leonard soothing and calming her and arranging for her meals—and the other influences that inspired her. Marcus argues that it was her mother—and the women who subsequently substituted for her—who played the role of muse for Virginia and stimulated and thrilled her rather than lulled her. This series of surrogate mothers encouraged her feminism—they hoisted her on their shoulders as it were—whereas what Leonard did was to refuse social invitations when it was not good for her to go out. Leonard only prepared the ground; but Dame Ethel Smyth,

Vita Sackville-West, Violet Dickinson, and various other women planted the laurel and the rose, inspired the writing, and provided the experience of the self that led to the art.

Woolf was adept at attracting women whose relation to her, as her mother's had been, was more like that of an ardent lover than that of a comfortable sturdy old shoe. The functions of enabling and inspiring—ego and id functions, roughly—are served simultaneously by most of the other "mothering" figures presented in this book. Mrs. Thrale seems to have done both for Johnson, and Toklas seems to have done both for Stein. It is interesting to speculate on what it means that Virginia Woolf separated and satisfied these needs with different figures—as if the needs themselves were dissociated, their impulses disconnected at the root. The other example in this book of a relationship built on the domestic without the erotic component is that of Watts-Dunton and Swinburne, discussed in the next section, a lifetime connection both faithful and celibate. Jordan tells us that, as with Leonard and Virginia Woolf, Watts-Dunton enabled but did not inspire Swinburne's poetry. I could speculate that, since neither Swinburne nor Woolf lived out his or her homosexuality fully, this separation is a symptom of renouncing desire. On the other hand, both Woolf and Swinburne were volatile personalities who simply needed more ballast in their daily companions, and for whom it was wiser to be habituated and calmed than further stimulated.

The final section, "Friends as Family and Family as Friends," examines three "mothering" relationships in which the enabling figure was neither lover nor spouse nor real-life mother, but in some other kin or kinlike relation to the writer. Algernon Swinburne's friend Watts-Dunton was something between a brother and a mother to the poet. A careful and conservative lawyer, he was thoroughly approved of by Lady Jane Swinburne as a surrogate to take care of her son. She approved the plan of "daily rest and exercise," regular habits, and temperance that Watts-Dunton arranged for Swinburne. Jordan argues that Watts-Dunton did not impose this regime on Swinburne so much as Swinburne, who knew he needed someone to regulate his life—perhaps as his mother had regulated it—adopted him in order to arrange proper conditions for writing. Swinburne was fond of his mother and kept in close touch with her until she died at eighty-seven. She, in turn, contributed financially to the household at Number 2 The Pines. Jordan tells us that the relationship with Watts-Dunton marked a symbolic rebirth for Swinburne, and that the poet wrote of their first three years together as his "soul's best birthdays." Watts-Dunton's capable presence permitted him to retain his boyish fire and romantic unconcern with the material conditions of life, allowing a "controlled regression," as Jordan calls it, to a self out of which he could continue to write poetry.

The influential figure in Emerson's life, Barish tells us, was his aunt Mary Moody Emerson. She gave him the tools of his trade—his language and his sense of mission. From her he learned a poetic diction which Milton had early inscribed on her consciousness. It was she who taught him to read the natural world for transcendental moral implications, to value intuitive knowledge over fact, and to stand outside society's categories of thought. Emerson mythologized her capacity for language and belief, learning in part from this eccentric and socially marginal woman the necessity of being self-reliant if he were to be a true poet. Their relationship, as much epistolary as face-to-face, tells us something about the relation of his writing and reading to his life, for the man who learned and passionately taught that "books are for the scholar's idle hours" had, on the contrary, earlier begun, like the aunt who influenced him greatly, by loving books and abstract ideas above all things.

Wordsworth, more than the other writers dealt with on these pages, seems to have self-consciously understood the role Dorothy played for him: "True companion who/ Maintain'd for me a saving intercourse/ With my true self." He did his best work during the period of her influence, just as Robert Browning's verse ripened in his years with Elizabeth Barrett. Vogler argues in his essay that the time at Grasmere constituted a psychic return for Wordsworth to a reconstituted preoedipal maternal symbiosis, after a symbolic oedipal episode abroad. This interpretation gives us another way of understanding Wordsworth's preoccupation with reviving and describing a preexisting and only intermittently perceived relation to nature as a way of fully realizing himself as a poet.

Like Emerson with his aunt, Wordsworth, we know, mined Dorothy's journals for observations, memories, and language. But as Vogler and Barish see these two relationships, Dorothy was for Wordsworth a twin self entirely in accord with his thoughts and predilections, another pair of eyes and hands with but one mind and will, whereas Mary Moody Emerson was a mentor for her nephew, a seer, a mysterious and free-spirited sibyl who showed him the way and tried to keep him on the right track.

These are the cases collected here, but there are many more instances that one could point to to illustrate the principle that creation is more collaborative than we have been taught to think, even though only one name may appear on the title page. In the lives of these fifteen writers—Locke, Swift, Johnson, George Eliot, Stein, Barrett, Browning, Marshall, Walker, West, Colette, Woolf, Swinburne, Emerson,

Wordsworth—their friends and lovers, wives, sisters, mothers, husbands, and aunts all played a significant part in producing the work the world so values. In this day and age we can no longer afford the mythology of the individual genius toiling alone to realize his solitary vision, oblivious to the rest of the world. It is time to reinstate the value of connectedness—of the artist to his or her family, to personal history, and to the person or persons who supported the work and encouraged its free expression.[25] It is time to recognize properly that without these "support" functions the creative impulse, which we so overrate in the individualist Western tradition, would have many times been overwhelmed by unhappiness, anxiety, poverty, illness, or just plain loneliness. This book constitutes a collective plea for the reading public to take utterly at face value the common ascription of debt on many a page of acknowledgments: "To my wife (husband), to whom I owe more than I can express." If we are to survive as individuals—a nation, a planet—we must learn to acknowledge our debts and dependencies not as weakness but as part of the fundamental human condition. In this spirit we wrote *Mothering the Mind.*

NOTES

I am indebted to P. W. Shaw for an unpublished paper presented in the MLA session "The Self in Writing: Teaching," December 1979, and for countless conversations about this subject. This essay has also been much improved by suggestions made by Taylor Stoehr, Evelyn Barish, Catharine Stimpson, and Thomas A. Vogler.

1. Sigmund Freud, "Beyond the Pleasure Principle" (1920), in *The Complete Psychological Works of Sigmund Freud,* ed. James Strachey, 24 vols. (London: Hogarth Press and The Institute of Psycho-analysis, 1955) XVIII, 16.

2. D. W. Winnicott, *Playing and Reality* (1971: reprint ed. Middlesex, England: Penguin, 1974), p. 15.

3. In her excellent article "Maternal Thinking," Sara Ruddick makes a similar point by distinguishing the mothering attitude she calls "holding" from a more directly appropriating "acquiring." Necessity loosens the maternal grasp even more, she adds, because "the 'holding,' preserving mother must, in response to change, be simultaneously a changing mother." *Feminist Studies* 6 (Summer 1980), especially pp. 350–52.

4. Tillie Olsen, a pioneer in this as in so much else, recognizes this role in the creative process in the chapter "Wives, Mothers, Enablers" in *Silences* (New York: Delacorte, 1978), pp. 218–23.

5. D. W. Winnicott, "From Dependence Towards Independence in the Development of the Individual" (1963), in *The Maturational Processes and the Facilitating Environment* (New York: International Universities Press, 1965), p. 86.

6. Winnicott illustrates this point with an anecdote about a baby girl who was brought to him because she was regularly seized with strange fits of crying. She became able for the first time to make up and enjoy a game (throwing away spatulas) while on his knee. After this, as if she had been able to learn how to play because of his nearness and her trust of him—and as if her fits had been a symptom of her inability to play—the child recovered and became "an entirely healthy, happy, intelligent and friendly child, fond of play and free from the common anxieties " (*Playing and Reality*, pp. 56–58).

7. D. W. Winnicott, *Playing and Reality*, p. 130. For an example of how another clinician adds in the element of "mirroring" by the mother in the process of analysis and treatment, see Heinz Kohut, *The Restoration of the Self* (New York: International Universities Press, 1977), pp. 1–52, especially pp. 8, 25, 50, 52.

8. R. D. Laing, *The Divided Self* (1959; reprint ed. Middlesex, England: Penguin, 1973), *passim*, especially pp. 34–36, 78–83, 119. Laing derived this and much else from Winnicott's work.

9. D. W. Winnicott, "The Capacity to be Alone," *International Journal of Psycho-Analysis* 39 (1958), 416–20.

10. In a less metaphysical way, another's presence often creates the conditions for creativity by sheer physical work—what Adrienne Rich calls the "activity of world-protection, world-preservation, world-repair—the million tiny stitches, the friction of the scrubbing brush, the scouring cloth, the iron across the shift, the rubbing of cloth against itself to exorcise the stain, the renewal of the scorched pot, the rusted knifeblade, the invisible weaving of a frayed and threadbare family life, the cleaning up of soil and waste left behind by men and children. . . ." "Conditions for Work: The Common World of Women," in Sara Ruddick and Pamela Daniels, eds., *Working It Out*, (New York: Pantheon, 1977), p. xvi.

11. D. W. Winnicott, "The Capacity to Be Alone," p. 418.

12. Ernest Tuveson's fascinating book *The Imagination as a Means of Grace* (Berkeley: University of California Press, 1960) is about the merging of these secular and religious functions in the eighteenth century.

13. Margaret S. Mahler, "On the First Three Subphases of the Separation-Individuation Process," *International Journal of Psycho-Analysis* 53 (1972), 335.

14. "Anaclitic" literally means "leaning against," and although such object choices are an obvious improvement over purely narcissistic self-involvement, a Freudian would still consider them immature. Freud explained such love as the conflation of sexual libido with the instinct for survival. In the first phase of development, he reasoned, the sexual instincts have no independent means of finding satisfaction and "prop" themselves upon the self-preservative instincts. Thus infants love the men or women who tend them and later in life may form anaclitic attachments in which the infantile conditions of love are fulfilled.

15. Sara Ruddick implies that women are conditioned to have intellectual predilections along these lines: "Women are said to value open over closed structure, to eschew the clear-cut and unambiguous, to refuse a sharp division between inner and outer or self and other." "Maternal Thinking," p. 352.

16. For the original source of this anecdote see H. D., *Tribute to Freud* (1956; reprint ed. New York: McGraw–Hill, 1974), pp. 47–49.

17. Virginia Woolf, *A Room of One's Own* (London: Harcourt, Brace & World, 1929), pp. 90–91.

18. This, of course, is the solution urged by Dorothy Dinnerstein to the multiplicity of problems arising from the fact that women do all the primary child care in the culture, with the result that formation of the self always involves a breaking of symbiosis with some female Other. See *The Mermaid and the Minotaur: Sexual Arrangements and Human Malaise* (New York: Harper and Row, 1976).

D. W. Winnicott and his disciples have contributed importantly to our thinking about the relationship of the developing self to that Other, by stressing that self-definition comes not from snapping the psychological umbilical cord but from incorporating it, not by differentiation from that Other but in relation to that Other. See, for instance, *Playing and Reality*, p. 96. This is a lesson that feminist social theorists have picked up and advanced in a variety of contexts. Nancy Chodorow has examined the implications of it in her excellent article "Feminism and Difference: Gender, Relation, and Difference in Psychoanalytic Perspective," *Socialist Review* 46 (July–August 1979), 51–69. One view of the implications for literary theory, particularly interesting for its comparison of Ellen Moers's notion of a female tradition in literature with Harold Bloom's notion of a male literary tradition, is Elizabeth Abel, "(E)merging Identities: The Dynamics of Female Friendship in Contemporary Fiction by Women," *Signs* 6 (Spring 1981), especially p. 433.

19. This fascinating relationship is sketched by Elzbieta Ettinger in her introduction to *Comrade and Lover: Rosa Luxemburg's Letters to Leo Jogiches*, ed. and trans. Elzbieta Ettinger (Cambridge, Mass.: MIT Press, 1979).

20. Erik H. Erikson, *Life History and the Historical Moment* (New York: Norton, 1975), p. 57.

21. While in the grip of this extraordinary creative fervor, Freud also realized how much he owed his old *Kinderfrau* (nanny)—"the old woman who provided me at such an early age with the means of living and surviving"—and he reported the debt to Fliess without any awareness of its echoes in their own relationship. At the same time, he noticed that he was beginning to work more like an artist and less like a methodical and unimaginative problem-solver. That is, he began to wait on inspiration rather than pushing ahead by rational will. Increasingly he relied upon his own inner sense of reality to focus and test elaborations of his theory. "I have to wait until things move inside me and I experience them," he told his friend Fliess. Ibid., pp. 69–70.

22. Quoted in Paul Colin, *Van Gogh*, trans. Beatrice Moggeridge (London: John Lane, 1926), p. 46.

23. Gertrude Stein, *Everybody's Autobiography* (New York: Vintage, 1973), p. 133.

24. Virginia Woolf, *A Room of One's Own*, p. 107.

25. R. C. Lewontin, in an article on the state of genetic research in biology, refers to a similar ideological bias in conceptualizing in that field, which he states as "the belief in the dominance of intellectual labor over mere production, of design over execution. We speak of Cheops 'building' the Great Pyramid and of Napoleon 'conquering' Europe, although of course laborers built the pyramids and French soldiers conquered Europe." *The New York Review of Books*, January 20, 1983, p. 35.

Female Muses
The Early Tradition

"My Idea in Your Mind"

JOHN LOCKE AND DAMARIS CUDWORTH MASHAM

Sheryl O'Donnell

The Masham
Residence at
Oates. Courtesy
of the Essex
Record Office;
Victor Gray,
MA, County
Archivist

⌒⊃T̲o his contemporaries, John Locke (1632–1704) was a highly secretive man. But he wrote hundreds of letters and kept meticulous records of his daily activities for modern scholars to pore over. Locke's papers contain the fascinating details of life with his most intimate friend and biographer, Damaris Cudworth Masham (1659–1708). They met in 1681, when Damaris, living among philosophers and theologians at Christ's College, Cambridge, questioned Locke's yet unpublished attacks on the theory of innate ideas. The forty-nine-year-old bachelor and the twenty-two-year-old daughter of Cambridge Platonist Ralph Cudworth felt an immediate and mutual affinity, which lasted almost a quarter-century. Taking the names "Philander" and "Philoclea," they exchanged some forty stunningly complex and playful billets doux, *recording their negotiations for mutual succor. When Damaris married old Sir Francis Masham and moved to Oates, his isolated Essex estate, she began a campaign for Locke's permanent company. After extended visits to Oates, Locke moved there, thus assuring Damaris Cudworth Masham the books, the company, and the intellectual stimulation she so longed for. And the father of British empiricism found the domestic detail he needed for his essays on human understanding and his thoughts on education.*

Schoolmen have always thought Locke's philosophy dangerous because it elevates the mundane world to the sphere of rigorous discourse. In the story of how Damaris Cudworth Masham wooed John Locke to Oates, and in the details of their life together there, we find a record of that discourse and a history of that world.

... it is not for Guilded Coaches, and Embroider'd Beds, Nor Yet the more important Considerations of a Familie, and Children, How Bountefully soever stor'd with Them that will with me make them give Place to those Others, There being no Inconsistencie I hope betweene being still the same Philoclea, and indeavoring to Acquitt my self as my Lady ——— But that is a Name to which we will lay aside if you Please till you are Better Reconcil'd to it, and Have seene (which I cannot but Hope you once will, and that ere very long) How Perfectly she Resembles your Governess.

—Lady Damaris Cudworth Masham to John Locke, September 15, 1685[1]

$\smash{\sim}\!\!\mathcal{S}$cattered throughout the Bodleian Library's Lovelace Collection of John Locke's writings are poems and letters by his most intimate friend and companion, Lady Damaris Cudworth Masham (1659–1708).[2] Since most of Lady Masham's papers apparently have been lost or destroyed, these documents offer a rare glimpse into the private side of what was essentially a public friendship between Locke and Lady Masham. But the many visitors to Oates, the Masham estate in Essex where Locke spent the last fourteen years of his life, knew most of the details of their association. In fact, the terms "public" and "private"—so helpful for illuminating the separate, sometimes gender-defined spheres of work and thought in postindustrial life—hardly apply to the privileged seventeenth-century milieu which Locke and Lady Masham shared. Their friendship was "aristocratic" in the best sense of the term: free from anxieties about the respectability of a married woman's sharing her home with a man other than her husband; unfettered by the enervating details of housework and child care; bound only by the leisured disciplines of thought and writing. From a modern vantage point, their friendship seems remote, even pastoral, a kind of high-minded domestic romance played out in a landscape where art (philosophy, theology) and nature (children, material comforts) are one. We read Locke's letters to find him basing his educational treatises upon observations of Lady Masham's son and other children who visited Oates at his invitation.[3] We sort through Lady Masham's legal papers to discover her following Locke's advice to circumvent her husband's and her

28

brother's legal claims against the estate she inherited at her mother's death.[4] But neither Locke nor Lady Masham had what we would consider heavy domestic responsibilities in a household of ten servants. And the wife of an English baronet who stood for Parliament, regardless of her diminished financial status in the eyes of the law, had world enough and time for several rooms of her own.

Any conclusions, then, regarding the household at Oates or the influence of domestic relations upon the intellectual lives of its occupants must be drawn from the facts of class privilege. Wealthy philosophers such as Locke and Lady Masham, attached as they were to the busy household of a Stuart landed family, no doubt would find the whole notion of "domestic arrangements" a contradiction in terms because it implies a life apart from home.[5] Why design a private life to accommodate one's public interests when the household is itself a center of European notoriety? Why regret leaving Cambridge to marry a dull man and join "the Countrey Ladies," as Lady Masham called them, if one's permanent house guest, the most prominent physician, civil servant, and philosopher in England, attracted the company of Sir Isaac Newton and the Earl of Shaftesbury? Why should intellectual discipline be separated from family or business affairs when one's essays on human understanding drew illustrative detail from domestic life? The friendship between Locke and Lady Masham was mutually nourishing because the dichotomy between public and private which has often isolated and denigrated mothers since the eighteenth century did not exist in their lives. As "modern," privatized women who loved men with public careers, Swift's Stella and Johnson's Mrs. Thrale were not mothered by the men they cared for. For a variety of reasons, their acts of encouragement, self-sacrifice, and propitiousness were not returned in kind. But such was not the case with Locke and Lady Masham. Judging from their personal correspondence, poems, household accounts, and miscellaneous papers, Locke and Lady Masham mothered each other for almost twenty-five years.

Lady Masham's biography of Locke, published in Jean Le Clerc's Amsterdam journal *La Bibliothèque universelle* shortly after Locke's death in 1704, gives his poor health (chronic asthma) as the reason for his residence at Oates:

> He had during the years '89, '90 and '91 by some considerably long visits with which he had obliged Sir Francis and me, made trial of the air of this place, which is something above twenty miles from London, he thought that none would be so suitable to him. His company could not but be very desirable to us, and he had all the assurance we could give him of always being welcome here; but, to make him easy in living with us, it was necessary he should do so on his own terms, which Sir Francis at last consenting

to, Mr. Locke then believed himself at home with us, and resolved, if it pleased God, here to end his days—as he did.[6]

Locke's "terms" are carefully recorded in his journal: He paid £1 a week for himself and his manservant, plus a shilling for his horse. He brought furniture, scientific instruments, clothing, and thousands of books to Oates, and the detailed inventories of his belongings—some by Locke and some by Lady Masham—suggest that the paraphernalia attached to this seventeenth-century philosopher gradually filled up the household.[7] But Lady Masham's biography of Locke mentions none of these matters, not because they were secret, but because they were inappropriate to her literary task.

What Lady Masham does in her biography is to downplay the intimacy of their early friendship at the same time that she mythologizes Locke's low origins. She tells the story of Locke's birth in a way that explains away the humbleness of the thatched Somerset cottage where he was born. Locke's mother, writes Lady Masham, "designing" to give birth in her own parish, was "surpris'd on her way thither" and "forced into a little house in a place call'd Broadwell Downs and was there deliver'd; . . . this is the Reason of her Sons Birth not haveing been Regis-ter'd."[8] But Maurice Cranston has shown that the cottage where Locke was born was his maternal grandmother's house, not the temporary shelter of Lady Masham's account. Cranston numbers this "entirely false story" among several other accounts concocted by "snobbish historians of Somerset" who, "appalled by the thought of so great a man as Locke being born in so proletarian a dwelling, glamorized the place out of all recognition."[9] Lady Masham at least cautions her readers that she was forced to rely on others for the facts of Locke's early life:

> But for the Events of Mr. Lockes life I am able to tell you but little of my own knowledge: My first acquaintance with him beginning when he was past the Middle age of Man, and I but young . . . tho' before his leaving England in the year 1683 I had for a great part of above two years convers'd frequently with him, and then he honour'd me sometimes with his correspondence dureing his continuance in Holland.[10]

This muted account is true enough. But by suggesting that she never knew Locke until 1689, Lady Masham diminishes the romantic aspects of their friendship. She reveals nothing of the passion we find in their early letters and poems because that "Idea" was neither lasting nor important to her. Her retrospective vision instead stresses Locke's humane intellect, his generous interest in all sorts of people. Locke insisted that experience provide authority for speculation and reflection, partly because he doubted the usefulness of rational methodologies and distrusted thought in codified systems. Lady Masham recorded his conviction that the life of reason depends upon the life of action in her biography of Locke:

> He had the greatest condescension in the world to the meanest of other men's capacities, and always, in his debates with any one, found all the strength in their arguments against him that could be conceived to be in them, had the thoughts of the proposers been better digested, or their sense more advantaged by their expression. He was alike conversible with all sorts of people, . . . from his real persuasion that he could learn something which was useful of everybody, together with a universal love of all sorts of useful knowledge; from whence, and from his custom of suiting his discourse to the understanding and proper skill of every one he conversed with, he had acquired so much insight into all manner of acts or trades as was to everybody surprising; for a stranger might well have thought that he had made each of these matters his study or practice, and those whose professions these things were often owned they could learn a great deal from him concerning them, and did frequently beg his direction or advice thereon.[11]

Since most scholars of Locke feel compelled to remark on his intolerance of opinions other than his own, Lady Masham's testimony seems uncritical when she writes that he sometimes spoke "a little warmly" to "disputants" who repeat the same arguments "after having been ever so often beaten out of them":[12] "No man was less magisterial or dogmatic than he, or less offended with any man's dissenting from him in opinion."[13] But she insists upon Locke's genuine interest in intelligent debate passionately conducted, and it is this characteristic which Locke most admired in her. He wrote to Limborch in 1691:

> I have already told you that I was acquainted with the daughter of Dr. Cudworth, and have spoken to you of her wonderful qualities. . . . The lady herself is so well versed in theological and philosophical studies, and of such an original mind, that you will not find many men to whom she is not superior in wealth of knowledge and ability to profit by it. Her judgment is excellent, and I know few who can bring such clearness of thought to bear upon the most abstruse subjects or such capacity for searching through and solving the difficulties of questions beyond the range, I do not say of women, but even of most learned men. From reading, to which she once devoted herself with much assiduity, she is to a great extent debarred by the weakness of her eyes, but this defect is abundantly supplied by the keenness of her intellect.[14]

Locke and Damaris Cudworth met in late 1681, perhaps at the London home of Edward Clarke, the husband of Locke's cousin Mary Jepp and the friend of Damaris's father, Ralph Cudworth, the Cambridge Platonist. Locke's journals and correspondence from this period show an immediate and mutual affinity between the woman of twenty-two who had been raised among philosophers and theologians at the Master's Lodge of Christ's College, Cambridge, and the forty-nine-year-old bachelor who was by this time a Somerset landowner, the confidential adviser to the first Earl of Shaftesbury, and an Oxford don with unorthodox—and as yet unpublished—views, which he loved discussing with friends.[15] Over the next seven years, John and Damaris exchanged more than forty letters, a series of philosophical *billets doux* delightfully contrived from the myriad interests of "Philander" and "Philoclea," as they styled themselves.

Some of these early letters, parts of which Locke copied into his journal, are debates that show Locke developing epistemological theories he would later publish in his *Essay Concerning Human Understanding*.[16] Locke had begun his essay in 1671, and by the time he met Damaris Cudworth he was sharpening his attack on the Platonic theory of innate ideas. His critique included an analysis of the powers of human reason unaided by divine revelation.

Since there remains no evidence that Locke ever met Ralph Cudworth, whatever direct contact he had with Cudworth's philosophy probably came through Damaris.[17] At her urging, Locke bought Cambridge philosopher John Smith's *Select Discourses* and began to read them, along with Ralph Cudworth's *The True Intellectual System of the Universe* (1678).[18] Both Smith and Cudworth describe the physical world as knowable only through the eyes of faith; nature is properly understood by minds at one with God. Locke rejected this claim as antirational, dismissing Smith's account of "The True Way or Method of attaining to Divine knowledge" as irrelevant to philosophy. "Opinions not founded on reason, if they concerne God and religion deserve the name of Enthusiasm," Locke wrote in his journal and later to Philoclea. "Whatever is known, however sublime or spiritual is known only by the natural faculty of the understanding and reason, however assisted."[19] He wrote Philoclea that Smith only enumerated various kinds of divine love, not the working of human reason. But he wanted to know how she understood the *Discourses*.

Philoclea answered, calling herself Philander's "Governess." Her characteristically witty reply reaffirmed Smith's major precepts by shifting the grounds of debate from Smith's *Discourses* to the writings of St. Paul, who also insisted that we see as through a glass darkly. Philoclea begins her defense of reason as a divine faculty with an indirect attack on Locke's trust in the powers of human discourse. In defending the school of philosophy her father led, she wrote:

That I have no Ill Opinion of the Platonists I confess, nor ought you to wonder at That seeing I have spent the Most of my life amongst Philosophers of that Sect in which I have always found the most Vertue and Friendship.[20]

She questions Locke's disparaging references to "Enthusiasm" and "Vision," using scriptural authority to make her claim against unaided human reason:

> I know not what you may call Vision nor how much you may attribute to the power of Reason, onely as I understand them it seemes to me that there may be something between these two things, there being (I think) such a Degree of Perfection to be attain'd to in this Life which the Powers of meere Unassisted Reason will never Conduct a Man. . . . I would faine know whether you think not that by imploying it the best one can, and by constantly adhereing to the Dictates of it, they may not at length come to be acted by a Higher Principle. Or whether it is by that alone that we are capable of becomeing those new Creatures so often spoken of, it seemes to mee I confess that it is not, and I beleeve that my Author [Smith] was of that mind, neither do I know how to understand several places in St. Paul (which seem'd not difficult before) if hee Himself were not as much an Enthusiast as this comes to.[21]

Philoclea caps her defense of right reason—reason aided by faith—with a slighting reference to her own frail physical health, thereby reaffirming her and Smith's conviction that the human mind, caged by mortal flesh, must be perfected by an Idea outside of itself. She makes her argument about the place of reason entirely intimate: For Philoclea, the Idea is Philander himself:

> But I shall tire you as I have alreaddie done my self, you know I cannot write short letters, but if you aske me questions they'll be twice as long. . . . You may be able to judge what I am like to do by this, since I am lame at present, and thought I could not have writt at all when I took the Pen in my Hand, haveing almost broke my Arm to day besides three or foure mischeifs more that I got all with a fall as I was standing still. . . . You see how careful a Governess you have of me, that I neglect you not withstanding all these disasters, but it is no more than you ought to expect from who is so much your friend and Servant. . . .[22]

The letter's closing, with its warm declaration by a "Governess" who is also a "friend and Servant," is typical of seventeenth-century *billets doux*. But as Philoclea's witty distinctions between mind and matter shade off into pointed casual references to her bad eyesight, bouts of depression, and mysterious fainting spells, literary convention gives way to personal testimony, which in turn is held in check by either of two rhetorical poses designed to elicit Philander's concern: mock anger or stoic resignation. With a few exceptions, letters between Philander and Philoclea are patterned by provocation, which invites rebuttal, commands restatement, or leads to acceptance or expression of concern. Their correspondence, contrived from philosophical debate and personal confession, springs from the central contradiction between desire for nurture and the longing for autonomy which characterizes the discourse of mothering.[23] The tensions created by simultaneous demands for freedom and shelter—demands expressed by both Philander and Philoclea as they strike various bargains with each other—are at once intimate and antagonistic.

One of the most striking examples of this discourse begins with Philoclea's mocking rebuttal of Philander's repeated requests for more news, for further comments on Smith's *Discourses* or more information about her fainting spells. Philoclea threatens to inundate the curious Philander with some questions of her own, insisting all the while that she has been inappropriately provoked:

> But why would you put me upon this againe when I told you in my last letter that you must not? were you not affraid that in Revenge I should have ask'd your advice about makeing me a New Petticoate? Have sent you an Account of all the new Fassions [*sic*] that have beene since you left the Town? told you what my new Manto is made of? and a Thousand things more of the like nature that I have all in store for you if you provoke me to it again. . . . Pray take care and remember that you are only freely and Plainly to tell me your thoughts of my Author [Smith] without ever examining mee about him, who am so far from being able to explain His Opinions that I cannot give you an account of my owne Actions which was the other thing that you desir'd of me, al that I know being only that I got such a Fall as I told you of, but which ways I cannot for my Life immagine.[24]

Reiterating her aversion to Philander's questions, Philoclea details her withdrawal from society, making the first of many complaints against unwelcome intrusions:

> I am the worst in the World at answeareing Questions. The Truth is, I have of late so Mortall an Aversion for it that twoo Hours practice every night is so far from reconcileing me to it that I almost wish sometimes that I were Dumb, and am in a Freight every time that any Body begins to speak to me. I thought the other Day that if I lock'd my self up in my chamber I should certainly be free from this trouble, when before I had beene at rest an Houre in comes your Letter and another of three sides of a sheet of Paper all questions from one t'other. . . .
>
> Write any thing to me rather then ask me one question more, since I am so far out of Patience that I prefer'd being sick last Night before it. I am almost so too now with the length of this letter. . . .[25]

The witty protest against curious intruders, the exaggerated wish for incapacity and solitude, is made against the very literal disclosure of physical pain. In the guise of the vexed Philoclea, Damaris Masham reveals her suffering to Locke. The mask and its maker are one.

Anna Grigg, one of Locke's more sanguine friends, called Damaris Cudworth a "fair and intolerably witty lady."[26] The historian Peter Laslett says that she was "certainly personable" but "excessively short-sighted, nervous, and excitable—perhaps the first bluestocking of them all."[27] Indeed, nearly all of Philoclea's letters and poems to Philander are complaints, as she herself frequently calls them. But they are designed for an intimate friend, who she claims "is much disposed to be in Choller" himself.[28] Anger gave the correspondents a common emotional vocabulary, enabling Philoclea to demand sympathy, encouragement, information, advice. Even when she wrote to ask him to send her some snuff, the tone was feisty and self-justifying. The rhetoric of invalidism, so commonly used by women needing freedom from continual demands made on them, is punctuated by threats of withdrawn attention, first to "Trigonometri," then to Philander:

> You will make no scruple I hope to give snuff to one that desires it, and that so importunately, that I can scarse find Patience to waite till it is Possible you should send it me. there is none in this Towne but what perfectly fuddles [intoxicates] me, and I fancie almost gives me the Palsie, though I find so much good in it too, as tempts me to take it notwithstanding. . . .
>
> If you would know now what it is that I ail, that makes it so necessarie for me, I should find it very difficult to tell you, since I can describe it no otherwise, but that without being so much Paine, it is something in my Head which is . . . depriveing me almost of the use of that little understanding which I us'd to have, so that at present there is no great danger of my applying myself much to the study of Trigonometri, at lest you will say with Likelihood of much success. . . . If you have any Pitty contribute what you can to help me out of this sad Condition, till then I shall not be able to apprehend any thing that you can say, or to write one Word of Answeare to all the Letters that you send me. . . .[29]

Reluctantly, Locke sent the snuff the following week; he disapproved of tobacco and alcohol, drinking nothing but water specially filtered through limestone.[30] He capitulated to the voice of Philoclea, sometimes impatient, sometimes urgent, always eager to report her "Quarrell with the World," her Platonic philosophy, and her wry conviction that, at Cambridge, "the Heart is one of the most useless things in the World."[31] Using the persona of an irritated lover whose genius is thwarted by the annoyances of mortality and daily life, Damaris Cudworth got the attention she needed from Locke.

Philoclea's favorite pose is one of Platonic distance from the material world, a sphere that came to include housewifery, husband, and
children. Before her marriage in 1685 she frequently wrote of her disdain for domesticity and of her longing for a more rarefied life. A poem
sent to Locke in 1682, beginning "When deaths cold hand shall close my
eyes," repeats some familiar tropes of Neoplatonic consolatory verse:
Only the ignorant and the vulgar fear death; our souls, freed from the
body's prison, will reveal our true selves; ancient philosophers will join
enlightened Christians in heaven, much to the chagrin of religious
bigots. But the poem's last five stanzas break from these predictable
themes to raise a feminist polemic against male arrogance and its con-
comitant strictures against female education:

> All Harsh opinions here [on earth] shall cease
> products of ignorance and pride
> where charity and good will and praise
>   no differences can ere divide
> All freely seeke each others good
>   where Pride, nor Envy's understood
>
> And our weake sex I hope will then
> Disdaine yt stupid ignorance
> wch was at first impos'd by men
>   their owne high merits to inhance
> And now pleade custome for pretense
>   to banish knowledg witt and sense
>
> Long have we now condemned been
> to Folly and impertinence
> but then it surely will be seene
>   There's in our Souls no difference
> When we no longer Fetter'd are
>   but like to them our selves appeare.
>
> These great advantages are sure
> a part of them we may propose
> When we Eternall life insure
>   and doe this Momentarie lose
> Enough are those to let us know
>   pity on death we will bestow.
>
> But Envy rather due does seeme
> But oh! who dares at fate repine
> or does not yt ye fittest deeme
> wch God sees best him to assign
>   nor life nor death my wish shall bee
>   but humbly to submit to Thee.[32]

Few of Damaris Cudworth Masham's other poems repeat this angry charge against men's sinful enlargement of their own images at
women's expense. But the relationship between right reason and Chris-

tian duty is a familiar theme in both of her philosophical works, *A Discourse Concerning the Love of God* (1696) and *Occasional Thoughts in Reference to a Vertuous or Christian Life* (1705), where she urges women to study the rational grounds of their religious faith. Part of one verse Philoclea sent Philander in 1686 includes this wry comment to an anonymous "Dear Sister," for whom the poet distinguishes marital duty from happiness in love. Like *A Discourse* and *Occasional Thoughts,* the poem mocks the "duty" of female submission to men by equating happiness with the proper exercise of reason:

> The Text you'l find is very Plaine
> Eve, was made onely for the Man,
> Then How can you your self Deceive
> And think you're not some Adams Eve?
> Or on the Man Look with a Frowne
> Who onely comes to Claime His owne?
> And Begs but that You would Restore
> The Ribb you Rob'd Him of before;
> And though for th' Hall of Westminster,
> The Man no Justice can have There,
> Yet surely Sister it is Plaine
> He ought to have his Ribb Againe.
> Then Haveing with our Duty done
> I to our Happiness go On,
> For if one Word will serve the Wise
> What I have said may well suffice.[33]

Philoclea asks Philander for an impartial judgment of her verse. Then she offers him a witty invitation to her home, naming the very source of "Happiness"—the public world of poetry and philosophy which Philander represents—at the same time she rejects her "Duty"—the private world of domesticity which he seeks and which she longs to escape. She will not send him the directions for making jam which he requested when she is writing "higher" lines: "you will see I am got now quite out of the Element of Houswifrie, and Therefore I hope will excuse me for Receits of Marmalade, and Puding, But let me see you in my Closet, and There you shall have Them All."[34] She implies that should he enter her home, she could have "All" as well: Talk of Plato and Descartes would transform material "Duty" into "Happiness."

By this time Damaris Cudworth was Lady Masham, married and expecting her first—and only—child. She had written Locke of her engagement to Sir Francis while Locke was in Holland, and connected her announcement to a series of queries and jokes about the Labadists, a quietist religious sect founded by Jean de Labadie in Weiwert.[35] Philoclea chides Philander for his disapproval of the Labadists, announcing that she had found one "on this side of the Water" to marry. "If the notion I have of them [Labadists] is right," she wrote Locke in 1684, "and there is any Happiness to be found in Marriage it must certainly be amongst them, who I suppose Consider nothing in it but to Please them selves, To Whom

> Joynter, Portion, Gold, Estate,
> Household, Householdstuff, and Land,
> (The Low Conveniencies of Fate)
> Are Greek they do not understand."[36]

At Damaris's request, Locke visited the colony in August of 1684, and he sent her a three-volume set of Labadie's religious writings, which she could not yet read, since she knew no Latin until Locke joined the Masham household seven years later. In January of 1685 she wrote that she was "but Half Arm'd against Matrimonie," asking "by which of my Halfs it is that I ought to be Determin'd," while hinting that "there is alreaddie a very great change wrought in me I can assure you."[37]

Inexplicably, she married Sir Francis in June 1685, writing Locke no wedding details except that the former "Mademoiselle C," as she called herself, had received his letter "in the very Church . . . and Almost at the very same moment that she was going to quitt that name for Another Under which you will Always find her as much your Friend as she ever was, or as you can Desire that she should be."[38] She makes Locke's letter the central event of her wedding, so that the literary lovers, Philander and Philoclea, take precedence over the mundane coupling of man and wife. Ideal love, Philoclea insists, will prevail.

The circumstances of Lady Masham's marriage to Sir Francis remain unclear. Perhaps she married this baronet, a widower with eight sons and one daughter by his first marriage, to ensure her own social position and to acquire the "low conveniencies of Fate" that would attract Locke back from Holland.[39] And her own mother lived at Oates after Ralph Cudworth died in 1688.[40] Whatever her motives, Lady Masham's subsequent letters to Locke always link marriage and children to earthly, and therefore, to her, more secondary matters, while associating Locke's friendship with the rarefied intellectual state which she desired. Of course these literary connections may be a rhetorical strategy designed to highlight their philosophical differences: As a Platonist, she quarreled with Locke's empiricism. But her letters bespeak her desire for Locke's company, for his physical presence:

> . . . there are so very Few People that I can Possibly have Any High Esteeme for; Not but that since I have seene you I have had the good fortune to be Knowne to Diverse Whom All the World that can Judge, speake of with Honour, and I have been Oblig'd to them for some Particu-

lar mayks of Respect and Good Will; . . . I am Certainlie Plac'd in the Wretchedest Neighborhood in the whole World and never had so Violent a Desire in my life as now to good Companie. Tis in Vaine that I think (and therefore Pray say nothing of it) of Suiting my Mind to my Condition, for Business and the Impertinent Concerns of a Mistress of a Familie will never have Anie Place in my Heart, and I can at most do no more then submit to Them.[41]

From the day of her marriage until he moved to Oates some three years later, Lady Masham wrote to Locke of her need for him. As early as August of 1685, a little more than a month after her wedding, she began her campaign for Locke's company while he remained in Holland. In a sense, marriage to Sir Francis made it possible for Lady Masham to live with Locke. It allowed her to "improve upon the Old Foundations"[42]—her Cambridge education and her proper marriage— by offering Locke the very domestic experience she hoped to transcend. Her letters repeatedly assure Locke of her high regard for him, urging him not to "think that the Spirit of Care, and Familie Affairs shall Intirely Possess" her.[43] She reminds Locke of her deep commitment to the life of the mind, defining knowledge in the same way that she would in 1705, when she published *Occasional Thoughts in Reference to a Virtuous Life*.[44] Knowledge, like friendship, is most useful when it is moral and spiritual: "The Love of my Friends Therfore and Best Kinds of Usefull Knowledge so far as I am Capable of it, will still Possess my Heart as much as ever They did. . . ."[45]

She anticipates Locke's pragmatic suggestion that she read in the country, then refutes it with a plea for his company:

You will perhaps Advise me to Converse with the Dead since Here are so few Living that are Worth it; I am indeed forc'd to do so more then I have of a long time done before But besides that I do not Naturally Love Reading My Eyes will not permit me to do it very much. The most Comfortable thing that you can say to me that I can Think of, is, still to Assure me you have some Esteeme for me. That Alone would make me think Life not Altogether Insignificant were there yet fewer things Pleasing in it to me then there Is; and Besides it will Continue in me some Value for my self which as Proud as I sometimes seeme I think I do at Others a little Want.[46]

Here, then, is the nourishment Locke could provide Lady Masham: confirmation of her highest powers, her rational self. Only intellectual life could sustain her against dreariness at Cambridge or London or Oates. In the boldest of language she chooses Locke among all men to live this life with her:

> Philander is a Name, that since I have seene you, has many times Recon-
> cil'd me to the World when nothing else would; When I have beene in This
> Place Plagu'd with Theire Pedantry and scholastick Arrogance; when in
> Towne with the Noisie Fops There; And when with the Insipid Coxcombs
> of the Countrey; But Above All I have made use of it (though whether
> with so much Reason, or No, You and Heaven Can Onely Tell) when I
> Have beene Tempted to Beleeve that there was no such Thing Below
> (amongst your Sex at least) as an Undesigning and Honest Friendship;
> free from Unjust Ends; and Little Interests; which when either Disap-
> pointed; or Serv'd; turns to Hatred, Malice, and Revenge; Or to Coldness,
> and Indifference. . . .[47]

Calling herself a "widow," saddened that she is "now out of the Land of
Philosophy," Lady Masham laments the debasing effects of rural life
upon her mind. She blames her exile in the country for her inability to
write:

> . . . Tis in Vain that you bid me Preserve my Poetry; Household Affaires
> are the Opium of the Soul and it is impossible for me to make use of that
> Preservative unless I can Recover first from this Lethargie that I am now
> in. Which that you may have some Hopes of However, Know that I am
> Present All alone in that Place I told you of except the Gentleman you
> Know of, a Young Man of 16, a Child of 5, and a Girl between both that
> speaks not yet a Word of English; For These last you may judge what
> conversation They are; and for the first the Business of this World Almost
> wholly imploys him when he is at Home, so that I have very little of His
> Company.[48]

But what was wasteful of time and energy for Damaris Masham was
grist for Locke's mill. What better place to live, when one based theories
of knowledge on domestic experience, than in a bilingual household
with young children? The domestic affairs that Lady Masham found
boring interested this intensely empirical thinker. Lady Masham, hun-
gry for talk of "the Platonists and Cartesians on whose Accounts [she and
Locke] have formerly had so manie Quarrels," teases Locke: "But you
will Perhaps, think now tis no longer pardonable for me (If ever it were
so) to Talk of Subjects of That Nature, and that Culpepper and the
Countess of Kents Receits afford more Suitable Speculation for a Countrey Lady who had Children and a Familie to look after."[49] She hints that
even Cambridge might please her now:

> . . . Remember that in the Learned Dulness of this Place [Cambridge] there
> is Yet more Societie then in the Countrey And that amidst the Impertinent
> Wranglings of the Schools One may sometimes Heare something more
> Edifying (at least more Diverting) then in the Repeated Entertainments of
> the Price of Corn, and the Best Management of a Dairie; and Conse-
> quently that I shall have more need now of the Conversation of my Absent

Friends then ever I have had Heare, How much soever I have formerly
Complain'd and that Justly enough too.[50]

She ends her letter with another invitation to Oates and a witty allusion
to Cowley, reminding Locke that she is "but within Half a Days Journey
of the Great World at any time, Nor much more from Hence: But you
know it is not Places I have ever lov'd; or Crouds that I have Thought
Company; Two, or Three, of my Friends therefore may bring the
Towne to me whenever they Please and leave London a Desert. . . ."[51]
Again, she sketches a seductive picture of her private life, drawing him
into the richly diverse world which seems so incomplete without him:

> . . . there is scarse any thing I would not give to see you Here in my Closet
> where I am now writeing to You; I can but Think how you would smile to
> see Cowley and my Surfeit Waters Jumbled together; with Dr. More and
> my Gally Potts of Mithridate and Dioscordium; My receits and Account
> Books with Antoninus's his Meditations, and Des Cartes Principles; with
> my Globes, and my Spining Wheel; for just in this order They at present
> ly, and tis not without Reason I think that I designe to Draw Curtains over
> this Fantastical Furniture.[52]

What better way to attract the world's foremost philosopher, physician,
educational theorist, and civil servant than to offer him these hidden
riches profusely displayed? Lady Masham's closet contained the world,
and welcomed Locke to it.

Finally he came. After extended visits to Oates in 1689, 1690, and
1691, Locke left the smoke and discomfort of London and moved to
Lady Masham's Essex estate, taking two of the best rooms on the first
floor of the modest Tudor manor house. Built in rough Gothic style,
battlemented in some parts and gabled in others, the red brick house
stood a little above a lake (now marshland). Locke's friends began to call
him "the gentleman now within the moated castle," referring no doubt
to the small moat encircling the house. But the phrase is also an apt
description of the way he and Lady Masham lived within a protected
space, each extending to each freedom that neither would have alone.

The voluminous details of daily life recorded in Locke's journals
give startling evidence of his meticulous attention to domestic life and
Lady Masham's concurrent avoidance of it. She read and wrote, learning
mathematics and Latin, arguing philosophy and theology, devouring the
nearly 5,000 books he brought to her home.[53] Locke managed some
household accounts and much of Lady Masham's business affairs, over-
seeing her loans and investments, buying her books and clothing and
spectacles, seeing to the cook's wages. In his journal he even preserved
some favorite recipes for pancakes and oatmeal pudding.[54]

He planted lime trees and filled the yard with new botanical speci-

mens brought from Holland. He spent as much time as he could out-
doors, reading in the garden or playing with the youngest Masham
children, Esther ("Dab") and Francis ("Totty"), for whom he wrote a
special edition of Aesop's *Fables* to teach them Latin.[55] He so filled the
house with books and furniture and scientific instruments that little
room remained for other guests, including Sir Francis's mother, who
lived nearby at Matching Hall, and Master Clarke, who was removed to
his parents' house after an eight-week stay at Oates.[56] Dozens of lists
made by Lady Masham mark the overflow of Locke's possessions
throughout the house. Records of this kind hint at what Locke and Lady
Masham's relationship must have been like: ritualized and intense, congenial but never diffident. The two philosophers shared the sort of
friendship Lady Masham had despaired of having with her husband, or
with any other human being. Now she had a friend and critic who
countered her Platonic idealism with the tenets of empiricism and a
rigorous practicality; a financial adviser and confidant who saw to her
property and her investments in land and the East India Company; an
educational theorist who supervised her son's reading and wrote deliberately playful advice to her stepdaughter; a physician who cared for her
elderly mother; a host who made Oates an international center of learning and culture.

Even a random sampling from Locke's journals written during the
last fourteen years of his life makes a startling union of money and love,
a pastoral that, by contrast, shows Pope's satiric portrait of Belinda's
jumbled dressing table as mean-spirited. Daily life at Oates mixed books
and parasols and fine wines into a dizzying list of Arcadian possibilities:

Friday June 24 1692
Received of Mr. Samuel Cudworth for my Lady Masham £4-10-0 and
then delivered up his bond for £50-0-0 due to my Lady which was in
her brothers name and taken a bond of him for the said fifty pounds in
my name which is to be countersigned to me for £50 of the £100 I lent
Sir Francis upon his bond upon this day below
Sent my Lady Masham by Lenham
a parasol
a split bongrace
6 pair of gloves
all bought for me by Mrs. R. Smithby

Tues. Jul. 18 1693
To Oates—paid by My Lady Masham to a carrier for bringing down
my load of books, maps, pictures
£3-6-0
green hamper little cabinet in it
a white hamper

my great hair trunk with drawers marked
My Table with drawers
a cane chair with arms
an iron furnace in a barrel with tongues to it

Thurs. Nove. 9 1963
for L Masham
18¾ yards of crepe
3 yards of black glazed Holland
1 pair of black silk stockings
1 pair of black shoes

Sat. Dec. 22 1694
To Oates
Delivered to my Lady Masham
Mrs. Astels Proposal to the Ladies
Mr. Norris's Letters

Friday Aug. 6 1703
Lent my Lady Masham 0-10-0 to pay for Franks letting blood. repaid

Friday Nov. 13 1703
Item paid Mrs. Masham for 6 doz bottles of cider sent by Mrs. Knight
0-10-8[57]

Shortly before his death in October 1704, Locke arranged a huge wedding feast at Oates for his closest relative, Peter King, and his new bride. The seventy-two-year-old philosopher served a sumptuous meal of pheasants and turkey, rabbits and woodcocks, lobster and crayfish and oysters. Wine sent down from London graced the table, and Locke's favorites, young Esther and Francis Cudworth Masham, were there. Lady Masham presided as hostess, while Sir Francis acted the guest in his own house. It is tempting to imagine what Locke and Lady Masham may have felt then, seated opposite each other at this wedding celebration. For more than two decades they had taken care of each other, meeting the challenge Philoclea had given Philander nearly twenty-two years before: "Surely no small a thing as my Idea in Your Mind could never have put You in so good Humor."[58] Locke and Lady Masham, who read and wrote and argued and toasted each other at the wedding feast in their moated castle, shared what Lady Masham called the "Sight of a Place where Love, and Business, may be so well reconcil'd."[59]

NOTES

1. E. S. DeBeer, ed., *The Correspondence of John Locke* II (Oxford: Clarendon Press, 1976), No. 830. All subsequent references to the letters are from this edition.

2. For a description of the holdings, see Philip Long, *Summary Catalogue of the Lovelace Collection of the Papers of John Locke in the Bodleian Library* 8 (Oxford: Bibliographical Society, n.s., 1956).

3. See Locke's letters from Holland to Edward and Mary Clark in *Correspondence* II, Nos. 777, 782, 799, 803, 807, 822, 829, 844–45; III, Nos. 929, 943, 999, 1098; IV, No. 1370.

4. Bodley MSS. Locke c. 16, fols. 18, 27; c. 24, fol. 189.

5. See Irene Brown, "Domesticity, Feminism, and Friendship: Female Aristocratic Culture and Marriage in England, 1660–1760," *Journal of Family History* 8 (Winter 1982), 406–24.

6. Universitiets-Bibliotheek Amsterdam Remonstrants' MSS. J. 57a.

7. Bodley MSS. Locke c. 25, fols. 57–60, 62.

8. Remonstrants' MSS. J. 57a.

9. Maurice Cranston, *John Locke: A Biography* (New York: Macmillan, 1957), p. 5.

10. Remonstrants' MSS. J. 57a.

11. Remonstrants' MSS. J. 57a.

12. Remonstrants' MSS. J. 57a.

13. Remonstrants' MSS. J. 57a.

14. March 13, 1691, *Correspondence* IV, No. 1375.

15. Locke's *Essay on Human Understanding* was first published in Jean le Clerc's *Bibliothèque Universelle* in 1688 and in England in 1690.

16. Bodley MSS. Locke, fols. 5, 6.

17. Cudworth's most important treatise, *The True Intellectual System of the Universe* (1678), was published four years before his death. Locke's journal for 1693 shows him bringing a copy of Cudworth's book to Mrs. Cudworth, who lived at the Masham estate during her widowhood (Bodley MSS. Locke, fol. 10).

18. Locke outlined his objections to Cudworth and Smith in his journal for 1682 (Bodley MSS. Locke, fol. 6).

19. Bodley MSS. Locke, fol. 6, and letter to Damaris Cudworth [February 21, 1682], in *Correspondence* II, No. 687.

20. March 9, 1682, *Correspondence* II, No. 690.

21. February 16 [1682], *Correspondence* II, No. 684.

22. February 16 [1682], *Correspondence* II, No. 684.

23. Jane Flax, "The Conflict between Nurturance and Autonomy in Mother-Daughter Relationships and within Feminism," *Feminist Studies* 4 (June 1978), 171–92.

24. February 27 [1682], *Correspondence* II, No. 688.

25. February 27 [1682], *Correspondence* II, No. 688.

26. Letter to Locke, April 20, 1685, *Correspondence* II, No. 820.

27. Peter Laslett, "Masham of Otes: The Rise and Fall of an English Family," *History Today* 3 (1953), 536.

28. April 20 [1682], *Correspondence* II, No. 699.

29. August 29 [1682], *Correspondence* II, No. 730.

30. Esther Masham, who was sixteen when Locke moved to the Masham estate, kept a 335-page notebook of 143 letters from friends and family, including 12 letters to her from Locke. She explains in a note: "Mr. Locke drank nothing but water. What he calls his Brewhouse was a Stone in the form of a great Mortar of so spungy a stone th[t] water being put to use to run throu in a very short time and Straind the water from any dirt th[t] might be in it." Newberry MS. Esther Masham, July 21, 1699.

31. July 1 [1682], *Correspondence* II, No. 720.

32. Bodley MSS. Locke c. 32, fol. 17, in the hand of Locke's amanuensis, Sylvester Brounower, except for eight initial lines in Locke's hand.

33. Probably written early in 1685, enclosed in a letter to Locke, March 13, 1686, *Correspondence* II, no. 847.

34. March 13, 1686, *Correspondence* II, No. 847.

35. Cowley, "Discretion," verse 2 modified, in "The Mistress" (1668), quoted in October 8, 1684, *Correspondence* II, No. 787.

36. October 8, 1684, *Correspondence* II, No. 787.

37. January 15 [1685], *Correspondence* II, No. 805.

38. August 14 [1685], *Correspondence* II, No. 827.

39. Sir Francis Masham was the grandson of a first cousin of Oliver Cromwell. His first wife, Mary Scott de la Mézangère, was the daughter of Sir William Scott, a knight seated in Normandy at Rouen. This connection was an excellent one for the Cudworths—and, by extension, Locke—to make, since Cromwell's relatives were active in English political life during the reigns of William III and Queen Anne.

40. Mrs. Cudworth died on November 15, 1695. Damaris, with Locke's help, managed her inheritance. Some of the Masham estate papers remain, including "An Account continued of the Entrusted Estate since the Management of it Came into my hands to the 25th of Januarie 1700," Bodley MSS. Locke c. 16, fol. 68. An inventory of Mrs. Cudworth's possessions, including a portrait of Damaris, is listed in Bodley MSS. Locke c. 16, fol. 40. To my knowledge this portrait has not been found.

41. January 17, 1687, *Correspondence* III, No. 895.

42. August 14, 1685, *Correspondence* II, No. 827.

43. August 14, 1685, *Correspondence* II, No. 827.

44. In 1696 Lady Masham published *A Discourse concerning the Love of God*, anonymously dissenting from the views of John Norris and Mary Astell in *Letters concerning the Love of God* (1695). Norris attributed the *Discourse* to Locke, and the two philosophers exchanged heated letters, which Lady Masham seems to have mediated. See her letter to Locke, April 7, 1688, *Correspondence* III, No. 1040, for a similar definition of knowledge as that which leads to piety or goodness.

45. August 14, 1685, *Correspondence* II, No. 827.

46. January 17, 1687, *Correspondence* III, No. 896.

47. October 9, 1686, *Correspondence* III, No. 870.

48. November 14 [1685], *Correspondence* II, No. 837.

49. [December 7, 1686?], *Correspondence* III, No. 882.

50. September 15 [1685?], *Correspondence* II, No. 830.

51. September 15 [1685?], *Correspondence* II, No. 830.

52. November 14 [1685], *Correspondence* II, no. 837.

53. Locke willed most of his money and half of his books to young Francis Cudworth Masham. The inheritance was placed in Lady Masham's care until Francis came of age (Bodley MSS. Locke c. 25, fol. 71). Locke deposited his will with Lady Masham on May 4, 1702. Bodley MSS (Locke, fol. 10).

54. Bodley MSS. Locke c. 25, fol. 85.

55. Locke called Esther Masham "Laudabridis" ("Dib" for short), and "Totty was a nickname" given young Francis Masham "when he was a boy" (Newberry MS., Esther Masham, December 8, 1694).

56. Letter from Locke to Edward Clarke, December 3 [1691], *Correspondence* IV, No. 1433.

57. Bodley MSS. Locke, fol. 10, pp. 114, 141, 196–98, 201, 251, 265, 557, 563.

58. October 28 [1682], *Correspondence* II, No. 740.

59. August 25 [1684], *Correspondence* II No. 784.

Jonathan Swift, c. 1718, by Charles Jervas. Courtesy of the National Portrait Gallery, London

Swift and Stella as teacher and pupil: a nineteenth-century imaginative portrait by Margaret Isabel Dicksee (1858–1903). Percy Fitzgerald, Laurence Sterne, *Days of the Dandies*, 15 vols. (London: Edinburgh Press for the Grolier Society, n. d.), II. opp. p. 131.

The Secrets of
Swift and Stella

⌁ *W. B. Carnochan*

Esther Johnson (Swift's
Stella), Irish School,
Eighteenth Century.
Courtesy of the National
Gallery of Ireland

$\smile$*Jonathan Swift (1667–1745) was born in Ireland of Anglo-Irish parents. His father died before he was born. His nurse took him from his mother, for reasons that remain obscure, when he was a year old and did not return him for some three years. His adult relationships with women seem to reflect natural uncertainties about his parentage. The author of* A Tale of a Tub, The Battle of the Books, Gulliver's Travels, *and* A Modest Proposal, *he became England's most famous satirist. As a young man he spent some years in England, and later played an active role in politics as a polemical writer for the Tories. His reward for his services was the appointment as Dean of St. Patrick's Cathedral in Dublin (Anglican) in 1713; he lived in Ireland almost all the rest of his life.*

In his early twenties he met young Esther Johnson (1681–1728), then eight years old. She was the daughter of a housekeeper to Sir William Temple, Swift's employer and patron, into whose household he had come to live. At first he took a pedagogical interest in her education. Later they became lifelong friends; it was at Swift's suggestion that she and an elderly companion, Mrs. Rebecca Dingley, moved to Dublin. Swift called her "Stella." In their deeply enigmatic relationship one thing is certain: Each profoundly relied on the other.

49

⌒In *Finnegans Wake* Joyce merges Stella and Vanessa, Swift's "other woman," into the split personality of Issy, whom he modeled on an actual case of multiple personality.[1] Joyce's maneuver accurately captures Swift's habit of projecting onto others, especially on Stella, the brilliant instabilities of his own imagination. He made her in his own image, and she was his best audience. Yet he both courted and excluded her, as he did the audience of his satires. With her he tested the limits of creation, of language, and of feeling; in a relationship bound by rigid, self-imposed constraints, he learned how far he could go.

Stella was not the first or only woman to enter Swift's life: Not only did he get caught in a complicated, pedagogical flirtation with Esther Vanhomrigh, whom he called Vanessa, but in his late twenties he became engaged to marry a woman named Jane Waring, whom he called Varina. In the long run, however, there was only Stella, though the relationship was almost certainly never consummated.[2] Her given name was Hester Johnson, but she was known as Esther or Hetty. She was probably the daughter of a housekeeper to Swift's employer and patron, Sir William Temple, in whose household she grew up. Swift very likely saw her first in 1689, when she was eight and he, at the age of twenty-one, had just entered Temple's service. He gives a spare, yet telling account of their first acquaintance: "[I] had some share in her education, by directing what books she should read, and perpetually instructing her in the principles of honour and virtue; from which she never swerved in any one action or moment of her life."[3] When Swift says he had "some share" in her education, he altogether understates his investment. That investment is clearer when he says he was "perpetually" instructing her and that the effects were permanent. "Perpetually" catches the obsessive quality of Swift's pedagogical habits. He was, in an astute characterization, an inveterate and sometimes "furious" headmaster, and Esther Johnson was the only one of his pupils "whom he caught young enough to mould completely into his system,"[4] even to the point of teaching her, by precept or example, to write a hand uncannily like his own. He instructed her and, eventually, worshiped and exploited her, asserting the control over another that springs above all from fears of loss. For much of his life Swift suffered from what was probably Ménière's disease, a syndrome of the inner ear affecting balance and perception. The disease eerily matched his personality, for he was forever putting his readers off balance, yet forever hanging on. Stella was the person whom, as an extension of himself, he could least bear to lose.

Swift returned to Ireland after Temple's death in 1699, and two or three years later he persuaded Esther to join him. Her companion, Rebecca Dingley, came with her, and the two of them lived the rest of their lives in Ireland. Sometime in the course of the long, enigmatic relationship, Esther became "Stella"; Swift preferred his women as fictional, even allegorical, creations: Varina, Vanessa, Stella. Stella's health was never robust, and she died in January 1727/1728, in her forty-seventh year. Swift survived her by almost eighteen years.

The relationship caused tongues to wag almost from the start, and speculation has never ceased. Was there a secret marriage? What were the psychosexual reasons that made Swift so reluctant to marry? Were he and Stella related by illegitimate ties of blood? Were he and Vanessa lovers? When Swift talks about "coffee" in his letters to Vanessa, does he really mean sexual intercourse?[5] In his letters to Stella between 1710 and 1714—collected later as the *Journal to Stella*—how should we weigh his obvious reluctance to speak of his visits with Esther Vanhomrigh? And so on. It is wisest to sidestep this morass of touchy and unanswerable questions and concentrate instead on the written record in the *Journal to Stella* and in the poems Swift wrote for Stella between 1719 and 1727. At the same time, Swift's discourse is often as veiled as his private life, and neither the *Journal* nor the poems provide anything like perfect revelations. Still, they are the best, because almost the only, places to look.

To set the stage, however, one early episode needs retelling. It displays Swift's passionate need to assert control, especially control by indirection. It is not a pretty tale. While Swift was away from Ireland in London in 1703 and 1704, the Reverend William Tisdall, Fellow of Trinity College, Dublin, and an acquaintance of Swift's, proposed marriage to Stella. Evidence of Swift's reaction survives in letters he wrote Tisdall. He was acutely uncomfortable, even panicky.[6] He was also gratuitously nasty:

> You seem to be mighty proud (as you have reason if it be true) of the part you have in the ladies' good graces, especially of her you call the *party:* I am very much concerned to know it; but, since it is an evil I cannot remedy, I will tell you a story. A cast mistress went to her rival, and expostulated with her for robbing her of her lover. After a long quarrel, finding no good to be done; 'Well,' says the abdicated lady, 'keep him, and stop him in your a—.' 'No,' says the other, 'that will not be altogether so convenient; however, to oblige you, I will do something that is very near it.'—*Dixi.*[7]

The application of the nasty anecdote is far from clear. What is clear, however, is the unlovely instinct to assert possession by indirection and, in this case, by violation. Swift warns Tisdall off his property by soiling the territory. He degrades Stella by proclaiming, in effect, "I'll say what I want to and do with her (at least verbally) what I will." Keep away, Swift says to Tisdall, all the while affecting indifference. Though he claims to have no remedy, the casual ugliness of his response is itself the remedy. Poor Tisdall, who seems to have been an inoffensive sort, can hardly be blamed for being unhappy.

Exactly what happened next is a matter of inference, but Tisdall accused Swift of being "unfriendly, unkind, and unaccountable," and Swift answered him with a mixture of self-proclaimed candor and covert foot-dragging: "if my fortunes and humour served me to think of that state, I should certainly, among all persons on earth, make your choice; because I never saw that person whose conversation I entirely valued but hers." He claims that it "never once entered into my head to be an impediment to you." But then he casts doubt once more on his disinter-est: "but I judged it would, perhaps, be a clog to your rising in the world; and I did not conceive you were then rich enough to make yourself and her happy and easy." Finally, he claims a neutrality that Stella, above all others, could hardly have interpreted as real:

> I appeal to my letters to herself, whether I was your friend or no, in the whole concern; though the part I designed to act in it was purely passive, which is the utmost I will ever do in things of this nature, to avoid all reproach of any ill consequence, that may ensue in the variety of worldly accidents. Nay, I went so far both to her mother, herself, and I think to you, as to think it could not decently be broken; since I supposed the town had got it in their tongues, and therefore I thought it could not miscarry without some disadvantage to the lady's credit.[8]

Swift's biographer makes a convincing comment on this last bit of disin-genuous pleading: Telling a woman like Stella that a broken engage-ment will damage her reputation is a good way to persuade her that her true interests lie elsewhere.[9] In any event, the engagement came to noth-ing. It was the only time Stella may have come close to breaking out of the magic circle Swift drew around her and around himself. Yet perhaps the issue was never in doubt. If Swift practiced magic, Stella was a willing apprentice.

As his apprentice, she was privy to some, but not all, of the sorcer-er's mysteries. In the *Journal to Stella*, Swift unburdens himself to her and to Rebecca Dingley, but he also keeps part of himself (and not only his flirtation with Vanessa) back. When he was writing the letters that com-prise the *Journal*, Swift was deeply engaged in the secretive business of politics. He was the friend of the chief ministers, Robert Harley (later Earl of Oxford) and Henry St. John (later Viscount Bolingbroke). He negotiated differences between them and was vital to the survival of their Tory ministry. To Stella and Rebecca, across the Irish channel, he played himself but also played the master. They were his audience, rapt apprentices, listening carefully.

Swift's dominant psychic strategy in the *Journal* is to play with secrecy. It is not just that he puts on a conspiratorial air when he talks about the intricacies of statecraft but that the air of mystery is thick throughout.[10] This is conspicuously true of his "little language," the combination of code and baby talk, half embarrassing and half endearing, that runs through the *Journal.* What were the uses of the little language? Intimacy, of course; and it has even been claimed that the frequent blottings out of passages in the little language were themselves part of a code that Stella would have understood, while Rebecca would not. Early in 1712 Swift wrote: "so adieu deelest Md Md Md FW FW Me Me Me Lele I can say lele yet oo see—Fais I dont conceal a bitt. as hope savd."[11] ("Md" = "My dear" or "My dears"; "FW" = "Farewell"; "Me" may stand for "Madame elderly," i.e., Rebecca Dingley; "Lele" is a puzzle here and elsewhere.) Among some other evidence, the claim here that "faith, I don't conceal a bit" led one scholar-detective, Émile Pons, to believe not only that the blottings out were part of a code, but that in this case the *lack* of any blotting out was the important thing. If one breaks the code, Pons concluded, Swift's secret marriage to Stella is revealed. "*Les ratures de Swift,*" he writes, "*sont une écriture de Swift,*" and we remember Derrida.[12] But in fact, Pons is probably wrong about the code. It is typical of Swift to claim openness in a language with concealment at its heart. The strategy exactly matches that of his satires, which implicitly claim frankness and ready meanings, yet baffle readers, and by design. Swift was intrigued by codes: In the "Voyage to Laputa," Gulliver explains that in the Kingdom of Tribnia (Britain), political plots are proven against the innocent by a spurious cryptography that deciphers "a Close-stool to signify a Privy-Council; a Flock of Geese, a Senate; a lame Dog, an Invader; the Plague, a standing Army; a Buzard, a Minister," and so on until, finally, "a running Sore" is artfully interpreted as "the Administration."[13] A spurious cryptography gives metaphorically accurate readings, yet the innocent are (presumably) not the less innocent despite the satiric accuracy of the interpretations. Behind Swift's codes lie still other codes. It must have pleased him to be able to correct Stella's spelling of "Secreet" (*JS* II, 392). As they read Swift's letters, the ladies in Ireland surely found themselves sometimes at a loss for understanding; Swift intended it that way.

Furthermore, the *Journal* has a dreamlikeness (part of its appeal to Joyce) that makes the familiar strange and must sometimes have made Stella uneasy.[14] On October 14, 1710, Swift tells her of his dream the night before. It is disturbing:

> Lord, I dreamt of Stella, &c. so confusedly last night, and that we saw dean
> Bolton and Sterne go into a shop; and she bid me call them to her, and
> they proved to be two parsons I know not; and I walked without till she was
> shifting, and such stuff, mixt with much melancholy and uneasiness, and
> things not as they should be, and I know not how: and it is now an ugly
> gloomy morning. [*JS* I, 56.]

Though it is all very well to unburden oneself of bad dreams by telling
them to a loved one, matters change perceptibly when that person is part
of the dream. How unsettling to be a sinister participant in someone
else's dream life. Swift catches Stella in a web of uncertainty, even danger, for which she is made to bear much of the responsibility: "I dreamt
of Stella . . . she bid me call them to her." Nothing is clear or stable. The
two clergymen turn out not to be who they seem. Stella's presence is
ambiguous: "I walked without till she was shifting . . ." "shifting" with
impatience—but Swift hints at some dreamlike metamorphosis of her
identity.[15] He knows something is wrong but cannot specify it: "things
not as they should be, and I know not how." Swift has drawn Stella deep
into the structure of his own anxiety. In fact, she is a scapegoat, having
bid him summon friends who were not who they seemed. Resentment
colors the dream, and Stella can hardly have missed the aggressive feelings that underlie Swift's anxiety. In the dream he replicates the conditions of his usual relationship, as satirist, with his reader.

But if his reader, whether Stella or ourselves, is partly an object of
resentment and an occasion for mystification, that same reader becomes
Swift's confidant—the person to whom he opens up his secret life. In the
Journal he is aggressive, petulant, engaging, boyish. The friend of ministers not only lisps in baby talk, he boxes the ears of his servant, chides his
superiors, tells dirty jokes, and behaves with the self-assigned privileges
of adolescence. What is more, he has a wonderful time doing so. His
servant Patrick, often drunk and disorderly, was a source of constant
annoyance, and once when Patrick had gone away with the house key,
Swift lost patience altogether: "Then came in Patrick. I went up, shut the
chamber-door, and gave him two or three swinging cuffs on the ear, and
I have strained the thumb of my left hand with pulling him, which I did
not feel until he was gone. He was plaguily afraid and humbled" (*JS* II,
375–76). This exuberant minor violence, ending with Swift suffering a
sprained thumb, mirrors the common structure of his satires, in which
the satirist, the instigator of violence, is himself satirized. A simple cuff
on the ears is an uncomplicated way of working out feelings that in other
situations take more intricate shape.

Swift was particularly touchy about his relationship with those in
positions of authority, and the *Journal* recounts incidents that show him

asserting a petulantly boyish independence. On April 11, 1711, he dined with the secretary of state, Henry St. John, who seemed, in Swift's words, "terribly down and melancholy" (*JS* I, 229). Brooding on what had happened, Swift decided to take it as a personal insult. The next time he saw St. John, he read him a lecture:

> I made him a very proper speech, told him I observed he was much out of temper; that I did not expect he would tell me the cause, but would be glad to see he was in better; and one thing I warned him of, Never to appear cold to me, for I would not be treated like a school-boy; that I felt too much of that in my life already. . . . [*JS* I, 230.]

The lecture went on in the same offended vein, and St. John must have been taken aback, but he seems to have known his man. "He took all right; said, I had reason, vowed nothing ailed him but sitting up whole nights at business, and one night at drinking," and then he asked Swift to dine with him to make amends. Swift could not bring himself to accept the invitation, and he seems puzzled and embarrassed by his own prickly recalcitrance: "I don't know, but I would not" (*JS* I, 230). He may claim not to know his motives, but we think we do, and so must have Stella.

In fact, much of Swift's private history can be read in and between the lines of his lecture to the powerful secretary of state. In the text of the *Journal*, following the telltale remark that "I felt too much of that in my life already," comes what is probably an editor's interpolation: "(meaning from Sir William Temple)." Interpolation or no, it is certainly accurate. Swift's father had died before he was born, he had been taken from his mother by a nurse at a very young age, and Temple was the first parent he had ever really known. But finding a surrogate father, especially a demanding one who sometimes treats you like a child at the age of twenty-one, is a mixed blessing.[16] The experience with Temple, combined with the deprivations of his childhood, seems to have fixed Swift's self-image as a boy asserting his manhood or, sometimes, playfully assenting to his childishness. And if Temple was once his demanding surrogate father, the Stella of Swift's creation served as a loving surrogate mother, in whose presence he could preen himself on his boyish good behavior as well as his boyish sensitivities. He writes her usually sitting in bed at night, as if she were there, like Gulliver's nurse in Brobdingnag, to tuck him in. "Your mother's cakes are very good," he tells her, "and one of them serves me for a breakfast, and so I'll go sleep like a good boy" (*JS* I, 105). Or, "I was to day with my Printer, to give him a little Pamphlet I have written. . . . if it succeeds I will tell you of it, otherwise not. we had a prodigious Thaw to day, as bad as rain, yet I walked like a good Boy all the way" (*JS* II, 605–606).

Yet what the boy Swift also needed, as much as a mother, was an accomplice in his naughtiness, someone willing to play with him on his own terms. Even Stella's misbehavior therefore endears her to him: "I have been scribbling this morning, and I believe shall hardly fill this side to-day, but send it as it is; and it is good enough for naughty girls that won't write to a body, and to a good boy like Presto" (*JS* I, 22). As the mother, Stella had to be pure of mind; Swift tells her he has received a letter from a woman friend "that has quite turned my stomach against her: no less than two nasty jests in it with dashes to suppose them" (*JS* I, 118–19). As the naughty girl companion, Stella has a mind as quick and dirty as Swift's, and he plays up to it shamelessly: "Why do you trouble yourself, Mistress Stella, about my *instrument?*" he asks with pseudo-gravity (*JS* I, 34). (His "instrument," shorn of italics, was the commission he had brought with him from Ireland to solicit for the Irish Church remission of certain ecclesiastical taxes.) And: "When I pass the Mall in the evening it is prodigious to see the number of ladies walking there; and I always cry shame at the ladies of Ireland, who never walk at all, as if their legs were of no use, but to be *laid aside*" (*JS* I, 270). And: "to-day, I was brought privately to Mr. Harley, who received me with the greatest respect and kindness imaginable: he has appointed me an hour on Saturday at four, afternoon, when I will open my business to him; which expression I would not use if I were a woman. I know you smoakt it; but I did not till I writ it" (*JS* I, 41). All these jokes implicate Stella and make her Swift's guilty partner, even the one who leads him astray. It is she who has so much curiosity about his instrument. If not exactly an Irish lady, she is a lady living in Ireland on whom he urged his own obsessional devotion to walking.[17] Worst of all, she catches the wordplay about opening the business to Harley before he does: Swift is the innocent victim of an errant pen; Stella has the nasty mind. She is also complicitous in another joke with Harley as its victim. Swift explains how well Harley has treated him, then contrives a situation that leaves his friend with the embarrassment of watching this difficult, sexually ambiguous brat exhibit himself. Like Gulliver in Book I of his *Travels*, Swift displays some of his private equipment to a receptive audience, at the same time as another audience is watching. Swift the exhibitionist and trickster is in charge.

The mystery and the exuberance of the *Journal* both reflect the heady feelings of Swift's years in London; in such a mood, he was a great performer. But when he was rewarded, near the end of the Tory ministry, with the deanship of St. Patrick's, Dublin, it was not what he had hoped for. He had wanted an English bishopric. And when the Tories went out of power on Queen Anne's death in 1714, Swift's career behind the political scenes came to an end. Being dean of St. Patrick's and being in Ireland meant a sad comedown, and the last thirty years of his life were increasingly a dark time. In these years he wrote *Gulliver's Travels* (1726), attended to his duties as a dean, railed against English oppression of Ireland, railed against Irish indifference, and alternately cursed his luck and made the best of it. The poems he wrote for Stella between 1719 and 1727 have mostly to do with aging and with prospects of death. They are more intimate than the *Journal,* for Swift no longer plays to a distant audience. Immediate and stark, they blend his ambiguous worship of Stella with still more private needs. And in the very last of them, he briefly achieves a self that is new for him, in that one instance overcoming his neediness and his impulse to exercise control. Finally he shares with Stella an equality of feeling. Taken all together, the poems make an extraordinary revelation of someone most reluctant to reveal himself.

In the first of them, Swift is still the sorcerer and the pedagogue, as well as Stella's reverent admirer:

> Stella this Day is thirty four,
> (We won't dispute a Year or more)
> However Stella, be not troubled,
> Although thy Size and Years are doubled,
> Since first I saw Thee at Sixteen
> The brightest Virgin of the Green,
> So little is thy Form declin'd
> Made up so largely in thy Mind.
> Oh, would it please the Gods to split
> Thy Beauty, Size, and Years, and Wit,
> No Age could furnish out a Pair
> Of Nymphs so gracefull, Wise and fair
> With half the Lustre of Your Eyes,
> With half thy Wit, thy Years and Size:
> And then before it grew too late,
> How should I beg of gentle Fate,
> (That either Nymph might have her Swain,)
> To split my Worship too in twain.[18]

In fact Stella turned thirty-eight in 1719, so the offhanded "year or more" of the second line is an understatement (probably intended as such, though Swift was seldom accurate when he referred either to Stella's age or to how long he had known her); he first saw her long before she was sixteen; but if he *had* first seen her at sixteen, and if her age had doubled, she would have been thirty-two. With this temporal muddle Swift wittily announces that he will not be captive to time and, therefore, neither will Stella. In treating the love poet's oldest theme, he vanquishes time by ridicule, not by direct challenge: the years have passed, and Stella has grown fat, but neither matters because the poet chases time offstage. He is still in charge.

Being in charge, Swift takes a risk even greater than pointing comically at Stella's waistline. In the enigmatic context of his relationship with her, the casual mock-pastoralism of line six, "The brightest Virgin of the Green," loses its innocence. There are only two possibilities: Either Stella is still a virgin at the age of thirty-something, or not. If not, we probably succumb to vulgar curiosity: Who? When? Surely not Swift? But in the more likely event that she is still a virgin, the pastoral compliment has a double edge. It is one thing to praise a woman, in early middle age, as having been the brightest virgin of the green, but if she is virginal still, the compliment may evaporate in irony; what was desirable then seems less evidently so now. Moreover, the poet in this case bears the blame, if it is a matter of blame. We may feel some cruelty in this playfulness, but it goes together with Swift's godlike handling of temporal reality in the poem. Indeed the "Gods" of line nine, whom he conceives as splitting Stella into two, are formed in the poet's own image: They manipulate the world, joke with it, alter it at will. They have sportive imaginations; they might (for example) have invented the little people and the big people of *Gulliver's Travels*. They also meet Swift's special needs by giving him two Stellas: the one to worship and the other to do with as he will.

Swift is never so lighthearted again in the poems, but even in his darkest moments he does not altogether despair. The grimmest of the poems is that of 1723/1724, "on the Day of her Birth, but not on the Subject, when I was sick in bed."[19] Swift asks: "Tormented with incessant pains, / Can I devise poetic strains?" (1–2). He remembers a better day "when I could yearly pay / My verse on Stella's native day" (3–4). And then, in two of the most painful lines he ever wrote, "But now, unable grown to write, / I grieve she ever saw the light" (5–6). There were times, and this is one of them, when Swift believed life so painful that it would be better never to have been born (or to have been sold for food at the age of a year, just as the modest proposer says). Here it is as if, having created Stella in his life and in his poetry and finding himself unable now to write and therefore to create, he has become her destroyer. Yet he had great resilience, and he draws back, "Ungrateful; since to her I owe / That I these pains can undergo" (7–8), to celebrate now not her birthday but her angelic ministering. Near the end comes a promise of recovery and an echo of boyish playfulness:

> Whatever base returns you find
> From me, Dear Stella, still be kind.

> In your own heart you'll reap the fruit,
> 'Tho I continue still a brute.
> But when I once am out of pain,
> I promise to be good again. . . . [29–34.]

Swift admits he is being very naughty but promises to behave himself better when the pain is gone. This reassertion, in pain, of his self-image as a little boy brings back, however faintly, the childish exuberance, as well as the childish dependency, of the *Journal to Stella*. Typically Swift recovers life, ironically, from the grip of negation.[20]

In the last of the birthday poems, however, written less than a year before Stella died, he sets aside boyishness, bantering, and his own needs. He speaks in a new voice:[21]

> This Day, whate'er the Fates decree,
> Shall still be kept with Joy by me:
> This Day then, let us not be told,
> That you are sick, and I grown old,
> Nor think on our approaching Ills,
> And talk of Spectacles and Pills;
> To morrow will be Time enough
> To hear such mortifying Stuff. [1–8.]

Notwithstanding the characteristic pun—"mortifying stuff"—the feeling here is direct and simple. As in the first of the birthday poems, almost ten years before, Swift announces victory over time: Tomorrow will be time enough to think about age, death, spectacles, pills. In this poem, however, it is not Swift the magician at work, for he shares Stella's lot, which is simply the human condition. Though sick and old, they are together, joined against the world and against time: "This Day then, let us not be told, / That you are sick, and I grown old."

Swift's sportive and ironic play, his imaginative sallies, his insistent childishness, his impulse to dominate—all the material of his friendship with Stella and of his quarrel with the world—were defensive gestures; by such means he insured himself against loss. To that extent, the liberty of wit, on which he prided himself, was itself a constraint. But here, coming face to face with loss, he manages to release himself from that last constraint and speak to Stella with a new freedom and security:

> Yet, since from Reason may be brought
> A better and more pleasing Thought,
> Which can in spite of all Decays,
> Support a few remaining Days:
> From not the gravest of Divines,
> Accept for once some serious Lines. [9–14.]

What follows in the poem is less satisfying; it consists of an effort to argue Stella into accepting the inevitable while also looking forward to a life after death. The trouble is that Swift himself does not seem totally convinced there will be another life. Yet he manages to sustain a joyfulness, if at a price:

> Yet you, while Time is running fast,
> Can look with Joy on what is past. [17–18.]

And:

> Virtue in her daily Race,
> Like *Janus*, bears a double Face;
> Looks back with Joy where she has gone,
> And therefore goes with Courage on. [73–76.]

The cost shows through the insistently logical "therefore." Swift presents Stella, as though in a rigid demonstration, with the need to go on courageously. To do anything else would be unworthy of her because illogical—but this is a dogged pedagogy at best. In fact, Swift the teacher had finally learned more of value than his pupil, for she enables him at last to step outside himself: "This Day, whate'er the Fates decree, / Shall still be kept with Joy by me."

During the summer of 1726, while he was on a visit to London, Swift heard that Stella had taken a very bad turn. He wrote the Reverend John Worrall: "ever since I left you my Heart hath been so sunk, that I have not been the same Man, nor ever shall be again, but drag on a wretched Life, till it shall please God to call me away."[22] A few days later he wrote another clergyman friend: "I think there is not a greater folly than that of entering into too strict and particular a friendship, with the loss of which a man must be absolutely miserable; but especially at an age when it is too late to engage in a new friendship."[23] These anticipatory cries of pain, addressed to expectations of loss rather than to Stella's suffering, seem to have released Swift from self-pity. She recovered for a brief time, he wrote the poem celebrating her last birthday, and when she died, he was in control of himself:

> This day, being Sunday, January 28th, 1727–8, about eight o'clock at night, a servant brought me a note, with an account of the death of the truest, most virtuous, and valuable friend, that I, or perhaps any other person ever was blessed with. She expired about six in the evening of this day; and, as soon as I am left alone, which is about eleven at night, I resolve, for my own satisfaction, to say something of her life and character.[24]

The price of control is a certain anesthesia of the heart, reflected in the conventionality, to the point of deceptiveness, of Swift's first account of Stella's "life and character." In that account Stella becomes a monument to his pedagogy and good taste, more a figurine than a real person. She is perfection. Though sickly until she was fifteen, she "grew into perfect health." She was "one of the most beautiful, graceful, and agreeable young women in London," although, as Swift has to confess, "only a little too fat." Never was a woman born "with better gifts of mind." Her advice was always "the best." Her gracefulness, "somewhat more than human in every motion, word, and action." And this Stella is not the same woman he wrote to in the *Journal*. Now he tells the world: "It was not safe nor prudent in her presence, to offend in the least word against modesty; for she then gave full employment to her wit, her contempt and resentment, under which even stupidity and brutality were forced to sink into confusion; and the guilty person, by her future avoiding him like a bear or a satyr, was never in a way to transgress a second time." Then he describes how Stella, annoyed by the "double meanings" of some would-be wit, lectured the poor fellow unmercifully, telling him that if ever she visited his house, she would be sure to ask at the door if he were home so that she might avoid him.[25] It does not seem likely Swift invented this episode; Stella's public behavior was probably as he describes it. Any deceptiveness in his account stems from the public front they both maintained before the world. If he had not found the right person to embody, and embrace, his public values, while at the same time maternally letting him act out, in private, his part as a vulgar-minded little boy, enchanted with double meanings, he might have broken under the strain. Perhaps the irreverent release his satires afforded would have been enough. Perhaps not.

Stella's funeral took place the evening of January 30, 1727/1728. Had Swift stayed in his bedroom in the deanery, he would have seen the light in the cathedral, where the funeral was held. He "removed into another apartment" so he would not have to see.[26] He is being very careful and secretive again, now that Stella is dead. For her part, Stella seems to have cherished that carefulness and, by doing so, to have opened avenues of expression to Swift that no one else could—even, briefly, to have enabled him to defy time and death directly and with a kind of joy. Whether it finally seemed worth it to her is another question, beyond the reach of our evidence.

NOTES

1. James S. Atherton, *The Books at the Wake* (New York: Viking, 1960), p. 117.

2. Irvin Ehrenpreis's biography is essential reading for anyone who wants to track the intricacies of Swift's relationships with women: *Swift: The Man, His Works, and the Age* (Cambridge: Harvard University Press, 1962–1983). See especially I. 165–68; II, 16–22; and II, 635–61. Ehrenpreis's view of Swift's character can only be called, at times, unsympathetic; e.g., "By attaching himself to an invalid [Stella], a man can relieve himself of angry impulses without openly admitting them, because the beloved is always suffering a punishment that he has not administered. Without feeling guilty, therefore, he can indulge a kind of sadism, even prolonging the existence of the woman in order to prolong his participation in her suffering" (II, 661). It is difficult, when thinking about Swift's life with Stella, to steer between the dangers of sentimentalism and dogmatic stringency.

3. "On the Death of Mrs. Johnson," in Herbert Davis, ed., *The Prose Works of Jonathan Swift* (Oxford: Blackwell, 1939–1968), V, 227.

4. Nigel Dennis, *Jonathan Swift* (New York: Macmillan, 1964), pp. 62, 63.

5. For a brief bibliographical introduction to these tangles, see Milton Voigt, *Swift and the Twentieth Century* (Detroit: Wayne State University Press, 1964), pp. 152–55.

6. Cf. Ehrenpreis, *Swift: The Man, His Works, and the Age* II, 138.

7. Harold Williams, ed., *The Correspondence of Jonathan Swift* (Oxford: Clarendon Press, 1963–1965), I, 41–42 (February 3, 1703/1704).

8. Ibid. I, 44, 45, 46 (April 20, 1704).

9. Ehrenpreis, *Swift: The Man, His Works, and the Age* II, 137–38.

10. Cf. Claudia Ruth Stillman, "Swift in Wonderland: The Language of Dream in the *Journal to Stella*," *Literature and Psychology* 25 (1975), 108–16.

11. Harold Williams, ed. *Journal to Stella* (Oxford: Clarendon Press, 1948), II, 529. Hereafter, *JS;* subsequent citations appear in the text.

12. Quoted by Harold Williams, *JS* I, liv. The blottings are normally explained as having been made later on by Swift, or an editor, to hide various intimacies (*JS* I, liii).

13. Davis, *The Prose Works of Jonathan Swift* XI, 191.

14. Stillman observes that "the predominant tone of the *Journal* is that of dream-fantasy." "Swift in Wonderland: The Language of Dream in the *Journal to Stella*," p. 109.

15. Ibid., p. 111: "As in dream, identities in the *Journal* are frighteningly fluid."

16. In a powerful essay on the *Tale of a Tub,* John Traugott studies Swift's relationship to Temple with much insight. See C. J. Rawson, ed., *Focus: Swift* (London: Sphere Books, 1971), pp. 76–120, especially pp. 83–93. Also see A. C. Elias, Jr., *Swift at Moorpark: Problems in Biography and Criticism* (Philadelphia: University of Pennsylvania Press, 1982).

17. Swift believed walking was therapeutic, but his devotion to it was even more than that of a health faddist. He regularly walked between his Chelsea lodgings and the house of Vanessa's mother, nearer to town. "I set out about

sun-set," he reports, "and get here in something less than an hour; it is two good miles and just five thousand seven hundred and forty-eight steps; so there is four miles a day walking" (*JS* I, 270)!

18. Harold Williams, ed., *The Poems of Jonathan Swift,* 2nd ed. (Oxford: Clarendon Press, 1958), II, 721–22.

19. Ibid. II, 754–55.

20. On the way in which Swift seizes being out of annihilation, see W. B. Carnochan, "The Consolations of Satire," in Clive Probyn, ed., *The Art of Jonathan Swift* (London: Vision Press, 1978), pp. 19–42.

21. *The Poems of Jonathan Swift* II, 763–66.

22. Williams, *The Correspondence of Jonathan Swift* III, 141 (July 15, 1726).

23. Ibid., III, 145 (to the Reverend James Stopford, July 18, 1726).

24. "On the Death of Mrs. Johnson," Davis, *The Prose Works of Jonathan Swift* V, 227.

25. Ibid. V, 227, 228, 234.

26. Ibid. V, 229.

Samuel Johnson, 1756, by Sir Joshua Reynolds. Courtesy of the National Portrait Gallery, London

"Under the Dominion of *Some* Woman"

THE FRIENDSHIP OF SAMUEL JOHNSON AND HESTER THRALE

⌒ Martine Watson Brownley

Mrs. Thrale and her daughter Hester (Queeney) in 1781, by Sir Joshua Reynolds. Gift of Lord Beaverbrook. Beaverbrook Art Gallery, Fredericton, N. B., Canada. Photo: Lewis Nadeau

In English literary history, the later eighteenth century is known as the Age of Johnson, after Samuel Johnson (1709–1784), the most famous literary figure of the time. In addition to his monumental Dictionary of the English Language, *Johnson was known for his poems, his periodical essays, the short fictional* Rasselas, *his edition of Shakespeare, and numerous biographical and critical works. Equally renowned for his conversation, which James Boswell immortalized in his great biography, Johnson dominated his age by the force of his personality as well as his writings.*

Early in 1765, during a period of acute physical and psychological crisis, Johnson met Henry and Hester Thrale (1741–1821), who gave him what became in effect a second home at their residences in Southwark and at Streatham. The amazingly reciprocal friendship of Johnson and Mrs. Thrale, which began when he was approaching fifty-seven and she was twenty-five, continued for almost twenty years, transforming the worlds of both. Two lonely people who seemed instinctively to bring out the best in each other, they collaborated on everything from poetry to chemical experiments and charitable projects. Her conversation, care, wit, and love produced an environment for Johnson that sustained him and allowed him to write the Lives of the Poets, *his last and greatest critical work. He in turn shaped her mind and was the major influence on her own subsequent career as an author. Although Johnson's and Thrale's friendship dissolved after her marriage to Gabriel Piozzi in 1784, its lasting results can be seen in the works of both.*

⌒ "It appears to me that no Man can live his Life quite thro', without being at *some* period of it under the Dominion of *some* Woman,"[1] Hester Thrale wrote in her diary in 1779. After mentioning Pope and Martha Blount as well as Swift and Stella, she proceeded to her own relationship with Samuel Johnson. The fact that part of Thrale's "Dominion" over Johnson involved maternal elements has long been recognized. Their contemporary Anna Seward attributed Johnson's feelings for Thrale partly to "cupboard love," the desire to be nurtured; recently W. J. Bate has shown how repressed elements of infantilism in Johnson's character emerged when he became close to Thrale.[2] Obviously the maternal element was only one among many which created the remarkable friendship that sustained both Johnson and Thrale for eighteen years. Like all good relationships, theirs functioned so well because each of them simultaneously filled several roles for the other. Yet because Johnson's need for the kind of physical and emotional care that mothering has traditionally furnished and Thrale's need to provide it were integral to the friendship, analysis of elements specifically maternal can offer some new perspectives illuminating the dynamics of their relationship. In particular, it is the maternal aspect of the relationship that most clearly shows the limits which ultimately destroyed it.

Although Thrale was a versatile women who in various circumstances showed considerable talents as a businesswoman, society hostess, author, and political assistant, her role as a mother was central to her character. She possessed a formidable model in her own mother, who, like Thrale herself, had been unhappy in her marriage and perhaps partly in compensation had devoted herself to her child. "For true Love of one's Mother & real preference of her to all human Kind, I believe I am a singular Example,"[3] Thrale wrote, and she tried to follow in Mrs. Salusbury's footsteps. She bore twelve children for Henry Thrale, only four of whom survived to adulthood. Her diaries show the enormous amount of time she spent "tutoring, caressing, or what is still more useful, . . . having one's Children about one."[4] In retrospect she could write that for twenty years she had "cared for nothing else" except her children.[5] She was greatly disappointed when after two miscarriages she was unable to have a child with Gabriel Piozzi, her second husband. Outside of her immediate family, she almost instinctively sought people to mother. She took in and cared for the children of friends, relatives, and servants.[6] She and Piozzi adopted his nephew, whom she wrote to as the "Son of my Soul."[7] Throughout her life Thrale kept adopting maternal roles; she instinctively responded both to actual children and to the children alive within the adults she knew. After her Johnsonian years, she mothered Mrs. Siddons. Still later she addressed the young actor William Augustus Conway as a son, and he responded by calling her "his adopted mother" and "his more than mother."[8] What Thrale did for Johnson is part of a larger pattern of mothering which marks her entire life.

Two major maternal figures stand out in Johnson's life before he met Thrale. His mother, Sarah, has sometimes received a rather bad press from critics, partially because blaming her is required for any standard psychoanalytical interpretation of Johnson. In addition, critics tend to find Michael Johnson, an energetic bookseller with some intellectual interests, a more congenial figure than the wife "unacquainted with books"[9] who looked down on her husband's family and who, without any understanding of business, constantly badgered her husband about his financial affairs. None of these traits necessarily produce a bad mother, and in fact Sarah Johnson was a devoted one. She assiduously watched over Sam even while he was under the care of a wet nurse. She exerted all her power to insure that his many childhood diseases received every possible attention; when he was sick, she spoiled him with expensive coffee that she could not easily afford. Despite her intellectual shortcomings, she was proud of her son's mind and fostered it, listening to his lessons and encouraging him when he found problems with Latin verbs. Noting that Sarah came from a family that included some educated and distinguished members, A. L. Reade suggests that Johnson's mental development was not due solely to his father.[10] His mother was an extremely pious woman, to whom the editors of Johnson's diaries give credit for "some ingenuity" in his religious education.[11]

Johnson himself in later years remembered his childhood as unhappy, placing the blame on poverty, parental incompatibility, and sibling rivalries.[12] Whatever domestic unpleasantness existed was hardly Sarah's fault alone. Her husband's financial ineptness created their poverty. Johnson described his father as "pious and worthy," but also as "wrong-headed, positive," and vain within the limits of his straitened circumstances.[13] Michael Johnson cannot have been an easy man to have at home. As a child, Johnson said, he was shown off by his father until he "absolutely loathed his father's caresses"; as a man he traced his terrible melancholy, what he described as his "morbid disposition both of Body and Mind," to his father, whom he also resembled in stature and build.[14] Johnson was never so overt in blaming his mother. Indeed, throughout his life he constantly expressed reverential affection for her. Nevertheless, when everything has been said in her favor as a conscientious mother, Sarah Johnson still emerges as a good woman severely limited

by the narrowness natural enough in a provincial housewife. Such limitations partly account for Johnson's statement that "I did not respect my
mother, though I loved her."[15] He could clearly have appreciated her
without desiring her company. However, deeper problems with her are
indicated by his failure to visit her for two decades after leaving
Lichfield, and particularly by his inability to return there to see her when
she was dying.[16] Unfortunately, the relatively scanty evidence now available on Johnson's early life remains extremely unclear about the actual
nature of his difficulties with his mother. Some critics have postulated
unresolved Oedipal conflict as the source of Johnson's well-known psychological problems and nervous disorders in later life,[17] but their con-
jectures, which would be fairly risky even if made by clinical analysts with
extensive experience, have so far been unsatisfactorily speculative.

Johnson's marriage to a woman twenty years his senior certainly
suggests a tendency to seek mothering, although other considerations
were also involved in the union.[18] His wife, who, like his mother, came
from a good family, was unlike Sarah Johnson physically and intellectually. Blond and buxom, Elizabeth Porter Johnson, whom Sam called
"Tetty," possessed literary acumen and considerable satirical wit. Like
Sarah, she had the piety which he prized in all of the women around
him. Her substantial dowry offered financial security for Johnson at
first. Despite their love for each other, the marriage was not entirely
happy. Ridiculed in various recorded comments of Johnson's contemporaries, Tetty, like Sarah, has received some rather rough treatment
from critics. Fortunately, W. J. Bate's balanced analysis in his recent
biography of Johnson has begun to set the record straight; he shows how
Tetty as well as Johnson suffered in a marriage marred by financial
difficulties, domestic differences, and sexual problems.[19] In spite of her
gradual withdrawal from him in later years of the marriage, Johnson
throughout his life expressed constant devotion to Tetty, just as he had
to Sarah. If neither had been a mother figure entirely satisfactory to
him, he remained grateful to both.

In Thrale, Johnson found a woman who combined many of the
best traits in his two former maternal figures, while lacking their negative qualities. Thrale's physical proportions and her general appearance
somewhat resembled Sarah Johnson's;[20] like Sarah, she anxiously pampered him. Although Thrale's social status, like Sarah's, was higher than
that of her husband, and though her diaries show her keen awareness of
birth, she never harped on her lineage to Mr. Thrale as Johnson's
mother had done at home. Thrale had the piety that characterized both
Sarah and Tetty. She possessed the financial acumen Sarah lacked, along
with intellectual interests. Though she had Tetty's excellent mind, she

never denied Johnson her companionship, as his wife had. She even showed traces of Tetty's tendency to play the coquette.

In addition to her resemblances to past maternal figures, it was important to Johnson that Thrale herself was actually a mother. When writing of his distress over her daughter's illness, he added: "I have much consolation from the maternal and domestick character of your dear letters."[21] Thrale as a mother gave Johnson access to a family life unlike any he had previously known. If Johnson appreciated Thrale's resemblances to and differences from his previous mother figures, he equally liked the way she mothered. Thrale saw her role as a mother in key ways that matched Johnson's interests and filled his particular needs.

For Thrale, mothering included a strong intellectual component. Following her own mother, who had energetically tutored her, Thrale devoted ceaseless effort and energy to educating her children. The nursery was for her always a schoolroom, and even after sending two of her girls away to boarding school, she commented, "When they come home they must be taught to think; a Lesson never learned in youth but of one's Mother."[22] In Thrale's mothering of Johnson, her intellect was also crucial, although obviously she was in no sense teaching him. However, sheer brainpower and scholarliness were never as important to Johnson as intellectual liveliness and range of interest, both of which Thrale possessed. Johnson tended to value brains in terms of the immediate company they provided for him, and this Thrale, with her ready colloquial wit and lively curiosity, abundantly supplied. They translated Boethius together, competed in turning epigrams and verses, and discussed the proof sheets of the *Lives of the Poets* together with the family over breakfast. Describing his "Congreve" in a letter to her as "one of the best of the little lives," Johnson added, "but then I had your conversation."[23] She shared Johnson's intellectual enthusiasm, if not his intellectual depth. Though probably never significantly shaping Johnson's ideas (which she also failed to do with her children), Thrale provided the kind of intellectual stimulation that led Johnson to compliment her for keeping "all my faculties in constant play."[24]

Thrale's mothering involved tending the body as well as the mind. She shared Johnson's interest in medicine, and the succession of childhood diseases in her family offered tragically ample scope for her talents. Indeed, when her *Children's Book* was published in 1977, it was reviewed in a British medical journal because it contained so much information about the Thrale children's physical problems and her remedies.[25] Thrale nursed her friends as assiduously as she did her children. When Fanny Burney was sick for a week at Streatham, Thrale recorded: "I gave her every Medicine, and every Slop with my own hand; took away her dirty Cups, Spoons &c. moved her Tables, in short was Doctor & Nurse, & Maid—for I did not like the Servants should have additional Trouble lest they should hate her for't."[26] For the constantly ailing Johnson, who noted to her in a letter that "it is indeed a great alleviation of sickness to be nursed by a mother,"[27] such care was a godsend. At Mrs. Thrale's, he wrote Malone, "I can use all the freedom that sickness requires."[28] His letters to her are filled with personal medical details, and she herself in the *Anecdotes* mentions her "ascendancy" over Johnson "in the things that concerned his health."[29] What her physical care of him meant can be seen negatively in the fact that friends unfairly blamed his death on her abandoning her care of him.

More than most forms of nonobsessive love, maternal affection traditionally has been viewed as unconditional. Thrale possessed the kindness, the patience, the adaptability, and the ability for self-effacement that allowed her—and in a sense compelled her—to offer this kind of love to those around her. From childhood she had been totally dominated by her mother, accustomed to conciliate her temperamental and unruly father, and encouraged to cater to rich relatives upon whom her family was dependent. She had thus been bred to attract and to please difficult and demanding people. She pleased them largely by cultivating an immense willingness to give to others at her own expense. When Piozzi accused her of spoiling her children, she replied that she loved spoiling people.[30] Her spoiling generally seems to have taken the form of offering the kind of selfless love that allows people to be wholly themselves. She accepted and loved Johnson as a human being rather than as a literary personality; as she wrote, "Would he not have been right to have loved me better than any of them, because I never did make a Lyon of him?"[31] With her and her children he could relax in amusing foolishness, indulging his lighthearted and frivolous side, which few others ever saw; Boswell sniffed in envious disdain that "at a very advanced age he could condescend to trifle in *namby-pamby* rhymes" to please Thrale and her children.[32] Johnson had received this kind of unconditional love from neither Tetty nor Sarah Johnson, and he ferociously tested Thrale's affection. She indicates that because of his "vehement lamentations and piercing reproofs," she would "sit quietly and make tea for him," often until four o'clock in the morning.[33] She submissively bore rebuffs from him that, in Fanny Burney's words, "would kill a stranger"; Frances Reynolds was amazed at how Thrale "would with much apparent affection overlook his foibles."[34] Thrale herself summed up their relationship as one "never infringed by one harsh Expression on my Part, during twenty Years of familiar Talk. Never did I oppose your Will, or control your Wish."[35] As Johnson found that he could rely totally on Mrs. Thrale's affection, he more unreservedly opened himself to her. She records one of his reactions in a conversation: "I cannot imagine says he on a sudden what makes me talk of myself to you so, unless it is that Confidence begets Confidence, for I never did relate this foolish Story to any one but to Dr Taylor & my Wife, not even to my poor dear Bathurst, whom I loved above all living Creatures."[36] When she found herself becoming, as she wrote, "more to him for Intimacy, than ever was any Man's Valet de Chambre," he finally entrusted to her his terrible fears of insanity, which she termed "a Secret far dearer to him than his Life."[37] She accepted the burden of this part of his personality as she had everything that concerned him, continuing to love and serve him, and commenting when writing of his fears of madness that "Johnson is more a Hero to me than to any one."[38] Secure in this affection, Johnson from that time relied on her care, sympathy, and company to help him deal with his crippling fears.

Mrs. Thrale's sustaining psychological care of Johnson, based on the relationship of trust which her unconditional love created for him, is responsible perhaps even more than her physical ministrations for the intellectual achievements of his final years. No one has yet argued with her own assessment of the case, which stresses the psychological:

> To the assistance we gave him, the shelter our house afforded to his uneasy fancies, and to the pains we took to sooth or repress them, the world perhaps is indebted for the three political pamphlets, the new edition and correction of his Dictionary, and for the Poets' Lives, which he would scarce have lived, I think, and kept his faculties entire, to have written, had not incessant care been exerted at the time of his first coming to be our constant guest in the country; and several times after that, when he found himself particularly oppressed with diseases incident to the most vivid and fervent imaginations.[39]

Credit for creating an environment out of which Johnson could write is of course due to both Henry and Hester Thrale, but the roles of each were clear from the beginning. In 1766, finding Johnson in despair in his room, Henry Thrale left Hester to convince their friend to move out to Streatham for better care. The order for Johnson's removal was Henry Thrale's. But it was Hester who carried it out, nursing Johnson and counseling him, particularly by giving him the kind of secure psychological environment that unconditional affection can create. Life at Streatham was based on Henry Thrale's physical resources and Hester Thrale's emotional ones, as Johnson seemed to recognize when he wrote to her at one point that Mr. Thrale "must keep well, for his is the pillar of the House, and you must get well or the house will hardly be worth propping."[40]

Along with the unconditional love that soothed him psychologically, one other maternal attribute of Thrale's encouraged Johnson to trust her and to allow her to be one who, as she wrote in connection with his feared insanity, "had him in her Power."[41] Thrale as a mother was a stern disciplinarian. With her ivory whistle always in her pocket to summon any erring child, and her "Salusbury fist" to enforce obedience, she kept her children strictly in order.[42] This kind of authority would have seemed particularly attractive to Johnson, who, as his diaries show, was incessantly trying to control himself and his life and always failing. During his nervous collapse in the mid-1760s, when he first became close to the Thrales, Johnson had almost abandoned hope of self-regulating what he described in his diary as "a life immethodical and unsettled."[43] With Mrs. Thrale he found someone to whom he could resign control, looking to her for an order which his own self-torment left him powerless to impose on himself. Thus in his letters he delighted in referring to her "government" of him, calling her his "governess" and himself her "slave" under her "Iron Dominion."[44] Thrale's character was ideal for the role. She was malleable and ductile enough to provide the altruistic love he could thoroughly trust. At the same time, she was not without spirit enough to seem a suitable disciplinarian. As Fanny Burney noted, Thrale "feared not Dr. Johnson; for fear made no part of her composition"; Burney also described Thrale's lecturing Johnson on his temper while he patiently listened.[45] It was a tremendous relief for Johnson to feel that he could surrender control of himself to such a woman. Confessing his fears of insanity to her, he could make his problems her own as she lightened for him the almost intolerable burden of himself. "When we get together again. . . ," he wrote to her in a letter, "you can manage me, and spare me the solicitude of managing myself."[46]

But the need for external order and control to escape himself was, of course, not Johnson's only drive. Equally strong was the sturdy independence and the integrity that made him finally unwilling to surrender his freedom. The characteristic tension between these two tendencies, a *discordia concors* clear in everything from his conversation to his prose style, accounts partly for his power as a writer and a personality. Johnson sought to submit to Thrale's "government" at least in part because the unique power status of a mother paradoxically offered him a way to fulfill simultaneously both of his conflicting desires. The maternal role has traditionally included almost total authority over children, along with relative powerlessness within the larger patriarchal society. This combination of complete power in a limited sphere and ultimate powerlessness in a larger context was particularly clear in Hester and Henry Thrale's relationship. "I know no man," Johnson told Boswell, "who is more master of his wife and family than Thrale. If he but holds up a finger, he is obeyed."[47] Henry Thrale left the nursery under Hester's control, but, from the kitchen to the grounds, he supervised all other domestic concerns. With Hester Thrale, Johnson could fulfill his need for order and control while retaining his independence, because the maternal power she represented was by its very nature limited. Like a traditional father, Henry Thrale, absent much of the time, left Johnson and his wife seemingly free to develop whatever relationship they wished. In reality, the limits of the relationshp were always governed by Henry Thrale. Together Hester and Johnson eagerly pursued chemical experiments, but when Henry unexpectedly arrived home and decreed an experiment in progress dangerous, the chemical enterprises abruptly ceased. Despite Johnson's expressions of submission to Hester, it was Henry Thrale whom he obeyed in matters of conversation, dress, and behavior. He did so at least partly because he could rely on his own considerable influence over Mr. Thrale. Hester Thrale's record of a conversation with Johnson about his desire to visit Chartreuse with her shows his recognition of the actual seat of power in the relationship: "We *will* go sometime that's certain, then replied I—whose Heart is set on very different Projects— . . . but are you willing to go? No Sir said I gravely: are you unwilling? Yes Sir,—in the same Accent: then says he I'll work up my Master to make you go, for go we will."[48] What had developed was a situation ideal for Johnson. On the one hand, he craved feminine company, affection, and "petticoat government"—Thrale noted that "*I* should not have the same Power myself over Johnson's *Spirits* . . . if I were not a Woman." At the same time, Johnson feared female power in certain ways: "Nature has given women so much power that the law has very wisely given them little"; "a Woman has *such* power between the Ages of twenty five and forty five, that She may tye a Man to a post and whip him if She will"; "Women . . . are less vicious than we, not from choice, but because we restrict them."[49] Johnson could submit willingly to Thrale's discipline without being threatened, because he knew that it was ultimately illusory. The unconditional nature of her love combined with the unique power status of a mother to produce circumstances perfect for giving Johnson both the security and the freedom that he wanted.

Because of the emotions that Thrale had repressed, it was necessary that her and Johnson's relationship be controlled from the outside. One important feeling she had managed to repress over the years with Henry Thrale was her growing ambivalence about her role as a mother. To a greater extent than most women, Thrale had been forced to see the costs of mothering. By the time of Henry Thrale's death, she had lost seven of her twelve children, a mortality rate high even by eighteenth-century standards.[50] Although three of them had died in early infancy, the rest had lived long enough for her to expend substantial energy rearing them. The sadness of their loss was exacerbated by the sense of the uselessness of her efforts: "I have really listened to Babies Learning till I am half stupified—& all my pains have answered so poorly—. . . . The Instructions I labor'd to give *them*—what did they end in? The Grave—& every recollection brings only new Regret."[51] Her growing disillusionment was shown by her decision not to educate her seventh child herself: "at Present I can not begin battling with Babies—I have already spent my whole Youth at it & lost my Reward at last."[52] Mary Hyde points out that after Thrale's *Children's Book* was filled in 1778, she lacked the heart to continue her separate record of her children, and the *Thraliana* began to take the place of the *Children's Book.*[53] The change is emblematic of Thrale's gradual movement away from maternal concerns toward personal ones.

The sense of futility created by her lost children was increased by problems with those who survived. Thrale received neither affection nor gratitude from her daughters as they grew up: "They are five lovely Creatures to be sure! but they love not me. Is it my fault or theirs?"[54] Acutely conscious of her daughters' dislike, Thrale could only feel that she failed as a mother. Only Johnson returned in any measure the affection she lavished on her household. Thrale's generous willingness to give to others was a strength that stemmed in part from her greatest weakness. The obverse side of her incessant need to please people was an insatiable desire for admiration, affection, and devotion. She admitted in the *Thraliana* that she was "a diligent & active Friend, who spares neither Money nor Pains to oblige, but who is soon disgusted if the Person obliged does not express the Sense of Obligation."[55] Mothering never provided her with the kind of appreciation she wanted. Even Johnson, so sympathetic in most ways, often treated her roughly. Moreover, as Patricia Spacks has shown, Thrale's keen feelings of maternal inadequacy were heightened by her sense of her own mother's inimitable perfections.[56] The incredible homage which she always rendered to Mrs. Salusbury undoubtedly made her feel doubly cheated when no one responded to her similarly. Living through and for others has generally been both the greatest reward and the ultimate temptation of traditional motherhood. Barred from the maternal rewards of emotional reciprocity and recognition, Thrale could only feel that she had succumbed to the temptations of motherhood, the classic power outlet for the powerless, in vain.

By the time Henry Thrale died, Thrale had too long put tremendous energies into mothering, which had failed to provide the rewards she sought. Partly because of the self-suppression required, the choice of the role of mother as it has been traditionally defined has necessarily limited other choices. Thrale in widowhood was almost ready to make these choices. If those she had mothered had not responded with the love she required, she thought that Gabriel Piozzi as a husband might. (Significantly, among the six reasons she listed in her diary for loving him was "his Duty to his Mother.")[57] After Henry Thrale's death, the most negative aspects of her mothering roles had become prominent; her daughters were even more unsympathetic than usual, and Johnson was so temperamental that he was driving others from her house. But motherhood was too deeply ingrained in her character to be abandoned without a fierce struggle; she wrote in the *Thraliana:* "My Children have a Claim to all that I can do & suffer."[58] She had easily left behind the other roles connected with her marriage, selling the brewery with delight, relinquishing political duties without comment, and even renting Streatham with little expressed regret. Her attachment to the role of mother was shown by the fact that she abandoned it only after one last effort to construct her life around it.

Dismissing Piozzi, she retreated to Bath with her daughters, where motherhood failed her for the last time. But the retirement to Bath revealed Thrale's ambivalence about mothering as well as her commitment to it. By leaving Johnson behind in London and never inviting him to visit, she in effect loaded her dice. Her final attempt at mothering would be made not with the one person who had offered substantial emotional reciprocity ("Nobody loves me as Johnson does at last—but then nobody has as much Soul to love one with"[59]), but with the daughters who had never satisfied her. Her action was probably instinctive at several levels. To continue to mother Johnson at this point meant abandoning her own plans; when writing of her desire to go to Italy, she noted that because she could not travel with Johnson and he could not bear to be left behind, "his Life or Death must determine the Execution or laying aside my Schemes."[60] Thrale was disillusioned with the constant sacrifices of herself to others that had been the essence of motherhood for her. Moreover, continuing to care for Johnson in his few remaining years would recapitulate her worst experiences as a mother: nursing children ceaselessly and hopelessly as she watched them die.[61] Thrale had suffered enough from death and from the insufficient emotional returns that had become inextricably connected in her mind with motherhood.

Ironically, it had been Johnson who had first encouraged Thrale to break out of her maternal role in some ways, criticizing her early in their relationship for devoting herself solely to her children and her mother and for failing to cultivate other interests. But he had never intended for her to leave mothering entirely, particularly not in his own case. He would never allow himself to recognize her ambivalence about motherhood, just as he refused to see her unhappiness as Henry Thrale's wife.

In both cases Hester Thrale's roles were too crucial to Johnson's own happiness for him to admit her ambivalences. Thus after Henry Thrale's death he wrote to her that God, who "has given You happiness in marriage to a degree of which without personal knowledge, I should have thought the description fabulous, can give You another mode of happiness as a Mother. . . ."[62]

This was precisely the happiness which Thrale had too long sought and found illusory. Uneasy with thinking of herself first, an action antithetical to the kind of mother she had been, she sought ways to free herself from Johnson as a dependent by retrospectively restructuring their relationship in her own thinking. In her diary she deliberately depicted her services to him in terms of his health: "I begin to see (now every thing shews it) that Johnson's Connection with me is merely an interested one—he *loved* M[r] Thrale I believe, that but only wish'd to find in me a careful Nurse & humble Friend for his sick and his lounging hours: yet I really thought he could not have existed without *my Conversation* forsooth."[63] She sought to view herself as unnecessary as a mother to his physical needs, and she reductively classed psychological care with physical concerns: "The original reason of our connection, his *particularly disordered health and spirits,* had been long at an end, and he had no other ailments than old age and general infirmity, which every professor of medicine was ardently zealous and generally attentive to palliate."[64] In addition to minimizing her contribution to Johnson's physical and mental well-being, she began to erect him into a symbol of priorities totally intellectual: "Johnson . . . desires above all other Good the Accumulation of new Ideas"; "he values nothing under Heaven but his own Mind."[65] She thus effectively relegated him to the one area in which he was not heavily dependent on her. Considering herself unnecessary to him as a nurse and intellectual companion, she wanted no further responsibilities for providing the "government" and the unconditional love that had created what she once described to Johnson as his "generous Confidence which prompts you to repose all Care on me, and tempts you to neglect yourself."[66]

Many complex circumstances caused Johnson and Thrale to part, but more than any other single factor, the maternal element produced the insoluble problems in the relationship. Because of the physical demands and the psychological constrictions on both parties, mothering cannot be a lifetime occupation. Continued for too long, it creates unhealthy dependencies on both sides. After Henry Thrale's death, Thrale was ready to free herself from the dependent state of motherhood to seek other outlets. Johnson refused to relinquish the most satisfactory mother figure he had ever known. Thrale could have kept Johnson as a friend, an intellectual companion, an adviser, a confidant. It was the demanding physical and psychological care of a dependent which drained her and thwarted her that she could endure no longer.

NOTES

An earlier version of this essay was presented at the Seventh Alabama Symposium on English and American Literature: "The Unknown Samuel Johnson," on October 10, 1980.

1. Hester Thrale Piozzi, *Thraliana: The Diary of Mrs. Hester Lynch Thrale (Later Mrs. Piozzi), 1776–1809*, ed. Katharine C. Balderston, 2 vols. (Oxford: Clarendon Press, 1942), I, 384. Hereafter cited as *Thraliana.*

2. Hester Thrale Piozzi, *Autobiography, Letters, and Literary Remains of Mrs. Piozzi,* ed. A. Hayward, 2 vols., 2nd ed. (London: Longman *et al.,* 1861), I, 255. Hereafter cited as Hayward. W. Jackson Bate, *Samuel Johnson* (New York: Harcourt Brace Jovanovich, 1977), p. 387. See also pp. 416, 436.

3. *Thraliana* I, 355.

4. Ibid. I, 158.

5. Ibid. II, 709.

6. See, for example, Mary Hyde, *The Thrales of Streatham Park* (Cambridge: Harvard University Press, 1977), pp. 111, 121, 207, 214.

7. Ibid., p. 288.

8. Review of *Letters of Mrs. Piozzi to William Augustus Conway (Unpublished), Athenaeum,* No. 1815, (August 9, 1862), pp. 169, 172.

9. Samuel Johnson, *Diaries, Prayers, and Annals,* ed. E. L. McAdam, Donald and Mary Hyde, in *The Yale Edition of the Works of Samuel Johnson* (New Haven: Yale University Press, 1958), I, 7. Hereafter cited as *DPA.*

10. Aleyn Lyell Reade, *Johnsonian Gleanings,* 11 vols. (privately printed, 1909–1952), III, 104.

11. *DPA,* p. 10.

12. Some perspective is placed on his negative views by Thrale's comment that his parents "did not however, as I could understand, live ill together on the whole: 'my father (says he) could always take his horse and ride away for orders when things went badly.'" *Anecdotes of the Late Samuel Johnson, LL.D.,* in George Birkbeck Hill, ed., *Johnsonian Miscellanies,* 2 vols., 1897 (reprint ed. New York: Barnes and Noble, 1970), I, 154. Hereafter cited as *Anecdotes.*

13. *Anecdotes,* p. 148; *DPA,* 6.

14. *Anecdotes,* pp. 148, 152–53; Frances Reynolds, *Recollections of Dr. Johnson by Miss Reynolds,* in *Johnsonian Miscellanies* II, 257.

15. *Anecdotes,* p. 163.

16. See James L. Clifford's discussion in *Dictionary Johnson: Samuel Johnson's Middle Years* (New York: McGraw–Hill, 1979), pp. 204–10.

17. George Irwin develops this point of view in *Samuel Johnson: A Personality in Conflict* (Auckland, N.Z.: Auckland University Press, 1971). He claims that

Johnson found in Mrs. Thrale "a mother-substitute under whose care he was able to relive and finally escape from the traumatic experiences of his childhood." His very problematical argument is that after failing to establish a "transference relationship," similar to that between patient and analyst, with his wife, Johnson succeeded with Thrale (p. 128). See also Katharine C. Balderston, "Johnson's Vile Melancholy," in F. W. Hilles, ed., *The Age of Johnson* (New Haven: Yale University Press, 1949), p. 4, n. 9; James L. Clifford, *Young Sam Johnson* (New York: McGraw–Hill, 1955), p. 25; Clifford's *From Puzzles to Portraits: Problems of a Literary Biographer* (Chapel Hill: University of North Carolina Press, 1970), p. 131.

18. At the age of twenty-five, he married only after obtaining his mother's permission. However, financial considerations may have dictated that Sarah Johnson be consulted.

19. Bate, pp. 150–53, 236–38, 261–65, 273–75.

20. Ibid., p. 415.

21. Samuel Johnson, *The Letters of Samuel Johnson, with Mrs. Thrale's Genuine Letters to Him*, ed. R. W. Chapman, 3 vols. (Oxford: Clarendon Press, 1952), III, 105. Hereafter cited as *Letters*.

22. *Thraliana* I, 465. Johnson would also have liked Thrale's religious instruction of her children: "My Children's Souls are in my Care, & all I can do for them is indispensible Duty." *Thraliana* I, 446.

23. *Letters* II, 362.

24. Chauncey Brewster Tinker, *Dr. Johnson and Fanny Burney*, 1912 (reprint ed. Westport, Conn.: Greenwood Press, 1970), p. 220.

25. Douglas Hubble, "Mrs. Thrale Keeping Notes," review of *The Thrales of Streatham Park*, by Mary Hyde, *British Medical Journal*, April 1, 1978, pp. 832–33.

26. *Thraliana* I, 413.

27. *Letters* I, 212.

28. Ibid. II, 463.

29. *Anecdotes*, 241–42.

30. Hayward, I, 349.

31. Ibid. I, 16.

32. George Birkbeck Hill, ed., *Boswell's Life of Johnson*, rev. L. F. Powell, 6 vols. (Oxford: Clarendon Press, 1934–1950), I, 179.

33. *Anecdotes*, 231.

34. Tinker, *Dr. Johnson and Fanny Burney*, p. 79; Reynolds, *Recollections*, pp. 272–73.

35. *Letters* III, 175.

36. *Thraliana* I, 161. See also *Anecdotes*, p. 158, where in recounting the story Thrale includes no mention of Johnson's wife.

37. *Thraliana* I, 385, 384.

38. Ibid. I, 385.

39. *Anecdotes*, 341–42.

40. *Letters* II, 139–40.

41. *Thraliana* I, 385.

42. Hyde, *The Thrales of Streatham Park*, p. 80; James L. Clifford, *Hester Lynch Piozzi* (Oxford: Clarendon Press, 1941), p. 113.

43. *DPA*, p. 162.

44. *Letters* I, 269, 399; II, 22, 40, 342, n. 1. It is of course this aspect of Johnson's personality which Katharine C. Balderston uses in "Johnson's Vile Melancholy" to argue for deep-seated erotic maladjustment. Whether or not one accepts the masochistic eroticism in her discussion, Johnson's famous French letter to Thrale and her reply clearly show Johnson's demands for external control and Thrale's providing needed reassurance and apparent control while actually encouraging Johnson to take care of himself.

45. Hayward II, 149; Tinker, *Dr. Johnson and Fanny Burney,* p. 129.

46. *Letters* II, 378.

47. *Boswell's Life of Johnson* I, 494.

48. *Thraliana* I, 187.

49. *Letters* II, 354; *Thraliana* I, 423; *Letters* I, 157; *Thraliana* I, 386; *Boswell's Life of Johnson* IV, 291.

50. Hyde, *The Thrales of Streatham Park,* p. 219. One more daughter was to die later.

51. Ibid., p. 163.

52. Ibid.

53. Ibid., pp. 219, 222.

54. *Thraliana* I, 504.

55. Ibid. I, 321.

56. Patricia Spacks, *The Female Imagination* (New York: Knopf, 1975), pp. 197–207.

57. *Thraliana* I, 549.

58. Ibid. I, 491.

59. Ibid. I, 418.

60. Ibid. I, 525, n. 2.

61. In addition, she had just spent two years worrying constantly over her husband's sicknesses, depressions, and erratic conduct as he inexorably ate himself to death.

62. *Letters* II, 415.

63. *Thraliana* I, 541, n. 1.

64. *Anecdotes,* 341.

65. *Thraliana* I, 492, 487.

66. Ibid. I, 384–85, n. 4.

Lovers as Nurturers

Robert Browning in 1858, by
M. Gordigiani. Courtesy of
the National Portrait Gallery,
London

The Domestic Economy
of Art

ELIZABETH BARRETT AND
ROBERT BROWNING

✑ Dorothy Mermin

Elizabeth Barrett Browning in
1858, by M. Gordigiani. Courtesy of the National Portrait
Gallery, London

*When Robert Browning (1812–1889) eloped with Elizabeth Barrett
in 1846, he had become notorious for the formidable obscurity of his long early poems
and had written verse plays with indifferent success, as well as* Pippa Passes *and some
fine short poems. The two poets settled in Italy, where Browning wrote many of his best
dramatic monologues and lyrics. When his wife died in 1861, he returned to London,
and the publication of* The Ring and the Book, *a series of dramatic monologues about
a seventeenth-century Italian murder, brought him substantial public success at last. He
became a bluff and cheerful frequenter of dinner parties and other social occasions, striking so acute an observer as Henry James as mystifyingly unlike a great poet in his appearance and behavior. Browning was less famous than his wife during her lifetime, but
his reputation rose as hers declined, and in his later years he was recognized, as he is
today, as one of the great poets of the nineteenth century.*

*By the time of her marriage, Elizabeth Barrett (1806–1861) had published an
epic in four books, a long philosophical poem, a translation of Aeschylus, two verse
dramas on biblical subjects, and various ballads and lyrics. After a happy childhood,
family tragedy darkened her life, and she had become an invalid, a recluse, and a mor-
phine addict when Robert Browning in 1845 initiated the correspondence that led to their
clandestine courtship. After marriage her major publications were* Sonnets from the
Portuguese, *which inaugurated a long tradition of amatory poetry by women, some
passionately committed poems about politics, which were sneered at for their unwomanly
subject matter and then forgotten, and* Aurora Leigh, *a popular verse-novel about a
woman poet, which is now considered her most significant achievement. Although the
story of her life has been distorted into a sentimental legend, she was a witty, hardworking, and tough-minded woman, who at the time of her death was generally regarded
as the greatest woman poet who had ever written in English.*

83

When Robert Browning and Elizabeth Barrett secretly married and eloped to Italy in 1846, he was thirty-four years old and she was forty. She was famous and widely respected as a poet and an unusually learned woman; he had achieved a more circumscribed but substantial literary success. Both were still living in their parents' homes and had always had the ordinary needs of daily life taken care of for them by others. Neither had ever earned a living or taken any responsibility for the management of a household. Elizabeth had only recently begun to recover strength after seven years of illness (probably pulmonary tuberculosis, then dormant) and to move outside of the one dusty, airless room in Wimpole Street to which illness had confined her. The elopement was an act of high courage for them both, since they thought that the unaccustomed exertion might prove fatal. When they reached Paris, Elizabeth was very happy but dangerously exhausted, and they immediately threw themselves on the maternal care of Mrs. Anna Jameson, a writer and friend of them both, who was also on her way to Italy and agreed to travel with them. Mrs. Jameson was astonished, delighted, but fearful. "I have . . . here," she wrote, "a poet and a poetess. . . . Both excellent; but God help them! for I know not how the two poet heads and poet hearts will get on through this prosaic world."[1]

In fact, they got on very well. They not only took very good care of each other, they took extravagant pleasure in doing so. Robert's anxious attention to his wife's health was entirely justified, but it often manifested itself in behavior strikingly like that of a parent to a very small child. They first set up housekeeping in Pisa, and Elizabeth's letters tell in joyous detail how he cajoles her to eat, lulls her to sleep, and gives her claret at dinner, "pouring it into the glass when I am looking another way, and entreating me by ever so much invocation when I look and refuse! and then I never being famous for resisting his invocations, am at the end of the dinner too giddy to see his face and am laid down at full length on the arm chair and told to go to sleep and profit by the whole." Her tasks as she describes them a month after their marriage seem strangely childish:

> Even the pouring out of the coffee is a divided labour, and the ordering of the dinner is quite out of my hands. As for me, when I am so good as to let myself be carried upstairs, and so angelical as to sit still on the sofa, and so considerate, moreover, as *not* to put my foot into a puddle, why *my* duty is considered done to a perfection which is worthy of all adoration.

Her appreciation is often faintly tempered, as it is here, by her sense of the ridiculous; some women, she notes, "might not like *the excess.*" She tells him not to talk so much of how she walks about, "as if a wife with a pair of feet was a miracle of nature." He was particularly insistent on carrying her: in and out of coaches and inns, and from room to room at home. "I am taken such care of; so pillowed by arms and knees . . . so carried up and down stairs against my will. . . ." She fears he will injure himself carrying her, and is "quite seriously angry"; "sins of this sort are his only sins against me." His quasi-parental protectiveness diminished as she became stronger, but it never disappeared and sprang back into life at her every illness. He was always watchful of her health, tried to protect her from overstimulation, scolded her for tiring herself. She could not visit her friend Mary Russell Mitford from London in 1852: Robert "would as soon trust me to travel to Reading alone as *I* trust Peninni [their son] to be alone here. I believe he thinks I should drop off my head and leave it under the seat of the rail-carriage if he didn't take care of it."[2] He nursed her through all her illnesses, and just before she died—in 1861, after fifteen years of marriage—she ate a little jelly to please him.

Browning's tender attentiveness to his wife was fairly matched by hers to him. She made less show of it than he did, but then there was less need for her to take care of him. When Robert returned from telling Mrs. Jameson of their arrival in Paris, Elizabeth characteristically thought of his exhaustion rather than hers and insisted that he lie down. Before they married, she fretted about his headaches and urged him to take care of himself so strongly and so often that one is sometimes in danger of forgetting, reading their correspondence, who was really the invalid. Love, gratitude, maternal impulse, the fearfulness generated in her by the death of her most beloved brother, could all account for her excessive solicitude, but it is probably also a matter of her resistance to Robert's parental behavior toward her. Marriage was her escape from an unnatural and unnaturally prolonged dependency on her father, and one suspects that she felt ambivalent at best about Robert's invitation to sink back into childishness. Her father was a tyrant to his nine children, benevolent when they bent to his will, but exacting absolute obedience. He allowed neither sons nor daughters to marry. Elizabeth explained that she had once said in jest:

> "If a Prince of Eldorado should come, with a pedigree of lineal descent from some signory in the moon in one hand, & a ticket of good-behaviour from the nearest Independent chapel, in the other"—?——
>
> "Why even *then*," said my sister Arabel, "it would not *do*." And she was right, & we all agreed that she was right.[3]

She loved her father with intense, unembarrassed devotion, but she knew that his behavior was neither right nor sane. When he would not make it possible for her to go to Italy, although her health and even her life seemed to depend on it, she ceased to believe in his love for her, and his hold on her was broken. She married and left. She still trembled at his wrath, hoped for his forgiveness, wrote him many letters (which were eventually returned to her unopened), and grieved at his death; but she never regretted her marriage, and she gloried in her freedom.

For Robert too, however, marriage marked the abrupt and very painful end to a prolonged dependency. His parents had loved, admired, and supported him, and although he said that they acknowledged his independence and "have never been used to interfere with, or act for me," he relied on them in many ways.

> There was always a great delight to me in this prolonged relation of childhood almost . . . nay altogether—with all here. My father and I have not one taste in common, one artistic taste. . . . what I mean is, that the sympathy has not been an intellectual one—I hope if you want to please me especially, Ba, you will always remember I have been accustomed, by pure choice, to have another will lead mine in the little daily matters of life. If there are two walks to take (to put the thing at simplest) you must say, "*This* one" and not "either." . . .

As this curious passage suggests, the deeper tie was to his mother. She was a devout, cultivated, strong-minded, and agreeable woman, fond of music and gardening, the center of a pleasant, peaceful household. Robert says little about her in the letters to Elizabeth, except that they had headaches at the same time—a "superstition," Elizabeth called it, but he insisted it was fact. He never saw his mother again after he went off with his wife, although Elizabeth said that he spoke of her every day, and his grief when she died in 1849 was prolonged and terrible. Elizabeth's explanation of his reluctance to revisit England in 1851 is suggestive: "The idea of taking his wife & child to New Cross [his parents' home] & putting them into the place of his mother, was haunting him day & night."[4]

When they married, each was eager to take care of the other, but neither wanted to make any assertion of will or power. Perhaps it was hard at first to break old patterns of behavior. Furthermore, they were both scornful of conventional marriages that functioned in terms of tyranny, submission, worldly values, and emotional emptiness, and were determined that their own would be different. But it took them a while to find their own way. When Robert admired Elizabeth for standing up to him in arguments, she admired his admiration. She had lived all her life under a preposterous domestic tyranny, and his refusal to exert any power over her, except in the form of loving persuasion—which generally succeeded—at first made her uncomfortable. "I am not very fond of praising men by calling them *manly*," she said in 1853; "I hate and detest a masculine man."[5] But such things are sometimes easier said than totally believed, and when she calls Robert "unmasculine" or tells him that he takes "the woman's part" one hears discomfort as well as pleasure and surprise. Eventually they did find their own way, however, in a combination of equal freedom, equal respect, and mutual nurturing.

Their manner of life made this relatively easy. They began housekeeping in idyllic simplicity, living in furnished rooms in Pisa, eating whatever the restaurant below chose to send them. Elizabeth's maid, Wilson, took care of her—when Wilson fell ill and Elizabeth had to dress herself, it was a notable event—and of routine household affairs. Elizabeth's early descriptions of their life in Pisa breathe forth delight and wonder, as if she were playing house. She never took responsibility for the household, then or later. "What would become of me (& of the house) I wonder," she wrote in 1858, "if I had a house to manage! It's a privilege on my part & an advantage on my husband's, that I have never ordered dinner once since my marriage."[6] Robert's part was harder: finding places to live in the many cities they stayed in (Pisa, Florence, Paris, Rome, Bagni di Lucca, Siena), arranging travel, keeping accounts, paying the bills. Choosing houses or apartments seems to have been particularly trying, since they often turned out to be unsatisfactory for his delicate wife, and he would frantically search for new ones; more than once they had to pay for lodgings that Elizabeth refused to occupy. (Her tendency to regret decisions once they were made—if not the choice of house, then the length of the lease—must often have made him uncomfortable.) But many of the responsibilities as well as all the actual work of the household were taken care of by servants. These made problems occasionally: one manservant proved smelly and unattractive, and in 1855 Elizabeth's maid, Wilson, married his replacement and caused some inconvenience by having a child three months later. But the Brownings were always taken care of. "'The kitchen' is an unknown horror to me,"[7] Robert had written feelingly before their marriage; neither he nor Elizabeth ever had to have anything to do with it.

The emotional focus of their lives and the balance of maternal solicitude shifted decisively when Elizabeth gave birth to a son in March 1849, after two and a half years of marriage. Thereafter their lives were much more complicated. Elizabeth was delighted—she had assumed that her age and ill health would make it impossible for her to have children—and took a much more active role. Her new maternal cares extended to her husband, too, for his mother died right after the child was born, and he plummeted from joy into extreme grief and months of depression. Elizabeth explained in a letter how she cajoled him back to health by appealing to his solicitude for her:

> My husband has been suffering beyond what one could shut one's eyes to in consequence of the great mental shock of last March—loss of appetite, loss of sleep, looks quite worn and altered. . . . I had the greatest difficulty in persuading him to leave Florence for a month or two. . . . I had to say and swear that baby and I couldn't bear the heat, and that we must and would go away.[8]

One feels some reluctance here—did she want to shut her eyes? She would have scorned such dissimulation earlier.

Robert eventually recovered his spirits and appetite, however, and then she could concentrate on her baby. She had disliked and avoided most conventional feminine pursuits since childhood, but for the baby's sake she bought a thimble; her own clothes never interested her much (her husband cared more for such things and sometimes insisted that she make herself more fashionable), but Pen, as the child came to be called, was lavishly clad in velvet and lace and feathers. On the way to Paris in 1855 they lost a box containing among other things some "ms. notes" for *Aurora Leigh,* but Elizabeth's chief anxiety was for Pen's clothes.[9] The note of excess recurs: Elizabeth adored her son, and Robert fussed and worried about him during his long widowerhood. The parents did little of the actual physical work of caring for the child—the doctors even insisted on a wet nurse, though Elizabeth wanted to nurse him herself—but they spent a great deal of time and thought on him. Elizabeth's letters are filled with beautifully drawn scenes of a childhood surrounded by love. One anecdote illustrates the new relationships in the household:

> Robert is very fond of him [the baby], and threw me into a fit of hilarity the other day by springing away from his newspaper in an indignation against me because he hit his head against the floor rolling over and over. "Oh, Ba, I really can't trust you!" Down Robert was on the carpet in a moment, to protect the precious head. He takes it to be made of Venetian glass, I am certain.[10]

They were gently parental toward the baby and toward each other, each evidently feeling like the only really responsible adult, the only fit mother.

As Pen grew older, his mother took the main responsibility for him: his clothes, his schedule, his social arrangements. But he never went to school, and both parents spent a lot of time teaching him. Instruction was sometimes difficult, since although he was always charming, he did not always apply himself to work, and they could not be severe. In 1859 they were each spending two hours a day, Elizabeth instructing him in language, Robert in music, and finding it burdensome. "We mean to have a master for him presently," Elizabeth wrote. "It won't do to give up our art for teaching—it is not good even for Peni." Teachers, when they came, did not relieve her entirely: "He doesn't work for his Abbé with his heart in it." she reports, "unless I sit by him." The drawback to being a mother, she found, was that it interfered with writing. In Paris in 1855, they were in a particularly bad apartment and it was hard for her to work, but the child came first. "I don't know how my poem [*Aurora Leigh*] is ever to be finished. It's as much as I can do, to get through Peni's lessons"—and then she cheerfully praises Pen's learning and his velvet hat. But such complaints are rare, and she did finish *Aurora Leigh*. Robert said later: "My wife used to write it, and lay it down to hear our child spell, or when a visitor came—it was thrust under the cushion then."[11] Robert usually had a room of his own for writing, but Elizabeth worked wherever she was.

They had time to devote themselves to their child, their art, and each other because they had essentially no other obligations. Neither worked for money, and living in Italy freed them from the social responsibilities they would have faced in England. Their social circles were casual and unrestricting: expatriate English and Americans, travelers, artists, single and quite emancipated women, and varied eccentrics. They were certainly not Bohemian, but they did not care to spend time upholding social forms or protecting their social status. Robert was the more conventional and sociable of the two, with time and energy to spare; he would have liked to live in Paris or London, but Elizabeth was never happy for very long except in the comparative isolation of Florence and the quiet towns nearby, where they sometimes spent their summers. Their letters are full of affectionate yearning and urgent invitations to relatives and dear friends to visit them, but they were happier alone; none of their sisters and brothers ever came to Florence, but once when numerous relations stayed with them in Le Havre, in the summer of 1858, they were both miserable. Elizabeth was always weary and depressed in London, where social obligations pressed heavily on them. On the whole, epistolary relations served her well enough. All her life she had jealously guarded the time she needed to read and write from the demands that society makes of women, just as Robert had refused to expend his powers in money-making or a career.

Money, however, was a serious problem both practically and emotionally for several years. Robert gave his wife more care and devotion than the world expected of husbands, but he could not give her the financial support that the world did expect. His father lent him a hundred pounds for their elopement but could give no more, and his writings earned nothing at all. They lived on Elizabeth's inheritance from her uncle, an allowance from her cousin, John Kenyon, and the income from her poetry. Life in Italy was marvelously cheap compared to London, but they were never financially easy until 1856, when John Kenyon died and left a substantial sum to each of them. Before they married, Robert offered to get a job, but she refused to let him sacrifice his genius to the world's opinion. She could never believe that money was really important, and her husband's carefulness in paying bills and avoiding debt amused and sometimes annoyed her. "There never was anyone who looked round a corner with a more imaginative obliquity, when the idea of money-difficulty is suggested in any form, than Robert does. It is we who remind our creditors of their claim on us. . . ."[12] Once they ran almost completely out of money while traveling with Pen and Wilson, and Elizabeth reported unsympathetically that "Robert [was] in a horrible fright all the way—he lets his imagination master him indeed."[13] His anxious and clearly necessary cares in this respect seemed to her honorable but superfluous, even unpoetical. She was inclined to believe that genius carried with it freedom from many social forms—from judgments on men's careers and restrictive notions of women's roles and powers—and liked to joke about the common notion that poetry and prudence are incompatible. Robert, however, thought that poets should behave like other people and managed their worldly business as properly and conventionally as he could.

At first they tried to live without the world, except by correspondence, and only slowly widened their social circle. Although they did not like to acknowledge it, they were reluctant to let each other go. In the early months of their marriage Robert insisted that they wanted no one to disturb their solitude, while Elizabeth urged him to go about and see things. The first time they *almost* spent a night apart was in July 1850, when Robert went to Siena to find a place to rent and could not get an early train back. "Such a day I passed, feeling as if I had lost my head—or something," Elizabeth reported with a nice ambiguity—but at three in the morning he returned after all. She did not in fact like him to leave her, despite her protestations, and her least attractive side appears in her petulant indignation whenever someone tries to call him from her: when his sister summons him to his cousin's funeral (he did not go) or their friends the Storys, distracted at the death of one child and the illness of another, ask for his company for a few days. Increasingly, however, their solitude was broken, especially in livelier cities than Florence. In Rome in 1859, Elizabeth was not well enough to go out much, and Robert "began by refusing all invitations to dinner—and he never dines out now— *except when he does.*" She was clearly more displeased than she liked to admit. "As to Robert he is lost to me and himself. If once a fortnight we have an evening together, we call it a holiday, both of us. . . . It pleases me that he should be amused just now (not but that he denies being amused very often); and I think it's good for him—in an occasional winter like this." "I believe I get some good for future lonely or quiet hours to digest," Robert explained glumly.[14] He for his part objected to many of his wife's visitors, either because they might tire her, or— especially when they shared her interest in spiritualism—because he thought they were taking advantage of her. They had many friends, but they both were wary and resentful of friendships that threatened to separate them or seemed to make inordinate demands.

Each was inclined to think the other too good-natured, too gener- ous, too susceptible and solicitous of others. The mothering qualities that upheld their marriage seemed less attractive when others were the object of them. Elizabeth professed astonishment that Robert's sister asked him to come from Paris to London for his cousin's funeral: "she understands nothing about Robert's susceptibilities"—"why, he would have had to go to the very cemetery, of course, where his mother's remains lie. . . . He is always a thousand times too good and tender."[15] Robert did not go, frightened by his wife's distress; but a few days later Elizabeth had a new complaint: He went to nurse an old lady, gave her medicine, was prepared to spend the night. Elizabeth, not unreasonably, thought this excessive.[16] Usually, though, it was Robert who tried to protect his wife from her own sensibility. When bad news was expected he intercepted her mail and dealt it out to her gently. He thought her much too trusting and generous and was particularly annoyed by her misplaced confidence in various practitioners of spiritualism, the one matter on which she refused to let him protect her.

The justification for all this anxious mutual solicitude, this selfishness *à deux,* was not just love, but also art. The Brownings pro- tected themselves from distraction, closed themselves up in their own world, and left their families, friends, and country behind them, so that they could work. The pattern of their lives together is reflected— sometimes with a strange obliquity—in their sense of themselves as poets and in some of the poems they wrote while they were married.

They admired each other's poems before they met, in terms that augured well for their meeting. When Elizabeth defended Browning's poetry to her skeptical friend Mary Russell Mitford, she always stressed maleness, passion, power. He is "very masculine," "eminently masculine and downright," "a true soul-piercing poet"; a scene "pants" with "power"; she feels "clenched passion . . . concentrated passion . . . burning through." Browning, reciprocally, chiefly praised and quoted her plangent ballads of love and longing. After reading her 1844 *Poems* he wrote the letter that began their correspondence: "I love your verses with all my heart, dear Miss Barrett," he began, ". . . the fresh strange music, the affluent language, the exquisite pathos and true new brave thought . . . and I love you too."[17]

They found in each other what they missed in themselves. Browning felt that his life had been dangerously happy and easy: "For when did I once fail to get whatever I had set my heart upon?—as I ask myself sometimes, with a strange fear." But everything he had so far set his heart upon had not been enough. He needed something else to want. He had ceased expecting to fall in love and declared himself tired of society, tired even of books. In her situation, her poems, and her letters he read a knowledge of suffering that was outside his own experience and is in fact rather conspicuously absent from his early poetry. For a long time she was afraid to let him meet her, marked as she was by age, illness, and sorrow. Then she distrusted his love and felt that she would be ungenerous to return it. She could teach him "nothing" she said, "except grief," and the suspicion that grief was what he wanted to learn made her uneasy. "I have sometimes felt jealous of myself . . . of my own infirmities, . . . and thought that you cared for me only because your chivalry touched them with a silver sound." Once he explained, rather awkwardly, how glad he was that the state of her health required her to go to Italy (and thus in effect to marry him): "Nor am I so selfish, I hope, as that (because my uttermost pride & privilege and glory above all glories would be to live in your sick-room and serve you,)—as that, on that account, I would not rather see you in a condition to need none of my service. . . ." The parenthetical assertion buried in this convoluted syntax is extravagant, but his behavior bore it out. He saw in her poems, moreover, not only deep feelings but also the ability to express them. In his second letter he compared his poetry to hers: "You *do* what I always wanted, hoped to do, and only seem now likely to do for the first time. You speak out, *you*,—I only make men & women speak. . . ."[18] He had already produced a substantial body of remarkable poetry, his reputation and his powers were alike increasing, and he had every reason to be sanguine. All that he seemed to lack was what Elizabeth Barrett had in abundance: dark experience of the inner life, and the ability to express it. Through his marriage, furthermore, he enacted the recurrent central myth of his poetry, Perseus' rescue of Andromeda.

And Elizabeth Barrett was ready to be rescued. Although she did not realize it, her illness was no longer active and her strength was returning. She was sick of isolation and did not cherish sorrow; she was ashamed of her nervousness, easy tears, and morbid terrors. Her early poetry expresses yearning, grief, and the pain of renunciation, but she had always tried to cultivate intellect in herself, not feeling. She had written at age fourteen: "My feelings are acute in the extreme but as nothing is so odious in my eyes as a damsel famed in story for a superabundance of sensibility they are carefully restrained!"[19] She had resisted in many ways the tedious demands that society made on upper-middle-class women, but now, she said, she had learned to value cheerfulness and society. She was desperately restless, longing to travel and know the world. Visitors wearied her, but she knew that solitude made her morbid and deprived her of the materials she needed for her writing. Browning coveted the knowledge she had drawn from introspection and inner experience, but she wanted to write about the world and valued his energy, strength, freedom, and knowledge of life. He wanted to be able to speak from his own subjectivity, and she hoped that he would; but for herself, she wanted to write something more impersonal, a novel-poem of modern times. She saw no attraction in illness, no heroism in caring for the ill. When all England honored Florence Nightingale in 1855, she resented the implication that "the best use to which we can put a gifted and accomplished woman is to *make her a hospital nurse*. If it is, why then woe to us all who are artists!"[20] One of her late poems, "A Court Lady," tells of a noblewoman who dressed herself up in court attire to visit soldiers in a hospital, praising their courage and exalting their patriotism and helping them by her majestic presence to die nobly. That was Elizabeth Barrett Browning's idea of an artist's proper role in a sickroom.

So it is not surprising that his attentiveness always quickened when she was sad or ill, and that her response to this was ambivalent. One sometimes feels something working a little against his overt will to make her strong and free; he carried her, nursed her, mothered her, tried to protect her from the world's folly and evil. She in turn sent him off to enjoy the sights of Pisa and Florence, the dinner parties of Rome, even when he said he wanted to stay alone with her. One does not want to stress this—he certainly did not want to keep her an invalid and was particularly eager to help her free herself from the opium to which medical advice had addicted her, while she was not pleased when he did start dining out. But the original basis remained: He was drawn to her weakness, she to his strength.

As writers, despite the differences that drew them together they were enough alike to help each other. They both wrote poems that were learned, innovative, difficult. They found in each other the sympathetic yet discriminating audience that Browning especially, whose works had met mostly with incomprehension, needed. The early part of their epistolary courtship was much taken up with her comments on his poetry, earnestly solicited and modestly offered. Her praise—subtle, just, accurate, unstinting—probably helped him more than her criticisms did. Her suggested emendations are mostly in the direction of clarity and smoothness, for she was anxious for his public success; an ear attuned to Browning's mature voice and to twentieth-century poetry will reject most of them.[21] She asked him to tell her in turn the faults in her poems, but although she was genuinely receptive to criticism and would not have taken offense, he put her off with lavish, rather awkward praise. He refused to be her teacher in poetry, although he helped her translate Greek. He must have helped her most, however, simply by taking her work seriously. Her father had been extremely proud of her precocious talents, but he always laughed, she said, "like Jove," at the idea that people could be "busy" with poetry.[22] Doctors tried to cure her nervousness by denying her the use of pen and paper (it is amusing to see her more than once offering Robert the same advice). Still, although he praises her genius and quotes her poems, it is *his* poetry, not hers, that the letters discuss.

Before they married she frequently urged him not to write unless he was feeling quite well, while he was occasionally seized with compunction and asked her not to neglect her own work for the sake of his. The terms of their solicitude changed after their marriage, when it became evident that she wrote much more fluently and happily, and moreover with greater public success, than he did. Her letters often return, lightly but insistently, to her worries about his work, reporting on Robert's application to his poetry and Pen's to his lessons in similar tones. She writes from Bagni di Lucca in the summer of 1853: "We are going to work hard . . . if Robert does not make good use of that cheerful little blue room with two windows, I shall give him up, I say." He did work hard then, but four years later, after the failure of *Men and Women* had discouraged him, she reports from the same place on a somewhat sharper note: "Robert has no models for his drawing, and no studio. Well—now poetry must have its turn, and I shall not be sorry for that. He has taken a passion for drawing, and . . . devotes himself to it too much, perhaps, neglecting his own art."[23] This comment is as near as she ever comes to criticizing him; it suggests that she is really worried.

Criticism might have been uncomfortable, since Browning did not become successful with the public until after his wife's death, although he was highly esteemed by those whose opinions really mattered. She was much more famous, and her work actually made money. When Wordsworth died in 1850, her name was mentioned for the laureateship; Robert's was not. In their Florentine circle she was the great writer, he the husband who graciously rejoiced in her success. Sometimes she seemed to feel some friendly rivalry, reporting to correspondents on their relative progress in writing. She was a little unhappy when she saw *Men and Women* reaching completion before *Aurora Leigh*: "It may be better not to bring out the two works together," she says, solacing herself, but adds, "If mine were ready I might not say so perhaps." The failure of *Men and Women,* which was not only the best book Browning ever published but also the one most likely to be liked and understood, was a terrible disappointment. *Aurora Leigh* got mixed responses from the critics, but it went into many editions. Robert's bitterness bursts forth in a letter to their publisher authorizing him to bring out the second edition of *Aurora Leigh;* he speaks of "we" and "us" and then catches himself up: "(*Us*—I am the church-organ-bellows' blower that talked about *our* playing, but you know what I do in the looking after commas and dots to i's)." But despite the errant judgments of the world, each believed absolutely in the other's greatness as a poet. Elizabeth understood with fine discrimination the consummate power of his work, while Robert asserted in 1871 that "*she* was the poet, and I the clever person by comparison." But she, it is clear, knew otherwise, and perhaps he did too, for he goes on to explain that one must "remember her limited experience of all kinds, and what she made of it."[24] In any case, his faith in her as a poet enhanced the value of her appreciation, and in the psychological economy of their marriage his genius must have balanced her success.

The effect of their marriage on the actual poems they wrote was, in general, to open up for each of them the territory represented by the other. His poems move from the monstrous psychological world of fanatics and murderers into realms of normal human feeling, exploring with particular zest and acuity various shades of love. Hers move from inwardness, literary themes, and legend to social and political scenes and subjects. The changes begin in the first poems they wrote after their marriage—poems in which they seem to go, in effect, too far, half assuming the other's identity and speaking as if in the other's voice. These early poems are in large part, curiously enough, about mothering.

Barrett Browning's "The Runaway Slave at Pilgrim's Point" is a contribution to the battle against slavery in America, a dramatic monologue spoken by a slave woman who has killed her infant because it had had "a look" like its white father's: "The *master's* look, that used to fall/ On my soul like his lash . . . or worse!"[25] She tells her dreadful tale of oppression and murder with the hallucinatory vividness, swinging energy, and crazily self-justifying logic of Johannes Agricola or Porphyria's lover, Browning's earliest dramatic monologuists. For Barrett Browning the poem had manifold personal relevance. Her family had been slaveholders in Jamaica and produced many children of mixed blood, including another Elizabeth Barrett;[26] her father, the family remarked, treated his children like slaves; she herself was dark; and in the eyes of her father and brothers she was a "runaway." Escape from her father into marriage with a man who explicitly refused to be "master" probably freed some long-repressed feelings and allowed her to write this cry of self-assertion against the tyranny of men and infants, the tyranny that is built into the structure of the family and disguises itself as love.

The first poem Browning wrote after their marriage was probably "The Guardian-Angel: A Picture at Fano." By a strange reciprocity with "The Runaway Slave," it expresses an infantile yearning for a protective maternal figure. The speaker addresses the angel, who is pictured with a praying child, and asks to take the child's place:

> And wilt thou bend me low
> Like him, and lay, like his, my hands together,
> And lift them up to pray, and gently tether
> Me, as thy lamb there, with thy garment's spread?[27]

Whereas "The Runaway Slave" is a dramatic monologue that resembles the poems Browning wrote, "The Guardian Angel" is explicitly personal, mentioning Browning's wife, their excursions, and his friend with accurate particularity. He seems finally to be doing what they had agreed that he should do: speak out in his own voice. But the voice sounds more like Elizabeth Barrett's at its worst than his own, with its paraphernalia of angels, wings, and children, the thinness, the stiff archaisms, the near-bathos of the diction, and the depressed and inhibited tone. Later Browning was to remark that his wife, unlike himself, took no "scientific interest in evil."[28] "The Runaway Slave" confronts evil, however, whereas Browning's speaker asks the angel to cover his eyes and make him see the world, "earth and skies / And sea," with "different eyes" (30–32).

> O world, as God has made it! All is beauty:
> And knowing this, is love, and love is duty.
> What further may be sought for or declared? [33–35.]

This is not his wife's view of the world, but it is a view that he sometimes hopes his love for her will help him discover.

The same excessive identification appears in *Christmas-Eve and Easter-Day* (1850), Browning's first important work after his marriage. Here he sets forth ideas on various religious topics, again apparently speaking quite openly, again yearning for a protective maternal figure. A vision of Christ appears to him in "a sweepy garment, vast and white" (*Christmas-Eve*, 438), to which he clings as he travels from one form of worship to another, and which saves him at the end, when he is "lapped again in its folds full-fraught / With warmth and wonder and delight" (1231–32), like the happy baby of a full-skirted Victorian mother. Elizabeth is usually blamed for the poem's form and doctrine, which resembles her own, but she had reservations about it; she "complained of the *asceticism*," and Robert replied that "it was 'one side of the question.' "[29] Still, the poem is tougher and more astringent in tone than "The Guardian Angel"; it marks the end of Browning's overt poetical dependency on his wife, as it marks his last show of yearning to be caught up and protected by maternal love.

Strong and ambivalent feelings about motherhood recur prominently, however, in Barrett Browning's later work. In *Aurora Leigh* all young women yearn for mothers. " 'When mothers fail us, can we help ourselves?' " (VI, 1229). The maternal breast repeatedly appears, often in very strange images, as the ultimate object of desire; Aurora turns to the hills of Italy, for instance, like a "sucking babe" to its sleeping mother (V, 1267 ff.). Throughout *Aurora Leigh,* however, mothers sometimes nurture but more often betray or destroy their children, while children both sanctify and consume their mothers. Marian Erle's mother had beaten and abused her, and Lady Waldemar's arrangements for taking care of her end in her being raped—a betrayal that Marian bitterly recognizes as " 'A motherly, right damnable good turn' " (VII, 10). Love for the child engendered by the rape saves Marian's life and spirit, but at the cost of everything else: " 'I'm nothing more / But just a mother' " (VI, 823–24). Aurora's story shows a similar doubling of love and hostility. Her mother died early—"She could not bear the joy of giving life, / The mother's rapture slew her" (I, 34–35)—and Aurora as a child is haunted by her dead mother's portrait, which seemed "by turns/ Ghost, fiend, and angel, fairy, witch, and sprite," Muse, Psyche, Medusa, "Our Lady of the Passion, stabbed with swords / Where the Babe sucked," Lamia . . . (I, 153 ff.). When Aurora becomes a successful writer, she imagines married life with similar though less lurid ambivalence, describing herself ironically as " 'a printing woman who has lost her place/ (The sweet safe corner of the household fire / Behind the heads of children)' " (V, 806–808), and thinking in a gloomy moment that she might have been happier with "chubby children hanging on my neck / To keep me low and wise" (II, 516–517). To love a child is to lose one's own life; this is the unspoken assumption behind the maternal cruelty that everywhere haunts the poem.

The poem tacitly insists, furthermore, that only women can nurture, protect, and feed, even though most refuse to do so. Marian, Aurora, and the structure of plot and imagery reject with astonishing violence Romney's repeated efforts to be, in effect, a mother. Near the end of the poem Romney recapitulates his disastrous career as a social reformer through a series of perverse maternal images. He had imagined the poor, he says, as prisoners inside the "Phalarian bull, society" (VIII, 388), which simultaneously holds them in its male womb and tramples them with its hoofs (VIII, 385 ff.). Then he saw them as the "great famishing carnivorous mouth" of a "huge, deserted, callow, blind bird Thing," which he tried to feed with worms (VIII, 395 ff.). The consequence of this misguided maternalism is that its ungrateful objects destroy his ancestral home, which he describes in terms—covered floors, "Carved wainscots, panelled walls, the favorite slide / For draining off a martyr (or a rogue) . . . stairs . . . slippery darkness" (VIII, 967 ff.)—that again suggest a womb. Aurora agrees to marry him only when he comes to her blind, defeated, humble, "like a punished child" (VIII, 362). Stripped of both masculine and maternal attributes, he accepts the role that Aurora had rejected for herself. "Work for two," he tells her, "As I, though thus restrained, for two shall love" (IX, 911–12). The general rebellion in *Aurora Leigh* against Romney's loving domination seems to amplify Elizabeth's strain of resistance against Robert and may suggest that although she did not consciously encourage his dependency on her, she did in some way desire it. The poem's insistence on the dark side of motherhood probably reflects the pain and fear of her pregnancies and miscarriages as well as a largely unconscious resentment of her adored, engrossing child.[30]

The Brownings expressed in their poems both the connubial affection for which they became famous and also other impulses—his to be dependent, hers to repel claims on her love—that were harder to acknowledge. Browning's need for mothering was partly satisfied by their marriage and issued in only a few weak poems. Barrett Browning's rebellious impulse, which was repressed and thwarted to a much greater degree, shows itself in more poems and is generally a source of energy—sometimes mawkish, sometimes surprisingly violent, but often suggestive, powerful, and strange. Insofar as it is possible to assess the total effect of their marriage on their writing, we can say with confidence that it was highly salutary. Freed from isolation and paternal censorship, Barrett Browning was able to write on contemporary public themes such as the role of women, prostitution, and the Risorgimento, which increasingly absorbed her attention. *Sonnets from the Portuguese,* her first major work and her last on a wholly private, erotic theme, was written during their courtship, and *Aurora Leigh,* her other major work, when Pen was little. Browning wrote all of *Men and Women* and some of *Dramatis Personae,* and partly conceived, though he did not execute, *The Ring and the Book.* He wrote less, quantitatively, in the fifteen years they lived together than he did before or after, but what he did write was much better. Almost all his best work comes from those years, and his characteristic weaknesses—excessive length, apparent shapelessness, opacity of language—hardly appear at all. Perhaps Elizabeth's salutary critical influence was responsible, or perhaps while she was with him he did not have to fill the emptiness of his time with writing. The Brownings' love story became a sentimental legend in their own lifetime and continues to repel some readers from their poetry and incite others to find flaws in their absurdly celebrated happiness. The subjects on which they disagreed—politics, Pen's clothes, spiritualism—have been made to suggest serious rifts, especially by critics who seem to imagine that an argumentative wife would be intolerable. They had many serious troubles, the worst being Elizabeth's miscarriages and illnesses. But they both *thought* they were very happy together, and Browning said many times that his wife was the source and inspiration of his best poetry. What they gave each other as poets, it seems, was a psychic space in which they could work freely, and the confidence to explore previously repressed or inaccessible desires and fields of experience.

NOTES

1. Gerardine MacPherson, *Memoirs of the Life of Anna Jameson* (Boston: Robert Bros., 1878), pp. 228–29. Barrett Browning's illness is analyzed by George Pickering in *Creative Malady: Illness in the Lives and Minds of Charles Darwin, Florence Nightingale, Mary Baker Eddy, Sigmund Freud, Marcel Proust, Elizabeth Barrett Browning* (New York: Oxford University Press, 1974), pp. 245–65. The Brownings' life together is discussed in many biographies; see Dorothy Hewlett, *Elizabeth Barrett Browning* (London: Cassell, 1953); Gardner B. Taplin, *The Life of Elizabeth Barrett Browning* (New Haven: Yale University Press, 1957); Alethea Hayter, *Mrs. Browning: A Poet's Work and Its Setting* (London: Faber and Faber, 1962); Betty Miller, *Robert Browning: A Portrait* (New York: Scribners, 1952); Maisie Ward, *Robert Browning and His World*, 2 vols. (New York: Holt, Rinehart, and Winston, 1967–1969); William Irvine and Park Honan, *The Book, the Ring, and the Poet* (New York: McGraw–Hill, 1974); and Edward C. McAleer, *The Brownings of Casa Guidi* (New York: The Browning Institute, 1979).

2. Leonard Huxley, ed., *Elizabeth Barrett Browning: Letters to Her Sister, 1846–1859* (London: John Murray, 1929), p. 11; Frederic G. Kenyon, ed., *The Letters of Elizabeth Barrett Browning*, 2 vols., 4th ed. (London: Smith, Elder, 1898), I, 306: *Twenty-Two Unpublished Letters of Elizabeth Barrett Browning and Robert Browning Addressed to Henrietta and Arabella Moulton-Barrett* (New York: United Feature Syndicate, 1935), p. 25; Kenyon, *The Letters of Elizabeth Barrett Browning* I, 427; *Twenty-Two Unpublished Letters*, p. 10; Huxley, *Letters to Her Sister*, p. 109; Kenyon, *The Letters of Elizabeth Barrett Browning* II, 85.

3. Elvan Kintner, ed., *The Letters of Robert Browning and Elizabeth Barrett Barrett, 1845–1846*, 2 vols. (Cambridge: Harvard University Press, 1969), I, 319.

4. Kintner, *The Letters of Robert Browning and Elizabeth Barrett Barrett* II, 1006, 960, 976; Peter N. Heydon and Philip Kelley, eds., *Elizabeth Barrett Browning's Letters to Mrs. David Ogilvy, 1849–1861, with Recollections by Mrs. Ogilvy*, (New York: Quadrangle/The New York Times Book Company, and The Browning Institute, 1973), p. 45.

5. Kenyon, *The Letters of Elizabeth Barrett Browning* II, 134.

6. Heydon and Kelley, *Elizabeth Barrett Browning's Letters to Mrs. David Ogilvy*, p. 136.

7. Kintner, *The Letters of Robert Browning and Elizabeth Barrett Barrett* II, 894.

8. Kenyon, *The Letters of Elizabeth Barrett Browning* I, 410.

9. Ronald Hudson, "Elizabeth Barrett Browning and Her Brother Alfred: Some Unpublished Letters," *Browning Institute Studies* 2 (1974), 147. On the intense and often problematic relation of the Brownings to their son, see Maisie Ward, *The Tragi-Comedy of Pen Browning* (New York: Sheed and Ward, and The Browning Institute, 1972), especially the introduction by Robert Coles.

10. Kenyon, *The Letters of Elizabeth Barrett Browning* I, 421.

11. Paul Landis, ed., *Letters of the Brownings to George Barrett* (Urbana: University of Illinois Press, 1958), p. 359; *Twenty-Two Unpublished Letters*, p. 85; Huxley, *Letters to Her Sister*, p. 233; Thurman L. Hood, ed., *Letters of Robert Browning* (New Haven: Yale University Press, 1933), p. 48.

12. Huxley, *Letters to Her Sister*, p. 73.

13. Letter to Arabella Barrett (June 26, 1851), in the Henry W. and Albert A. Berg Collection, The New York Public Library, Astor, Lenox and Tilden Foundations. Quotations from letters in the Berg Collection are published by permission of The New York Public Library and John Murray.

14. Huxley, *Letters to Her Sister*, p. 125, 307, 305; Edward C. McAleer, ed., *Dearest Isa: Robert Browning's Letters to Isabella Blagden* (Austin: University of Texas Press, 1951), p. 36.

15. Letter to Arabella Barrett (May 25, 1852), in the Berg Collection.

16. Letter to Arabella Barrett (May 29–30, 1852), in the Berg Collection.

17. Betty Miller, ed., *Elizabeth Barrett to Miss Mitford: The Unpublished Letters of Elizabeth Barrett Barrett to Mary Russell Mitford* (New Haven: Yale University Press, 1954), pp. 241, 251, 179, 80, 172; Kintner, *The Letters of Robert Browning and Elizabeth Barrett Barrett* I, 3.

18. Kintner, *The Letters of Robert Browning and Elizabeth Barrett Barrett* I, 25, 87, 247; II, 757; I, 7.

19. "Two Autobiographical Essays by Elizabeth Barrett," *Browning Institute Studies* 2 (1974), 130.

20. Kenyon, *The Letters of Elizabeth Barrett Browning* II, 189.

21. See Bernice Fox, "Revision in Browning's *Paracelsus*," *Modern Language Notes*, 55 (1940), 195–97, and Edward Snyder and Frederic Palmer, Jr., "New Light on the Brownings," *Quarterly Review* 269 (1937), 48–63.

22. S. R. Townshend Mayer, ed., *Letters of Elizabeth Barrett Browning Addressed to Richard Hengist Horne*, 2 vols. (London: Richard Bentley and Son, 1877), II, 145–46.

23. Landis, *Letters . . . to George Barrett*, p. 187; Huxley, *Letters to Her Sister*, pp. 276–77.

24. Heydon and Kelley, *Elizabeth Barrett Browning's Letters to Mrs. . . . Ogilvy*, p. 115; William Clyde DeVane and Kenneth Leslie Knickerbocker, eds., *New Letters of Robert Browning* (London: John Murray, 1951), p. 97; McAleer, *Dearest Isa*, p. 365.

25. *The Poetical Works of Elizabeth Barrett Browning* (Boston: Houghton Mifflin, 1974), XXI. All references to Barrett Browning's poems are to this edition.

26. See Jeannette Marks, *The Family of the Barrett: A Colonial Romance* (New York: Macmillan, 1938), for the history of the Barretts in Jamaica.

27. Browning, *The Poems*, ed. John Pettigrew, 2 vols. (New Haven: Yale University Press, 1981), "The Guardian-Angel," ll. 18–21. All references to Browning's poems are to this edition.

28. Richard Curle, ed., *Robert Browning and Julia Wedgwood: A Broken Friendship as Revealed by Their Letters* (New York: Frederick A. Stokes, 1937), p. 137.

29. Kenyon, *The Letters of Elizabeth Barrett Browning*, I, 449.

30. For a survey of Barrett Browning's poetry about mothers and children that takes a somewhat different point of view, see Sandra Donaldson, "'Motherhood's Advent in Power': Elizabeth Barrett Browning's Poems about Motherhood," *Victorian Poetry* 18 (1980), 51–60.

George Eliot in 1865 (age
forty-six), from a chalk
drawing by Sir Frederic
Burton. Courtesy of the
National Portrait
Gallery, London

On Exile and Fiction
THE LEWESES AND
THE SHELLEYS

⌒U. C. Knoepflmacher

George Henry Lewes in 1867 (age fifty), from a drawing by Rudolf Lehmann. By permission of the Trustees of the British Museum, London

Mary Ann Evans, (1819–1880), better known by her male pseudonym, "George Eliot," first exhibited her intellectual powers and radical tendencies as essayist and translator of D. F. Strauss's controversial Das Leben Jesu (1846), a work which challenged religious orthodoxy. She did not achieve her full literary eminence until she moved to London from the English countryside she recreated so lyrically in her novels. She wrote for and managed the Westminster Review, the most advanced intellectual journal of the times, until 1854, when she and George Henry Lewes, (1817–1878) an essayist and scientist whom she had met at the Westminster, eloped to Germany as a married couple, even though he could not obtain a legal divorce from his adulterous wife. The liaison between the two writers lasted twenty-four years, until Lewes died of cancer in 1878.

George Eliot adopted her mate's first name in her pseudonym, and fiction became a means through which a woman ostracized by Victorian social conventions transformed herself into the era's leading voice. She followed Scenes of Clerical Life (1858), a collection of three novellas, and Adam Bede (1859), the full-length novel that established her reputation, with six more novels, two volumes of poetry, and a collection of essays. The union was also productive for Lewes. Though accepting a subsidiary role to his companion, he published his well-received Life of Goethe (1855), served stints as editor of the Cornhill and Fortnightly Review, and embarked on a series of ambitious treatises on physiology and psychology, the last of which was carefully prepared for posthumous publication by George Eliot.

In May of 1880, much to the shock of some of her friends, George Eliot married John Walter Cross, twenty years younger than herself. She died that same year and was buried next to Lewes at Highgate Cemetery in London. The Leweses lie not too far from the grave of another Victorian exile, Karl Marx, whom they had briefly met in their days at the Westminster.

$\sim \bigcirc A$s a major novelist's retrospective attempt to account for the freeing of her imagination, George Eliot's "How I Came to Write Fiction" fully deserves the attention of her readers. In reproducing this document, biographers from John Cross in 1885 to Gordon S. Haight and Ruby Redinger in our times have rightly stressed its importance.[1] Yet "How I Came to Write Fiction" still requires further analysis. For in it George Eliot not only casts considerable light on the process of her creativity but also underscores the role played in the liberation of that creative process by George Henry Lewes, the partner whose first name she incorporated in her male pseudonym. This double aim also links, whether consciously or not, "How I Came to Write Fiction" to the account in which another female novelist looked back at the "origin" of her fiction-making and at the "inciting" influence of her male mate—the 1831 Preface to *Frankenstein*. Despite some recent efforts to connect George Eliot to Mary Shelley,[2] our minds seem determined to keep the two writers apart. George Eliot has forever become the preeminent emblem of a mature and thoughtful realism, the author of works, as Virginia Woolf put it, written for grown-ups. Mary Shelley, on the other hand, seems frozen as the author of *Frankenstein,* that product of an adolescent's fixed fears and fantasies. Though helpful, the juxtaposition remains oversimplified, and needs to include a full consideration of the roles played in each novelist's development by their respective mates, Shelley and Lewes.

George Eliot begins "How I Came to Write Fiction" on the same note of self-depreciation and doubt that marks Mary Shelley's 1831 Preface. She admits, as her predecessor did, her long-standing ambition to write a novel. But, unlike the Mary Godwin who was not yet nineteen, still a "young girl,"[3] when she turned to her first long work of fiction among the Swiss Alps, the Mary Ann Evans who eloped to Germany with Lewes in 1854 at the age of thirty-four was no neophyte but a skilled translator, editor, and essayist. It was her creative imagination that remained blocked, as she realized later, upon looking back at the "*shadowy* conception of what [her intended] novel was to be . . . from one epoch to another." Her despondency, she thus insists, was endemic: "I lost any hope that I should ever be able to write a novel, just as I desponded about *everything else* in my future life."

At this point in "How I Came to Write Fiction," George Eliot shifts, rather too abruptly, to her exile in Germany after her elopement with Lewes: an early sketch "*happened to be* among the papers I had with me in

Germany, and one evening at Berlin, *something* led me to read it to George." The vagueness and passivity which the writer claims for her own aspirations yield to an account of Lewes's gentle but determined preeminence; he is, we are told, "struck" by the "concrete" power of her descriptive abilities, warns her that he distrusts, indeed disbelieves in, "my possession of any dramatic power," thus implicitly confirming her own earlier self-estimate. And yet Lewes also begins to think "that I might as well try, some time, what I could do in fiction." Portrayed as an empiricist, Lewes thus seems to be willing to wait for further evidence before he will be ready to pronounce, "It is worthwhile for you to try the experiment." Only after his companion has shown a "greater success than he had ever expected in other kinds of writing," does he encourage her "to see how far my mental power would go towards the production of a novel." Though still quite guarded, he now chooses to speak "very positively" for the first time. His mate, however, reverts to her earlier resistances when she procrastinates over her first story, "after my usual fashion, with work that does not present itself as an absolute duty."

One morning, while "lying in bed" and "in a dreamy doze," George Eliot—or rather Mary Ann Evans still—takes a distinct step forward: "I imagined myself writing a story of which the title was—'The Sad Fortunes of the Reverend Amos Barton.'" Ever alert, Lewes seized the opportunity for a stronger dose of encouragement: "I was soon awake again, and told G. He said, 'O what a capital title!'" The approval proves to be exactly right, "and from that time on I had settled in my mind that this should be my first story." It is noteworthy that the female dreamer should immediately associate being "awake" with Lewes (who was probably lying next to her in bed). Although a determined antifantasist who had recommended to Charlotte Brontë that she saturate herself in the works of Jane Austen, this realist knew exactly how to mediate between a dreamy projection and its actualization. He enthusiastically applauds the chosen title, yet also reminds the reassured dreamer that the story itself still remains to be written. For all his encouragement of her creativity, he will not betray the reality principle to which she, like himself, must subscribe. He therefore carefully spreads out for her all possible contingencies. The story, he warns her, "may be a failure. . . . Or perhaps it may be just good enough to warrant your trying again. . . . You may write a chef d'oeuvre at once—there's no telling."

George Eliot's decision to reproduce the various stages of development in this genetic account is as noteworthy as the account itself. In its apparent faithfulness of detail, "How I Came to Write Fiction" adopts the "sincerity" which her coexperimenter, Lewes, had upheld both as the literary critic who, in his very first essay, professed to admire Percy Shelley "because he was eminently sincere"[4] and as the physiologist who, in those "Seaside Studies" that ran in *Blackwood's* concurrently with George Eliot's first fictions, insisted on a rigorous process of documentation and verification. By the time Lewes appeared in Mary Ann Evans's life, "sincerity" had also assumed a personal significance for him. No longer the dandy who once boasted himself "next to mad with love and its fallacies,"[5] Lewes had shed the flippancy and theatricality that marked some of his earlier incarnations—the garrulous drama critic "Slingsby Lawrence," the irrepressible *farceur* in Dickens's company of "splendid strollers," the wishfully self-dramatizing author of *Ranthorpe* (1847), which, as his first novel, he dedicated to his wife, Agnes, for lightening "the burden of an anxious life." Indeed, by 1854 Agnes Lewes had contributed to his anxiety, as well as to his maturer notions of "sincerity" and realism. It was she who led him to reconsider his earlier enthusiasm for a community based on free love, when she presented him with several children fathered by Thornton Hunt, the same friend whom Lewes had once urged to write down his early recollections of the Shelley both men worshipped.

Lewes understood that his new relationship to Mary Ann Evans had to be cemented on wholly realistic grounds. The woman who had on her own resolved to see life without any opiates of self-delusion demanded nothing less. His refusal to yield to falsification or to brush away her very own doubts about her "dramatic power" thus helped her, paradoxically, to overcome her mistrust of the gifts so apparent to others and allayed her intense fear of her creative energies. Interested in play as well as in the psychology of the imagination, Lewes seems to have fully fathomed the relation between creativity and regression. He regarded the portions on "Childhood" and "Schooltime" as the finest sections of *The Prelude* and implied that the "marvellous vividness" of Dickens's imagination stemmed, like the novelist's "overflowing fun," from a childlike capacity to believe in the fantastic and hallucinatory.[6] Yet he also derided the philosophic underpinnings of *The Prelude* as absurd and deplored Dickens's presumed lack of intellect. It thus seems unsurprising that he should emerge as an unusually sober adult superego in "How I Came to Write Fiction." Only the exuberant exclamation "O what a capital title!" suggests some of the playfulness that others continued to notice in Mary Ann Evans's vivacious, yet "sincere" mate. The childlike qualities that George Eliot would later impute to those two fictional male mothers, nurturers of adopted daughters, the grotesque Silas Marner and the droll Rufus Lyon of *Felix Holt,* are notably absent in her characterization of "George."

Sickly, despondent over his adulterous wife, Lewes gratefully leaned on the sympathy his new mate so fully extended to him after she pierced the veneer of his former Bohemian reputation. But he was also fully capable of being "primary caretaker"[7] for her own unfulfilled imagination, as "How I Came to Write Fiction" eloquently shows. His caring supervision of his three legitimate sons and his steady devotion to his long-lived mother, Elizabeth Ashweek Lewes Willim (she died in 1871, at the ripe age of eighty-three), suggest Lewes's appreciation of the necessity for "mothering" and his own ability to do it. Yet unlike the Percy Shelley who insisted in adopting a position of superiority in urging the daughter of Mary Wollstonecraft and William Godwin to prove herself "worthy" of her "parentage" and, by extension, improve her "ideas in communication with his far more cultivated mind,"[8] Lewes never infantilizes his "Polly" in urging her to try the identity of a novelist. She is not a recusant child, but a clear-eyed adult whose diffidence might be justified. A "chef-d'oeuvre" requires the full use of her mature powers, as the author of the immature *Ranthorpe* and *Rose, Blanche, and Violet* (1848) can himself testify.

Some elements in George Eliot's "How I Came to Write Fiction" remain deliberately screened, of course. When John Cross reproduced her account of the "dreamy doze," he stripped it of all sexual overtones by prudishly deleting the phrase "as I was lying in bed." In so doing, he may well have detected an inference which later male biographers, not privy—as he was—to George Eliot's marriage bed, should probably just as discreetly avoid. Still, the likelihood that George Eliot herself connects her latent creativity to her sexual intimacy with Lewes need hardly be discounted in her description of the dreamy doze. The tiny, ugly, pockmarked man, so un-Victorian and seemingly un-English in his lack of reticence, at first struck Barbara Leigh Smith as an "extremely sensual man." Smith, who distrusted her own passion for John Chapman (Mary Ann Evans's seducer), and who would soon marry the cold Eugène Bodichon to escape that passion, welcomed George Eliot's reassurance that "in their intimate relationship [Lewes] is unsensual, extremely considerate."[9] But the reassurance, proffered to a friend whose loyal friendship was essential to George Eliot, and veiled, as it is, by a triple layer of transmissions, only seems to suggest that the "intimate relationship" of the couple was extremely healthy indeed.

More tantalizing, however, is George Eliot's elliptical suggestion that her elopement with Lewes had reactivated earlier emotional traumas that her fiction would both tap and master. The phrase appearing early in her account, "just as I desponded about everything else in my future life," remains unlocalized in time and hence may seem descriptive of a self-doubting tendency we know to have been habitual with her even after each of her immense successes. Yet, since the phrase is followed by the quite explicit allusion to her 1855 stay in Berlin, several months after her elopement to Weimar, the effect is to yoke the general despair she felt about ever becoming a novelist with the specific anxieties about her future identity as Lewes's companion in exile. For in 1855 the identity of London journalist, editor, translator, and valued member of the Victorian intelligentsia that Mary Ann Evans had so strenuously fashioned for herself had suffered a shock that threatened to be more profound and damaging to her than all her previous crises put together.

Each of her earlier ruptures with the past had been severe. Her father's death and the dubious freedom that ensued, her antecedent clash with both Robert and Isaac Evans on the issue of her break with Christianity caused her considerable anguish. But most traumatic of all, if we are to believe Ruby Redinger, was her estrangement as a small child from the ailing mother she so wanted to but could not incorporate. Though Redinger, like Cross, forgets that Christiana Pearson Evans's decline was probably accelerated by the birth and death of twin sons in 1821, sixteen months after Mary Ann's own birth, there is no need to discount the suggestion that the girl magnified her "role in her mother's prolonged illness."[10] It is true that George Eliot's guilt never assumed the dimensions of Mary Shelley's self-castigation for having been the unwitting cause of her own mother's death. Still, by attributing Mrs. Evans's neglect to invalidism and by blaming herself as its cause, the child could deflect from the more painful inference that her mother did not really much care for either of her two daughters. For, even while healthy, Mrs. Evans had shown a similar indifference toward her older daughter and namesake, Christiana (or "Chrissey"), born in 1814. Whereas both girls were promptly sent off to boarding school at the early age of five, their brother Isaac, born in 1816 and "his mother's pet,"[11] was allowed to remain at home until the age of eight. Unable to obtain her mother's love, and bereft of her older sister, Mary Ann transferred her attachments to the two male members of her immediate family. Both her father and Isaac apparently returned her love. And by eliciting her brother's love the little girl could at least indirectly identify with her mother. It was a psychic pattern that would allow her to accept further compensating substitutions in her later life.

Nonetheless, as her portraits of deficient mother figures would later show,[12] George Eliot never fully weathered the withdrawal, at such an early stage of her development, of that maternal "warmth" she poignantly dramatized in "Self and Life," a poem which Redinger rightly reads as "one of her most personal utterances." In that dialogue, "Life" insists on a symbiotic fusion between mother and child: "I was thy warmth upon thy mother's knee / When light and love within her eyes were one; / We laughed together by the laurel tree." But an individuated adult "Self" bemoans its separation and exile: "Soon I knew thee more by Fear / And sense of what was not, / Haunting all I held most dear; / I had a double lot: / Ardor, cheated with alloy, / Wept the more for dreams of joy."

Both as a girl and as a growing woman, Mary Ann Evans struggled to accept the "alloys" of compensation for the early severance she had suffered. Yet the child who first turned to her rigid father and older brother as surrogates for the withdrawing Christiana Evans continued, as an adult, to find her emotional needs unsatisfied by a series of deficient male mentors and suitors. In 1854, at the age of thirty-four, she had at last discovered a man who could amply satisfy those needs. Ironically enough, however, her elopement with Lewes painfully reactivated all her earlier losses. She had entered a relation ideal in its finely balanced interdependence of needs and satisfactions. Yet the elopement also raised anew the old specter of total unrelatedness, of a solitude every bit as devastating as that which besets the loveless Shelleyan protagonist of her 1859 horror story, "The Lifted Veil."

Though Redinger properly stresses the blissfulness of the "dual solitude" that George Eliot would find after her elopement with George Henry Lewes, she also severely underestimates, I think, the depth and intensity of the fears unleashed by the decision to share his life. Once again, fusion was followed by separateness, the monster that an alienated little girl had never fully learned to slay. All past gains seemed in danger of becoming obliterated. By eloping with a married man, Mary Ann Evans had not only become irrevocably estranged from her brother Isaac, her father's stolid and conventional heir, and from her timid, tubercular sister Chrissey, her mother's namesake and fellow invalid, but also seemed to have deprived herself, just as irrevocably, of the much-coveted recognition of older friends such as Harriet Martineau, whose biography she now was never to write, as she had intended.[13] Would she—could she—ever again be accepted by Victorian society, when even some of its most free-thinking members seemed eager, in Barbara Bodichon's words, to "spit at" her?[14] All evidence seemed to deny that likelihood. The readership she had gained as thoughtful reviewer and editor at the *Westminster* might also now be lost. It was for this reason, apparently, that Lewes advised her to persist "in other kinds of writing" before venturing into the new province of fiction.

That George Eliot should choose, amidst these dire and uncertain circumstances, to show Lewes the old draft that somehow "happened to be among [her] papers" during their sojourn in Berlin thus seems doubly significant. Her phrasing strikes the only chord of disingenuousness, however slight, in "How I Came to Write Fiction." Surely both she and Lewes, expert weighers of consequences that they were, had carefully anticipated that their projected flight to the Continent might result in a resurfacing of old torments. Their decision to go had hardly been a matter of thoughtless impulse. The possible recurrence of her earlier anxieties must thus have called for some precautionary measures. It therefore seems deliberate that, whether consciously or only half-consciously, George Eliot chose to scoop up the old manuscript, "an introductory chapter describing a Staffordshire village and the life of the neighbouring farm houses." As an imaginative fragment of a lost but recreatable past, it could be a talisman against impending change.

The fragment had unquestionably been written to resist earlier bouts of dejection. If Gordon Haight is correct in his conjecture that it dates from 1846, it was composed at a time when Mary Ann Evans was finishing her influential translation of David Friedrich Strauss's *The Life of Jesus, Critically Examined*. At the time she reportedly told her friends the Brays that "she was Strauss-sick—it made her ill dissecting the beautiful story of the crucifixion, and only the sight of her Christ-image [a cast of Thorwaldsen's *Risen Christ* in her study] . . . made her endure it."[15] Not only the visible cast of Thorwaldsen's Christ but also her mental recasting of a solid Midland locality may have been needed on that occasion to allay her "dreadfully nervous" state, her worries about the book's impending publication and about her father's rapidly failing health. Despite her "pale sickly face and dreadful headaches," she was, significantly enough, also reported to look "very happy and satisfied at times with her work." Writing—whether the translation of "leathery Strauss" or the composition of her "introductory chapter" for a novel—had clearly become a welcome means of defense. In her later career as a novelist, her habitual migraines would miraculously cease whenever her pen began to flow.

It is not at all unlikely, therefore, that Lewes himself had actually encouraged her to take along the eight-year-old descriptive fragment. It was a portable bit of space, "a paradise within," to which the would-be pastoralist and lover of Wordsworth's poetry-of-return might therapeutically resort. It was soon to be extended as the "dramatic power," doubted and despaired of, gradually began to assert itself through Lewes's careful coaxing and through his mediations with *Blackwood's Magazine*, upon their return to England. In his own *Blackwood's* piece on "The Novels of Jane Austen," Lewes loyally puffed "the works of Mr. George Eliot," a writer whose "culture, reach of mind, and depth of mind," he avowed, exceeded Austen's. Although George Eliot must have relished this private bit of solicitude, she could also count on Lewes's characteristic candor. Ever the truth-teller, he allowed that "in the art of telling a story" the new novelist still "seems to us inferior" to Austen.[16]

His sincerity paid off. If the static quality of the description he had read in Berlin was still evident in "Mr." George Eliot's evocation of Shepperton Church in "Amos Barton" or of Cheverel Manor in "Mr. Gilfil's Love-Story," her rendering of the Hall Farm and its dairy in *Adam Bede* was far more dynamic (and impressed Queen Victoria so greatly that she commissioned a painting of Hetty Sorrel and Arthur Donnithorne next to the churning butter vats in the dairy).

By *The Mill on the Floss* (1860), when her gender and identity could no longer remain hidden, George Eliot had fully learned how to infuse description with drama. In the masterly opening of the novel, the solid and inert structures of the earlier fictions have been replaced by the ever-moving river. The little girl who stands on the bridge that connects Ripple to Floss may think herself shut off "from the world beyond," as sheltered and immune as the ducks "dipping their heads into the water here among the withes, unmindful of the awkward appearance they make in the drier world above."[17] But if the child stands arrested on that "one February afternoon many years ago," the adult intelligence of the narrator who witnesses the scene must bestir itself into motion (p. 8). The narrator cannot lose herself in the landscape that proves to be so hypnotic. In diction that reminds one of the "dreamy doze" in "How I Came to Write Fiction," George Eliot makes the narrator of *The Mill on the Floss* conscious of having "dozed off" in a reverie, of having "been dreaming" (pp. 8, 9). Though tempted to linger with Maggie, her fellow dreamer, the narrator must bestir herself to acknowledge a painful world of change, alienation, and loss. Unable to find fulfillment with either the brother who takes her father's place or with the unworthy surrogate with whom she vainly elopes, Maggie Tulliver herself must drown.

If a harsh world of change claims Maggie the dreamer, Maggie's creator manages to complete the metamorphosis denied to her heroine. We know that George Eliot wept bitterly while writing the last pages of *The Mill on the Floss.* Yet in depicting the drowning of Maggie and Tom, fused only in the ecstasy of death, the novelist also signified her imaginative transcendence of the stifling ties that stunted the growth of this incarnation of her earlier self. She had at last found the freedom to move beyond a fixation with the past and beyond her attachment to a Tomlike brother whom she regarded as her living link to that past. The newly integrated identity she had fashioned for herself could be shared with an alert mate far more supportive than the Stephen Guest who reproaches Maggie for seeing "nothing as it really is" (p. 420). By unleashing her long-delayed "dramatic power" in *The Mill on the Floss,* George Eliot paid tribute, however indirectly, to the fellow exile who had aided her in the transition from a dreamy doze to that dream's realization. Unlike Maggie, the exiles in her next two novels, Silas Marner and Romola Bardi, would, like their creator, find the strength to survive.

On August 2, 1863, Robert Browning impulsively dashed off a short note to "My dear Mrs. Lewes." He had just finished reading the second volume of her *Romola* and wanted to express his "gratitude for the noblest and most heroic prose-poem I have ever read." Possibly aware that George Eliot's eagerness to be acknowledged as "Mrs. Lewes" was matched only by her desire that her mate be accorded the same respect she was now receiving, Browning made sure to add his parting "regard to your Husband."[18] On reading the final installments of *Romola* a sobered Browning would privately retract his high estimate of the novel. But his intention may well have been to honor the writer of *Romola* more than the "prose-poem" itself. If so, the gracefulness of his tribute could hardly have failed to produce the desired effect; deeply as she must have valued finding *Romola* praised by a fellow artist noted for his own imaginative incursions into the Italian Renaissance, George Eliot would have especially cherished Browning's parting salutation. Although her literary reputation was by now more than secure, there were still those who privately harbored doubts about the reputableness of "Miss Evans" and "her elective affinity." One of these doubters, until won over by *Adam Bede* and *The Mill on the Floss,* had been Elizabeth Barrett Browning herself.[19] Her widower's letter, two years after her death, thus carried an added poignancy.

By 1863, the companionless Browning was well able to appreciate the benefits the Leweses had reaped from their creative partnership. In a further gesture of kinship, two years later, he invited the couple to 19 Warwick Crescent. George Eliot's journal entry for October 15, 1865, conveys her profound emotions: "15. Sunday. In the evening walked home with Browning, went into his house, and saw the objects Mrs. Browning used to have about her, her chair, tables, books, etc. An epoch to be remembered. Browning showed us her Hebrew Bible with notes in her handwriting, and several of her copies of the Greek dramatists with her annotations."[20] George Eliot's awed response to these memorabilia seems deeper even than Browning's own excitement at meeting one who once "saw Shelley plain." It was around this time that she, who had once praised *Aurora Leigh* as a "work exhibiting all the peculiar powers, without the negations, of our sex,"[21] had begun to entertain the notion of casting *The Spanish Gypsy,* that other woman-centered epic, as a verse poem. But it was the domestic setting of that October evening that must have made it, for George Eliot, an epochal ritual "to be remembered."

For a writer so wonderfully attuned to all shades of human relationships, a writer whose fiction relied on the continuous transposition and modification of the major relationships in her own life, a literary mother-sister was kept alive through the loving devotion of a surviving brother-mate. The copresence of Browning and Lewes was thus essential for her own fullest identification with the dead Barrett. Without these male figures, who were at once as capable of extending as of receiving a "mothering of the mind," George Eliot's heightened sense of the affinities between her artist-sister and herself would have remained incomplete.

Neither Browning nor his two visitors had to be reminded that Elizabeth Barrett's 1846 elopement with him to Italy had yielded strikingly similar results to the Leweses' own flight to Germany in 1854. As Dorothy Mermin shows so well in her essay in this volume, both *Aurora Leigh* and Barrett's later poems owe much to Robert Browning's impact. But unlike Barrett, who had been a famous poet long before her elopement, Mary Ann Evans had not really tapped her true creative powers during her years as translator, editor, and essayist. Whereas Barrett resembled the later Aurora Leigh in her emotional subjectivism and lyrical unselfconsciousness as a poet, the *Westminster* intellectual had only, like the younger Aurora in her years of apprenticeship, "learnt the use / Of the editorial 'we' in a review." Her creative identity thus depended far more fully on the chemistry of her exile with Lewes.

Even the circumstances of these two exiles were only superficially alike. Both women, to be sure, came in conflict with Victorian domestic mores: Just as Isaac Evans cut off all communication with his straying sister, so did Edward Moulton-Barrett bitterly sever all familial ties to his oldest daughter; the same Harriet Martineau who acidly denounced Lewes and George Eliot had earlier withdrawn her friendship from the Brownings on hearing of their flight. But life for the Brownings was relatively frictionless. As Mermin reminds us, they were more financially secure and did not require a market for their writing. The Leweses, on the other hand, were professional writers who had to rely on their pens, not just for their own living, but also to support Lewes's three legitimate children as well as Agnes Lewes. Unlike the Brownings, they could not afford to stay abroad in a foreign haven, but had to reestablish themselves in the literary marketplace. Nor could they resort to the games, creative but often hyperbolical, which the Brownings loved to act out with each other. The Brownings delighted in mythical poses, but the Leweses were forced to face sobering consequences unknown to the other pair. There was no possibility for them of casting Lewes as a rescuing St. George or of pretending that they were a reincarnation of Perseus and Andromeda. While the Brownings rummaged through archetypes, George Eliot and Lewes confronted facts. She had not eloped with a wealthy bachelor, as Barrett had, but with a married man weighed down by responsibilities and disappointments. The Brownings could have a child of their own to join them as playmate in their Florentine bower. George Eliot, however, could not afford further affronts to Victorian propriety. She was obligated to remain the surrogate *Mutter* to Lewes's three growing sons.

The feelings of kinship that connected the Leweses to Browning as they inspected his dead wife's mementos were undoubtedly genuine and finely felt. Yet beneath this bond lay another tie that would have remained suppressed, for to acknowledge it would have complicated even further their respective images of a realized marriage of true minds. That link was to still another pair of literary exiles, to Percy Shelley and Mary Wollstonecraft Godwin, whose own elopement to the Continent on July 28, 1814, had furnished a joint precedent for both Victorian couples.

The Shelleys provided Browning and Barrett with one further mythic wrapping in which to envelop their romantic relationship, as their letters to one another in 1845 and 1846 so eloquently show. Eager to emulate the "sun-treader" he had so steadfastly worshiped since his youth, Robert saw himself as reenacting the chivalric behavior of a Percy obsessed with tyrannical fathers and imprisoned daughters in distress. (Shelley had married his first wife, Harriet Westbrook, when she was sixteen years old, to protect her from her father's outrage at opinions which she had imbibed from Shelley himself.) As a young poet's muse, Elizabeth could, in turn, identify with the Mary Shelley whose *Frankenstein* and *Last Man* she so greatly admired.[22] In the letter written on the very eve of his elopement, Robert made sure to include an obligatory reference to Shelley's poetry; earlier, in opting for Italy as their destined haven, he had borrowed Elizabeth's copy of Mary Shelley's *Rambles in Germany and Italy* (1844) and noted his disappointment on finding that their heroine, "the 'Mary dear' with the brown eyes, and Godwin's daughter and Shelley's wife" had become a "commonplace" journalist.[23] Elizabeth, for her part, twitted Robert when she found Shelley's youthful novel *St. Irvyne* to be a banal production, yet professed to find comfort in the fact that it was written before the poet had reached "the maturity of his genius" and had been able to secure the help of "Godwin's daughter," the better novelist.[24] It was one of their poses. It was not until 1851, according to Betty Miller,[25] that a horrified Browning would discover the full facts of Percy's desertion of Harriet when he eloped with Mary—his proposal that all three should live together, with Harriet as his sister and Mary as his wife, and his leaving Harriet and their children entirely when she refused the menage. In the interim, the

Shelleys could act as a mythical archetype for the Brownings' own relation; even Pen Browning could be seen as a reincarnation of that other
Florentine child, Percy Florence Shelley, the only survivor of Percy's
seven children.

For the Leweses, the exile of the Shelleys also seemed buried as a
disturbing personal paradigm. Yet the precedent was not one that either
of them, and especially not George Eliot, was particularly eager to acknowledge. For this couple, unlike the Brownings, fully understood the
darker implications of the analogue. Like Mary Shelley and unlike
Elizabeth Barrett, Mary Ann Evans had eloped with a man legally married to another; but whereas the drowning of Harriet Westbrook Shelley
permitted Mary Godwin to assume the name of "Mrs. Shelley," George
Eliot had to drown an aspect of her own rebellious, Maggielike self in
order to find a tenuous acceptance as Lewes's second wife. For her, as
for the still unwed author of *Frankenstein,* fiction provided an outlet for
her hunger for relations. "Was I then a monster, a blot upon the earth,
from which all men fled, and whom all men disowned?" asks the Creature before pleading with Frankenstein that he create a "creature of
another sex, but as hideous as myself," to join it in "exile," cut "off from
the world."[26] That the Monster's plea—and emotions behind that plea—
had a special resonance for George Eliot is evident from her own experiment with the mode of the horror story in "The Lifted Veil," which she
wrote between *Adam Bede* and *The Mill on the Floss.*

When George Eliot sent John Blackwood, her publisher, the manuscript of what she called "the dismal story," she was unusually self-
deprecating. It was, she insisted, "a slight story of an outré kind—not a
jeu d'esprit, but a *jeu de melancolie.* . . . I think nothing of it, but my private
critic says it is very striking and original."[27] Supportive as always, Lewes,
her "private critic," must nonetheless have been shocked. For not only
did George Eliot completely contravene the canons of realism he and she
had so far jointly espoused, but she also dramatized the same sense of
desolation that beset a Mary Shelley who had turned to *Frankenstein*
upon discovering that her mate could not fill her need for "mothering"
any more than her father and stepmother had.[28] Latimer, the male protagonist of "The Lifted Veil," is as irrevocably alienated as Shelley's
Monster. Indeed, some of Latimer's wails of self-pity seem directly lifted
from *Frankenstein:* "I have never unbosomed myself to any human being," he complains; "I have never been encouraged to trust much in the
sympathy of my fellow-men." Shelley's Monster protests: "I am an
unfortunate and detested creature; I look around, and I have no relation or friend upon earth." George Eliot's Latimer echoes: "I have near
no relatives who will make up, by weeping over my grave, for the
wounds they inflicted on me." If the Monster, like Mary Shelley herself,

is born motherless, Latimer is, as George Eliot was, deprived of his "tender mother" as a "sensitive child." If the Monster is rejected by the father-creator who escapes his "detested form," Latimer is at odds with an "unbending" father who prefers his complacent older son to this abnormal child. If the Monster kills a brother figure in little William, Latimer profits from the death of the brother whose "small patronizing ways" had "irritated" him as much as Isaac Evans's ways had irritated George Eliot, recently returned to England from the Continent.

George Eliot invokes Mary Shelley's *Frankenstein* in the Genevan setting of "The Lifted Veil," the Shelleyan title, the portrayal of an experiment in animation, and, as Gilbert and Gubar have rightly noted, in the name of Bertha Grant, Latimer's vampiric mate. Yet George Eliot goes beyond Mary Shelley in her questioning of the surrogate relationship of "mothering." Bereft of kinship, the motherless Monster, who has admired the portrait of the maternal Caroline Frankenstein, asks Victor to "create a female" for him. "*Grant* my prayer," he vows, and promises to live in peaceful exile with his monstress-mate. It is George Eliot, however, not Mary Shelley, who grants such a mate; but Bertha *Grant*, whom Latimer desires as much as the Monster had desired a female fellow exile, only helps to confirm the impossibility of such a fusion. George Eliot's sudden doubts about the possibility of joining, not just the male and female genders, but also the male and female components of her own psyche seem dramatized by Latimer's predicament.

I have elsewhere noted that the localities Latimer and Bertha visit—Munich, Vienna, Prague, and Dresden—correspond exactly to the itinerary of George Eliot and Lewes after their own departure from Munich, where she had written much of *Adam Bede*. Even the crucial description of the Jewish cemetery at Prague, which ends the first half of the story, contains details factually recorded by the two tourists in their respective journals.[29] But the full emotional import of this analogy has remained unanalyzed. Upon returning to England, George Eliot seems to have called in question for a second time the self-sustaining, protective interdependence with Lewes, the "dual solitude" which, according to Redinger, was achieved on their first elopement to the Continent. That her doubts, soon laid to rest by his continued support of her creativity and by her continued rise to fame, were encased in a Shelleyan story leads us back to the significance the failed relationship of the Shelleys held first for Lewes and then for herself.

In his youth, Lewes had been as ardent an admirer of Shelley as Robert Browning. In 1841, a bare six weeks after his marriage to the beautiful Agnes Jarvis, not yet perceived as a Bertha Grant, he published a forty-one-page essay on the poet in the *Westminster Review*. Though ostensibly Lewes's aim was to review Mary's editions of Percy's poems and essays, his actual intention seems to have been to convince the poet's widow of his ideal qualification as Shelley's biographer. He repeatedly compliments her and naively praises Shelley's presumed feminism, which he, in still another compliment, credits quite dubiously to the influence of "Mary Wolstoncraft" [*sic*]. His praise of that "high-minded woman" (quite different from George Eliot's own later essay on Wollstonecraft and Margaret Fuller) is designed as a tribute, not just to her daughter, but also to the children of Swynfern Jervis, whose emancipated daughter Agnes had been brought up on a Shelleyan belief in free love unconstrained by legal or religious trammels. Lewes's paean to Shelley's presumed perception that "women are neither slaves nor angels—but women" is distinctly intended for the eyes of his own bride; "if a wife be meant to be a *partner* of your life—a sharer in your spiritual hopes and successes, as well as in your material ledger successes, then it is in Shelley that you will find the true ideal woman."[30]

In 1841 Lewes earnestly selected Shelley as a model because, like Browning, though in a different way, he was still eager to enact Shelley's presumed role as a champion of femininity, "the 'poet of women.'" He originally regarded Agnes as a fellow writer, a productive journalist who could help their "material ledger" with translations from French and Spanish, in short, such a woman as the editor and translator he would, years later, help convert into "George Eliot." By 1851, however, the year in which Mary Shelley died and in which Mary Ann Evans published her first *Westminster* essay, Lewes was more than ready to close his Shelley and open his Goethe. He could now add himself to the list of Byron and Shelley as "unhappy husbands" cited in his 1841 essay. The erotic pluralism that had once fascinated a Percy Shelley who tried to have T. J. Hogg share a common "treasure" in Mary had lost its mythical appeal when Agnes gave birth to the first of several children by Thornton Hunt. What is more, Percy's image had itself become badly tarnished; he was no longer the "gentle, brave, and generous" angel of his widow's guilty and distorted memory. Victorian reality had displaced Romantic mythology.

Thus, when Lewes eloped with Mary Ann Evans, almost exactly forty years after Percy had fled with Mary Godwin and Claire Clairmont, his new bride also differed markedly from the young bride he had so idealistically celebrated by implicitly linking her to Mary Shelley in his 1841 essay. Agnes had long ago ceased to be the "true ideal woman" who, according to Lewes, had inspired Shelley's best poetry. This later incarnation, though not sixteen, as Mary had been, nor so beautiful, was nonetheless much truer to Lewes's earlier, now matured, ideal. Yet the situation was also cruelly parodic: The eloping couple were not Percy and Mary speeding across the Continent with Claire; instead, a Frankenstein monster, at last awarded his desired mate, settled exhaustedly, not in the South American rain forests but in Goethe's sedate Weimar.

A consciousness of their Shelleyan antecedents seems to have been engraved in the minds of the newest pair of exiles much as it had been present in the minds of the Brownings. Like the Shelleys and unlike the Brownings, however, the Leweses returned to England some months after their elopement, when the same malicious calumnies that, according to Lewes's 1841 essay, were heaped on Shelley by "men calling themselves Christians" now deeply threatened Lewes's companion. As a Shelley-like agnostic and as a woman who had offended Victorian codes of conduct, she rightly feared a clash with the patriarchal society in which Lewes could still freely move, for all his feminism and unconventionality.

Small wonder, then, that in 1858, just before *Adam Bede* secured the reputation of the pseudonymous "Mr. Eliot," George Eliot should have become greatly unsettled by a strident attack, in the very *Westminster Review* to which she and Lewes had contributed, on Shelley's detractors.[31] Her prompt rejection of the author's clumsiness and "false sarcasm" betrays her need to distance herself from the Shelleyan precedent that she and Lewes had redefined. Yet her fears of total isolation, as the fable of "The Lifted Veil" so eloquently shows, were not easily allayed. Only Lewes's continued support (even of that "dismal story") and her gradual winning over of the public, who came to regard her as a "Mrs. Lewes," permitted her to continue to tap her creative genius. Fusion again became possible.

George Eliot's diary entries after Lewes's death on November 30, 1878, are most painful to read. And painful, too, for her Victorian admirers, was her hasty marriage to the younger John Cross. A widowed state was not as possible for her as it had been for Robert Browning. Nor could she, as Gertrude Stein would, find the masculine component she needed within her own selfhood. Stein, who drew on *The Mill on the Floss* for the title of one of her earliest essays, "Red Deeps," could move, as Catharine Stimpson shows in her essay in this book, from mother love through brother love to sister love. In 1880, the year of her marriage and death, George Eliot seems to have deliberately rejected such a possibility when she discovered that the young Edith Simcox, who had posed as her quasi-daughter, demanded more than mother love. When Edith kissed her repeatedly and "hung over her caressingly," she gently chided her as a "silly child." As Simcox later reported:

Then she said—perhaps it would shock me—she had never all her life cared very much for women—it must seem monstrous to me—I said I had always known it. She went on to say, what I also knew, that she cared for the womanly ideal, sympathised with women and liked for them to come to her in their troubles, but while feeling near to them in one way, she felt far off in another—the friendship and intimacy of men was more to her.[32]

Read in one fashion, this graceful rebuke was a justification for George Eliot's preference of the young John Cross as an object of her own "mothering." But it was also one last tribute to the dead Lewes and to the economy of their relationship. Lewes's special sympathy for women had led him to nurture and care for "the womanly ideal," a sensibility George Eliot attributed to several male characters in her fiction.

Mary Shelley's *Frankenstein* ends in an orgy of male destructiveness. At the end of *The Mill on the Floss,* however, the "strength, inspired by mighty emotion," which allows Maggie to rescue her brother, leads to a "sense of reconcilement."[33] Although Maggie and Tom, like the mateless Monster and Victor, can only be mated in death, their apocalyptic drowning allowed George Eliot to affirm the integrated powers of an imagination she had questioned in "The Lifted Veil." In *Middlemarch,* a novel embedded with Shelleyan allusions,[34] the novelist went even further. If Maggie clasps Tom's hand as they go down in "an embrace never to be parted," Will Ladislaw seizes Dorothea's "hand with a spasmodic movement." "A vivid flash of lightning" illuminates their faces; "and so they stood, with their hands clasped, like two children, looking out on the storm, while the thunder gave a tremendous crack and roll above them, and the rain began to pour down."[35]

Love, for George Eliot, happened in those moments of overcoming the separateness she just as intensely felt. Like the Dorothea who overcomes her momentary alienation from the mercurial Will Ladislaw, George Eliot may have, at certain junctures of her life, been beset by doubts about the steadfastness of a relation that had shaped her creative identity. But her internal integration depended on her determination to fuse with an "other," a male mate who had replaced her parents, brothers, and tutors. The "ardent" Dorothea Brooke, who misplaced her affection on Mr. Casaubon, attains fulfillment with the reformed Shelleyan worshiper of the feminine, a Will whose Slavic name is pronounced "Lady's Love." Yet Dorothea, whose creativity is spent in "channels of no great name," must efface herself and subordinate herself to her male companion. The novelist whose "great name" incorporated that of her "husband," George, fared considerably better.

NOTES

1. See J. W. Cross, *George Eliot's Life as Related in Her Letters and Journals* (London: William Blackwood, 1885), I, 414–16; Gordon S. Haight, *George Eliot: A Biography* (New York and Oxford: Oxford University Press, 1968), pp. 206–207; Ruby Redinger, *George Eliot: The Emergent Self* (New York: Knopf, 1975), pp. 4, 83, 290, *et passim.* "How I Came to Write Fiction" is also reprinted in Gordon S. Haight, ed., *The George Eliot Letters* (New Haven: Yale University Press, 1954–55, 1978), II, 406–10; hereafter this edition will be referred to as *GEL.*

2. See in particular Sandra M. Gilbert and Susan Gubar, *The Madwoman in the Attic: The Woman Writer and the Nineteenth-Century Literary Imagination* (New Haven and London: Yale University Press, 1979), pp. 455–58; George Levine, "The Ambiguous Heritage of *Frankenstein*," *The Endurance of "Frankenstein,"* George Levine and U. C. Knoepflmacher eds., (Berkeley, Los Angeles, London: University of California Press, 1979), pp. 23–25; and U. C. Knoepflmacher, *George Eliot's Early Novels: The Limits of Realism* (Berkeley and Los Angeles: University of California Press, 1968), pp. 138–43.

3. Mary Wollstonecraft Shelley, *Frankenstein, or, The Modern Prometheus,* ed. James Rieger (Indianapolis and New York: Bobbs-Merrill, 1974), p. 222.

4. "Percy Shelley," *Westminster Review* 35 (April 1841), 313.

5. William Bell Scott, *Autobiographical Notes* (London, 1892), I, 133; quoted in Edgar W. Hirshberg, *George Henry Lewes* (New York: Twayne, 1970), p. 22.

6. Hirshberg, *George Henry Lewes,* pp. 111, 90.

7. See Ruth Perry's Introduction to this volume.

8. Shelley, *Frankenstein,* pp. 222, 223.

9. Haight, *George Eliot: A Biography,* p. 205. The statement—and Bodichon's remark that Lewes's "manner" to Mary Ann was "delightful"—was relayed to Gordon S. Haight by Mrs. Belloc Lowndes, noted for destroying, as late as 1942, Bodichon's letter describing the Lewes's contraceptive practices.

10. Redinger, *George Eliot,* p. 43.

11. Ibid., p. 33.

12. Ibid., pp. 40–41. See also Bonnie Zimmerman, "'The Mother's History' in George Eliot's Life, Literature, and Political Ideology," in Cathy N. Davidson and E. M. Broner, eds., *The Lost Tradition: Mothers and Daughters in Literature* (New York: Frederick Ungar, 1980), pp. 81–94; and U. C. Knoepflmacher, "Unveiling Men: Power and Masculinity in George Eliot's Fiction," in Janet Todd, ed., *Men by Women, Women and Literature* 2, n.s. (New York and London: Holmes and Meier, 1981), pp. 130–45.

13. When the hypochondriacal Martineau circulated the rumor that she was near death, George Eliot asked John Chapman to allow her to become Martineau's official biographer. Martineau's *Autobiography,* an unduly neglected confessional masterpiece, appeared in 1877, a year after her actual death.

14. *GEL* III, 56.

15. Ibid. I, 200.

16. *Blackwood's Edinburgh Magazine* 89 (July 1859), 104.

17. George Eliot, *The Mill on the Floss,* ed. Gordon S. Haight (Boston: Houghton Mifflin, 1961), p. 8; subsequent references are given in the text.

18. *GEL* IV, 96.

19. See Helen Cooper, "Mrs. Browning and Miss Evans," *Nineteenth-Century Fiction* 35 (December 1980), 257–59.

20. *GEL* IV, 205.

21. Ibid. II, 278. George Eliot reviewed the poem in the opening of her "Belles Lettres" section in the *Westminster Review* 67 (January 1857), 307, and apparently reread it (with Lewes) thereafter.

22. See Elvan Kintner, ed. *The Letters of Robert Browning and Elizabeth Barrett Barrett: 1845–1846* (Cambridge: Harvard University Press, 1969) I, 179 ff., 189 ff., 218–19, 278.

23. Ibid., 189.

24. Ibid., 218–19.

25. Betty Miller, *Robert Browning: A Portrait* (New York: Scribners, 1952), pp. 169–70; but see Hall Griffin and C. H. Minchin, *The Life of Browning* (London: Methuen, 1910), p. 185, for a different dating of this event.

26. Shelley, *Frankenstein*, p. 142.

27. *GEL* III, 41.

28. See U. C. Knoepflmacher, "Thoughts on the Aggression of Daughters," and Peter Dale Scott, "Vital Artifice: Mary, Percy, and the Psychopolitical Integrity of *Frankenstein*," in Levine and Knoepflmacher, *The Endurance of "Frankenstein,"* pp. 88–119 and 172–202.

29. See Knoepflmacher, *George Eliot's Early Novels*, pp. 133–35.

30. "Percy Shelley," 331.

31. The essay on Shelley (*Westminster Review* 59 [1858], 97–131) was by John Richard de Capel Wise; his glib handling of the relation between Shelley and the society which had ostracized him offended a George Eliot eager to become reconciled to the readership of her early fiction: "I have long ceased to feel any sympathy with mere antagonism and destruction," she wrote her friend Sara Sophia Hennell after reading Wise's piece (*GEL* II, 421).

32. Quoted in K. A. McKenzie, *Edith Simcox and George Eliot* (London: Oxford University Press, 1961), p. 97.

33. George Eliot, *The Mill on the Floss*, p. 453.

34. See Roland A. Duerksen, "Shelley in *Middlemarch*," *Keats-Shelley Journal* 14 (Winter 1965), 23–31; the Gothic elements in the novel are discussed by David R. Carroll, "*Middlemarch* and the Externality of Fact," in Ian Adam, ed., *This Particular Web: Essays on "Middlemarch"* (Toronto: University of Toronto Press, 1975), pp. 77–84 *et passim*.

35. George Eliot, *Middlemarch*, ed. Gordon S. Haight (Boston: Houghton Mifflin, 1956), p. 593.

Gertrude Stein. Courtesy of Yale University Library

Gertrude Stein and Alice B. Toklas at Culoz in 1944. World Wide Photos

Gertrice/Altrude[1]

STEIN, TOKLAS, AND THE PARADOX OF THE HAPPY MARRIAGE

Catharine R. Stimpson

Alice B. Toklas.
Courtesy of Yale
University Library

∽*G*ertrude Stein *(1874–1946) was born in Pennsylvania but spent her adult life in Paris, where she died. Beginning to write seriously after 1900, she became a powerful figure in avant-garde and bohemian circles. Among her closest friends were Pablo Picasso and Ernest Hemingway. She was a unique theoretician about language and literature, and a modern writer so radically innovative that critics are only now measuring her achievements with full accuracy. She has been called a literary "cubist." Such works as* Three Lives *and* The Making of Americans *are marked by her manipulations of traditional narrative structure and syntax;* The Autobiography of Alice B. Toklas *remains her best-known work.*

Alice B. Toklas (1877–1967), a Californian, met Stein in Paris in 1907. They became lovers and inseparable lifelong companions. After Stein's death, Toklas nurtured her reputation. Toklas also started to write books that have their own idiosyncratic pungency, wit, and style: memoirs, cookbooks, and letters that were published posthumously.

ertrude Stein and Alice B. Toklas are legends and icons now. They have achieved that cottony apotheosis of later capitalism, imprinting on a T-shirt. Red outlines on blue cloth, they sit, behatted, on some steps in Venice in the plaza of St. Mark's. Stein is front and center, Toklas behind her to her right. Pigeons graze on the stones before them. Tourists, soldiers, and a little boy move between them and the church. Stein and Toklas seem wary but alert; self-contained but together.

Because legends and icons are inimitable, because of changes in social practice, and because of their own temperaments, Stein and Toklas may not have generated a life that many people can readily follow. Stein, who thought about repetition, would have understood. In her triumphant return to America in the 1930s, she mused: "There also is the important question of repetition and is there any such thing. Is there repetition or is there insistence. I am inclined to believe there is no such thing as repetition."[2] Despite their singularity, Stein, a woman of genius, and Toklas, a woman of gifts devoted to genius, are a Byzantine example of the conditions in which genius can fulfill itself and gifts freely bestow themselves.

People still prefer to gossip about them as personalities rather than to graph Stein's radical texts. Mistakenly, some of the people who knew Stein asserted that because her fame was the result of her personality, it would not survive her death.[3] Even now, literary professionals may honor and teach the simpler books and neglect the more extraordinary ones.[4] Yet as bohemian styles have been a part of modern culture, so the life of Stein and Toklas was a base for her work.

They met in Paris in September 1907. Stein was thirty-three, Toklas thirty-one, both past the age when women were to marry. In theory, they were strangers, but Stein had secretly read the letters that Toklas had written to a mutual woman friend. The one who later would seem to have power over the other first knew the other—through deception, inseparable from her sexuality, and through language, inseparable from her intellect and ambition. They also shared a social milieu. They were introduced formally at the home of Sarah and Michael Stein, Gertrude's oldest brother and his wife.

Nor in many ways were Stein and Toklas each other's psychological Other. Though Stein had more formal education than Toklas, both were cultivated women. They both admired the Henry James who so elegantly explores the nuances of consciousness, including that of the young American woman in Europe. Though Stein was born in Pennsylvania and Toklas in California, both spent much of their youth in the spacious American West. Both had, as children, traveled to Europe and to the Paris that they were later to mythologize as the city where a New Woman with purpose, resolve, individuality, and artistic interests had to go. Both were Jews, Gertrude the more orthodox, who had undergone the rites of secularization. Though both had some family financial backing, neither could count on an easy affluence. A friend and collaborator later said of Stein, ". . . about money, [she] did not joke."[5] Finally, both were lesbians.

Yet they differed in ways that influenced their passion, domesticity, and adventures. Stein was the last of five children. A plump, prodigal baby, she liked the privileges of that position, no matter how disorganized her family was to become. Her mother died of cancer when she was fourteen; her father when she was seventeen. Later, her comments about parents were laconic: "Fathers are depressing . . . Mothers may not be cheering but they are not as depressing as fathers."[6] One of Stein's most brilliant critics concurs:

> Her mother was an ineffectual invalid, gradually draining in her bed until, even before she died, she was emptied out of the world. Her father was a nuisance: stocky, determined, uneducated, domineering, quarrelsome, ambitious, notional, stern.[7]

Stein had three brothers and a sister, to whom she gave one virture: Bertha bore an interesting son.

Toklas, an only daughter with one much younger brother, was compelled to recognize the domestic obligations of that position, particularly after her mother, a charming woman, died, also of cancer, when Toklas was nineteen. Her father, benignly quiet, accepted his daughter's homely services without patriarchal bombast. Though Stein created many women characters, Toklas was the more involved in women's activities, traditional or not, before and after she met Stein. In 1957 she wrote:

> As a little girl I was allowed to meet Susan B. Anthony when she came to San Francisco. She was the first great woman I met and she made a lasting impression on me. She was beautiful and frail and quite naturally dominated the group of women who had been asked to meet her.[8]

On that American tour, Toklas insisted that the couple meet some women writers. In England, Stein describes her as ". . . at present most interested in the curtains that is what she finds most exciting that and everything else done by women." (*EA,* p. 316).

Moreover, by 1907, settled in Paris, Stein finally had a vocation. She had finished some novellas in which she had exorcised an unhappy lesbian affair. She was in the middle of *The Making of Americans: The Hersland Family,* in which she was to appropriate her family, transform it into her linguistic territory, and exorcise it as well. More than a writer, Stein was a person of language. She used, tested, and pushed it to its limits of both concrete precision and abstract spaciousness. She read and spoke voraciously: "When people were around she would talk and listen, ask questions. She talked with anybody and everybody."[9]

In 1907 Toklas, despite her brains and musical talents, had no vocation. Stein became her work. Toklas began as an apprentice, reading proof and typing—a skill she taught herself. She ended as the master of a special guild. Much later, when she was old and sick, Toklas once confessed that perhaps her expatriation was deeper than Stein's: "Gertrude never left home in the same way I did. She was always at home through the language, but I was at home only through her."[10] Yet her meeting with Stein was an exalted engagement with warmth and power, an experience resonant with a sense of rebirth. After Stein's death, she said, "It was Gertrude Stein who held my complete attention, as she did for all the many years I knew her until her death, and all these empty ones since then."[11]

Within a year they must have been lovers. In Italy, as Toklas wept, Stein proposed that they live together as man and wife. Paradoxically, as their naked erotic impulses broke boundaries, they clothed them in language that redrew those very lines. As they violated the rules of sex, they obeyed those of gender. As they discarded heterosexuality, they enforced the codes of marriage. They were at once defiant and submissive, traditional and modern. In the spring of 1909, Stein invited Toklas to join her and her brother Leo, for whom Toklas also typed from time to time, at the famous 27, rue du Fleurus. However, before they could fully realize their desires, they had to maneuver to dislodge others: Harriet Levy, the woman with whom Toklas had been sharing an apartment, and Leo, the brother with whom Stein had been sharing a home.

Harriet Levy, with encouragement, returned to California. In September 1910, Toklas took up full residency at "27." Biographers still puzzle over the relationship of Leo, Gertrude, and Alice—in part because any couple, any "two," with a history as intense as that of Gertrude and Leo leaves a residue that escapes analysis; in part because both Gertrude and Leo, those two Talmudic reasoners, had a fine defensive capacity for denial. Despite her frights and anxieties, Gertrude could declare firmly, "Any life you look at seems unhappy but any life lived is fairly cheerful, and whatever happens it goes on being so" (*EA*, p. 101). As if ideology were psychic reality, Leo could state, as firmly:

> From childhood on our private lives were entirely independent. At a very early time before our teens we had come to an explicit understanding not to interfere with each other, and this developed in many implicit ways.[12]

Despite such claims of independence, Gertrude and Leo had ties as intricate as the needlepoint Toklas later was to do. They were conceived because their parents had wanted a family of five, and after two babies had died, they needed replacements. An apprehender of the null and void, Gertrude once wrote: ". . . there were to be five children and if two little ones had not died there would be no Gertrude Stein, of course not" (*EA*, p. 115). Joining brother and sister, then, were a survivor's guilt and a substitute's sense of privilege and of the precarious. Both bright and verbal, they went to the same schools, lived in the same American cities, and went into a happy exile in the same house.

Yet commonalities are not the same as samenesses. Gertrude may have been incestuously attracted to Leo, and he may or may not have reciprocated. Virgil Thomson suggests that before Gertrude found Alice she was ". . . certainly tormented by amorous emotions not only toward certain women but also, I have reason to believe, toward her brother Leo."[13] Gertrude also permitted Leo to be her scout. He acted; she followed. She talked frankly about the pleasure, a common word in her vocabulary, of having an older brother to do "it all for and with you" (*EA*, p. 70). Though a passion for glory consumed Stein even in the early days in Paris, she let Leo be the "genius." He spoke about art; she listened.

Apparently serene, Leo gave up one of his rooms for Toklas. By 1913 he had left all of "27." Even after Gertrude and Leo's final "dis-aggregation," a suspiciously Latinate word for such a rupture, he wrote that Toklas's presence had been a "godsend as it enabled the thing to happen without any explosion."[14] Doubtless Toklas was too shrewd to become an ostensible cause of trouble between brother and sister, but equally doubtless, she was, at most, a secondary cause.

For Leo hated Gertrude's increasing command of public speech. Until his death, he loathed and satirized her writing and condemned the quality of her mind. She healthily resented his disdain. Again showing how much her identity was interwoven with language, she used the metaphor of deafness for his response to her refusal to be mute. She once wrote that, although Leo learned to read before she, "reading was something we never did together. Reading is something you have to do alone, and it was something I always did completely alone" (*EA*, p. 71). (She did, however, once read the letters of Queen Victoria aloud to Toklas.) That youthful, autonomous sense of self as reader surely prefigured her eventual assumption of Leo's role of speaker, which only one person in their twosome apparently could play.

In contrast, Toklas wholly endorsed Gertrude as genius, another touchstone in their mutual vocabulary, and as a man of language. Stein had also found, in Picasso, another, and more egalitarian, brother. He was perhaps the most compelling of the men, like Hemingway, who were, in overlays as complex as the facade of St. Mark's, to serve as surrogate brothers, sons, and, on occasion, as sexually charming Adonis figures for the older Stein. Less obviously, Joyce, Stein's rival, was to loom as the bad brother about whom one can barely speak, yet whom one can never eradicate.

Together for nearly forty years, Stein and Toklas were open about their lesbianism with each other and with some trusted friends. They were close-mouthed with everybody else. Friends respected the point where silence replaced speech. For example, the sculptor Janet Scudder in her autobiography blandly mentions Stein as "the discoverer of Matisse and the inventor of a new literature."[15] As discreetly, Scudder refers to her own friend—a "Mrs. Lane."

Though the literary prowesses of Stein and Scudder are dissimilar, they had to confront the same impossible problem in autobiography. To write one, they had to say something about their domestic life. To do *that,* they had to mention a realm and people whom they also wished to protect. Devising their strategies of mingled admission and concealment, they gave much of the game away though writing about it at all. Refusing to tell a reader that Mrs. Lane's first name is Camille hardly renders her invisible. Torn between exhibitionism and fear, a Scudder, with fewer technical tricks to distract a reader than a Stein, produces a page that lacks both interesting declarative statements and blankness. It tempts the invasion of the innuendos she so hoped to avoid.

Few, if any, printed references to Stein and Toklas's sexuality appeared until the end of World War II, when Stein died.[16] Most notoriously and dankly, Hemingway proclaimed it, his words a final weapon in his sad, bitter war with them.[17] As culture has become less rigidly heterosexual, people have explored their erotic bond far more carefully.[18] Perhaps the danger now is not that we will avoid their wedding and their bedding, but that we will linger there too long. Confusing attention and voyeurism, we will inadvertently extend the error that defines women either as chaste creatures, incapable of sex, or as promiscuous creatures, capable of nothing else.

Stein and Toklas must have given each other permission to release desire, fantasy, urge, tenderness, and play. They dissolved each other's repressive armor and solidified a gratifying ardor. Stein, who liked explanations, could rationalize that sexuality. Like some male theoreticians of her period, she linked homosexuality to artistic strength. She also celebrated lesbianism as an activity that fused sensuality and purity. Hemingway, who may not be reliable, tells of an encounter in which she rebuked his homophobia. However, she agreed that male homosexuals do "ugly and repugnant things," possibly an allusion to fellatio and to anal intercourse, in which the organs of eros, urination, and excrement are spatially so close. Then, negating her habitual association of self and maleness, she separated male homosexuality from female, and implicitly declared herself female. For women ". . . do nothing they are disgusted by and nothing that is repulsive and afterwards they are happy and they can lead happy lives together."[19]

If Stein and Toklas refused to defend their sexuality more explicitly or publicly, they had reasons other than guilt and cowardice. They endorsed a social code that both valued privacy and fit easily with a cautious, realistic assessment of the world's attitude toward lesbians. In 1912 neither sexual nor literary experimentation won awards.[20] Maturely summarizing her attitude toward her life, Stein told another young admirer:

> We are surrounded by homosexuals, they do all the good things in all the arts . . . I like all people who produce and Alice does too and what they do in bed is their own business, and what we do is not theirs . . . most of our really good friends don't care and they know all about everything. But perhaps considering Saint Paul it would be better not to talk about it, say for twenty years after I die, unless it's found out sooner or times change. But if you are alive and writing then you can go ahead and tell it, I would rather it came from a friend than from an enemy or stranger.[21]

In spite of, or perhaps because of, her reticence, Stein took more from her lesbianism than erotic satisfaction. Her alienation from the life of an ordinary woman provided perspective, "a critical distance that shape[d] her understanding of the struggle to be one's self."[22] Her sexual identity may not be "at the center of . . . [her] questioning of language,"[23] but the exploration of differences that engaged her is consistent with the sexual difference that she and Toklas efficiently learned to manage.

So doing, they often displayed exotic, even eccentric, manners: Stein in her brocaded vests, Toklas in her decorated hats; Stein reading palms, Toklas chain-smoking. What Richard Kostelanetz respectfully says of Stein might be true of them together: "Not unlike other American geniuses, Stein walked the swampy field between brilliance and looniness."[24] Structuring their life, they set up a number of interlocking dyadic roles. We, who value freedom and options and flexibility, must accept the possibility that the very firmness of their roles helped them to surmount the difficulties of their deviancies. Most problematically, Stein was that husband, Toklas that wife. Not only did Stein write, and Toklas type and edit,[25] but Stein ate, and Toklas cooked and served. Such acts, which Toklas taught herself to do magnificently, were literally and symbolically nourishing. Stein drove the Ford cars she loved. Toklas was driven. Stein hoed the garden and, during World War II, chopped wood. Toklas supervised the garden and, during World War II, rationed food and furiously prepared rooms for the officers of the armies of occupation that were billeted in their country homes.

Not surprisingly, given the period, the marriage was Victorian. The bluffer, bigger, more athletic Stein could do more, think more, say more. When provoked, she swore. The tinier, more ladylike Toklas was more restrained. Another of the young men who entered their lives once wrote, "Alice was every inch a lady in the pleasant Victorian sense of the word, and she set limits to her curiosity."[26] Others, rummaging for metaphor in more distant ages, found Stein a Roman emperor, Toklas the gatekeeper and guide to his emotional states. The most persistent anecdote about their marriage arises from their entertaining, the mixing of a public and a domestic life. As Gertrude talked to the men, particularly to the smart ones, Alice talked to the wives. Another American expatriate recalls:

> I knew the rules and regulations about wives at Gertrude's. They couldn't be kept from coming, but Alice had strict orders to keep them out of the way while Gertrude conversed with the husbands . . . I couldn't see the necessity for the cruelty. . . . Curiously, it was only applied to wives; non-wives were admitted to Gertrude's conversation.[27]

When Hemingway complained that Stein talked a lot of "rot," his wife answered, "I never hear her . . . I'm a wife. It's her friend that talks to me."[28]

To oversimplify the Stein/Toklas marriage and ménage is stupid. Toklas was also a willful woman whom Stein sought to please. In "Bonee Annee," Stein has Toklas say, "This must not be put into a book."[29] If this shows Toklas's linguistic inhibitions, the line's imperative mood also marks her power. So does a phrase in the middle of the 2,000 or so lines of "Lifting Belly," the most audacious, pungently lyrical, witty text ever published about lesbian sexuality: "Husband obey your wife." If Toklas appeared to be "Pussy," the guardian subordinate, the salon keeper, the watchful servant of "Lovey's" needs, she chose that role. She knew that in that role she would have something to guard, a salon to keep, a way to serve her needs as well. Thomson concludes:

> Alice had *decided* [italics mine] long before that "Gertrude was always right," that she was to have whatever she wanted when she wanted it, and

that the way to keep herself always wanted was to keep Gertrude's writing always and forever unhindered, unopposed.[30]

If Toklas was a cordial, gracious hostess, her fiber also frightened some. She was a sly, rapid conversationalist, a subtle, elegant, amusing literary stylist. She provided Stein with a stable but contrasting sensibility against which Stein could measure herself and from which she could borrow. If Stein was elliptical, Toklas was condensed; if Stein was aural, Toklas was visual.[31] Stein also praises Toklas's objectivity, impartiality, and accuracy; Toklas is "always right so much" (*EA*, p. 123)—cognitive virtues a genderizing culture has attributed to men.

Yet the Stein who wrote the biting "Patriarchal Poetry" and who deplored patriarchal excess did claim the prerogatives of the male. In effect, she distinguished between overweening fathers, whom she rejected, and good husbands, which she became; between dumb men, whom she disliked, and genius, which she wanted. Psychologically, because of her long involvement with Leo, she might personify a theory of Karen Horney, the revisionary psychoanalyst who was her contemporary. Horney mentions cases in which the "illusion of being a man" is a dynamic part of the self. She speculates:

> . . . in them a conspicuous degree of identification with a specific man— generally the father or the brother—has taken place, on the basis of which development in a homosexual direction or the formation of a narcissistic attitude and orientation occurs.[32]

Sociologically, Stein's husbanding of her energies shows the limits of her imagination. She knew plenty of women artists, writers, and intellectuals. Yet at heart she was apparently unable to picture a world in which men, and an exceptional woman, did not plumb language and define culture. Such a conservative attitude was consistent with many of her other political analyses. She once declared, "Writers only think they are interested in politics, they are not really, it gives them a chance to talk and writers like to talk but really no real writer is really interested in politics."[33] For better or worse, often for worse, Stein talked. During the Depression, she commented on the servant problem, "It is curious very curious and yet not at all unreasonable that when there is a great deal of unemployment and misery you can never find anybody to work for you" (*EA*, p. 10). She generalized vapidly about national and racial characteristics. Her comments about "Negroes" are fearful, ignorant, and embarrassing. A biographer, whom Toklas was to revile, said, "Revolutionary in her art, she was reactionary in politics, and the liberal outlook did not appeal to her."[34] A friend phrased it more affectionately, ". . . Miss Stein was a hard-rock Republican."[35]

Modulating the familial roles of husband/wife was Stein's simultaneous status as polymorphous baby. Neither father nor mother, but parent, Toklas both disciplined and conjured up a sense of boundless security. She also handled difficulties that Baby might find upsetting. "Even in her later years . . . she was inclined to let Alice dispose of sticky personal problems."[36] Stein's reassuring sense of the boundless could, reversing itself, fall away into nothingness. She was a sophisticated thinker about identity and a woman anxious about her own. Who was she if her little dog stopped knowing her? The adult Toklas could renew boundlessness and the firmness of boundaries. Baby's mind was not infantile, but Baby could be productively infantilized.[37] Unsurprisingly, the couple seems to have thought little of real babies,[38] or even surrogate daughters, who might have interfered with the fantasy. They could be conscientious godparents, but they did not romp readily with infants in their salon. As a medical student, Stein disliked obstetrics and the process of biological birth. The surrogate sons—whom Stein advised, whom Stein and Toklas welcomed, and with whom they sometimes quarreled—were adults, at least on the calendar.

As lover, wife, and parent, Toklas reassured Stein about her writing. Some may interpret Stein's jealousy of other writers and her need for praise as narcissism, and Toklas's need to praise as self-effacement. However, the public consistently ignored, misunderstood, or mocked Stein's work. Until 1933 and the appearance of *The Autobiography of Alice B. Toklas,* only a few supporters knew that she was more than a bohemian character, an art collector, a language freak, or a joke. After 1933, though she delighted in her fame, she legitimately queried the reasons for her new success. The support that Toklas built for Stein was less a mutual indulgence than a coping mechanism for an innovator.

Toklas did more than minister to an ego. Socially, she administered the homes in which Stein talked out her ideas and received stimulus and esteem. From 1930 to 1933, Toklas oversaw the Plain Editions, five Steinian texts that the sale of a Picasso underwrote. Before and after Stein's death, Toklas organized the notebooks of unpublished work. She was an efficient secretary, agent, editor, archivist, and publisher. Stein could be grateful: "Alice B. Toklas is always forethoughtful which is what is pleasant for me so she said she would make copies of all my writing not yet published and send it to Carl Van Vechten for safe keeping" (*EA*, p. 11). She could also treat Toklas's efforts with casual aplomb. If Stein was dependent, Toklas was dependable. In America a photographer asked for pictures of Stein doing anything:

All right I said what do you want me to do. Why he said there is your airplane bag suppose you unpack it, oh I said Miss Toklas always does that oh no I could not do that, well he said there is the telephone suppose you telephone well I said yes but I never do Miss Toklas always does that, well he said what can you do well I said I can put my hat on and I can take it off and I like water I can drink a glass of water all right he said do that . . . [*EA*, pp. 218–19.]

Toklas was a muse as well, Stein's memory, prod, and inspiration. Stein wrote both out of and about her immediate world. Toklas supplied that world with raw material: events, tales, domestic details, tension, sexuality, and flair. Stein returned those materials to her as comparatively finished texts. The first of their transactions, which Toklas could distrust, was the early portrait "Ada." Symbolically, Stein read it to Toklas one evening while she was preparing supper. Ada (the Toklas figure) has a passive father, a younger brother, and a dead mother whom she loved, and with whom she shared some stories. However, Ada has had other stories, presumably sexual, that she could not tell. Resentful of having to take on her mother's role, Ada instead takes some inherited money and goes away. She then meets another (the Stein figure), who listens utterly, who is chivalrous, and who generously gives her a new life. As the portrait moves from psychological sketch to sweet romance, its language becomes more and more lilting and euphonious. For Ada comes "to be happier than anybody else who was living then . . . who ever will be living."[39]

"Ada" was only the beginning of hundreds of transactions. Critics are deciphering, with increasing subtlety, Stein's erotic poetry, the record of her fluid, interrogated, sustaining lesbianism.[40] Her rhythmic and musical skills animate such work. "As A Wife Has A Cow: A Love Story" uncannily replicates the rising waves, the gasps of the excitement that culminates in the female orgasm. Yet as Toklas was everywhere in Stein's life, so she is everywhere in Stein's writing, in the erotic texts and elsewhere. For example, people have correctly said that "Susie Asado" imitates a Spanish dance. It begins and ends, "Sweet sweet sweet sweet sweet tea." But "tea" puns on "T," and "T" is Toklas, a common joke for Stein. In the penultimate line—"What is a nail. A nail is unison"—Stein, among other things, alludes to the fingernails that Toklas frequently manicured. The nail is her nail and a synecdochal delegate for the hands that might toil for Stein and touch her.

Stein's experiments with grammar articulate the unison that "Susie Asado" declares. Her wiping out of quotation marks in passages of dialogue makes the flow of speech between people more important than their separate statements. Her syntactical ambiguities fuse persons and roles. For example, in "Lifting Belly," "lifting," as a participle, modifies the belly that is being lifted, so deliciously. Lifting, as a gerund, signifies both the act of lifting and the actor who is lifting the belly, so deliciously. The word merges lover and beloved. Simultaneously, Stein blurs genres. "Fact," what she sees and does, glides into "fiction," what she thinks, imagines, and remembers, and what she does to "fact" through her juxtaposition of perceptions and events.[41] As she writes, she is often self-conscious about it. In the middle of "As A Wife Has A Cow," she mentions "the fifteenth of October," when T. S. Eliot was to publish a portrait in *The Criterion*. She even concludes "Lifting Belly" with "In the midst of writing there is merriment."

Stein and Toklas had their merriment-stopping fights. Some of Stein's last lines might have been her "means of having a final word in one of her spats with Alice, who was still transcribing her daily writing into legible form."[42] Stein was probably lazy and flirtatious, Toklas fussy and jealous. Both could manipulate. Yet, anxious without each other, they never left each other. They visited in lesbian circles in which monogamy was a trifle. They were apparently hugely faithful. Not for Stein "the matings and rematings that went on among the amazons."[43] Even after Stein was a celebrity, her name in lights, they stayed together. They pleased each other. In Bilignin, their country home, *les mesdemoiselles américaines* were capable of ". . . a great racket . . . shouting at once, or laughing. . . ."[44] If they were symbiotic, "complete and complemented,"[45] they saved each other—Stein from a far less productive career, Toklas from a far greater marginality.

Stein died of cancer in 1946. Leo was to die of the same disease a year later. Like an after-image, Toklas's widowhood showed the quality of her marriage. As she had been warily alert to people devaluing her as Stein's "companion," she now feared their desertion. As she had guarded Stein's work, she now nurtured its reputation and sought to insure its historical standing. In 1957 she joined the Catholic Church. As Stein had been her husband, she now found solace and happiness in priests and patriarchal structures. As she had been faithful, she now found compensation for her loss and a promise of seeing Stein again in a new faith. She wrote, in part for money, but *The Alice B. Toklas Cook Book* also fulfilled a scene with Stein. Returning to Europe after their American trip, the couple talked with a third person about Toklas's "career," rather as if she were a housewife thinking about reentry. Toklas decided that she would produce a cookbook. Stein concurred and noted in a comic throwaway that would become a prophecy, ". . . of course this she would not let me do for her and with reason" (*EA*, p. 296).

Toklas's intelligence and toughness began to fill the foreground Stein had once occupied. She could be pithy. "Gertrude," she once said, "was not deep, but she could insert herself in a fissure. So she was very near to things."[46] She thought she had to be Stein's witness. A friend reports that if she was asked what Stein had thought, and if she began to give her own opinion, ". . . she would suddenly cease, as if with a sense of heresy or as if she were contributing to apocrypha. . . ."[47] Yet, never a Jamesian captive of another's will, she showed more and more of her own. Despite this, she must have been lonely. She spent her last three years in an apartment she and Stein had never shared, and when she died in 1967, I suspect she was relieved.

Obviously, to understand Stein and Toklas means to remember the period in which they lived. It was, Karen Horney politely but firmly says, one in which "woman's efforts to achieve independence and an enlargement of her field of interests and activities continually met with skepticism."[48] Hemingway, unhappily, spoke for the culture whose skepticism they had to besiege. Remembering Stein, he wrote, "There is not much future in men being friends with great women although it can be pleasant enough before it gets better or worse, and there is even less future with truly ambitious women writers."[49] Beating down their time, Stein created Stein the writer. Toklas helped immeasurably, and in the process created Toklas too. Their tightly organized lesbian marriage was one of their strongest weapons. Perhaps ironically, it continually meets with skepticism now. To egalitarians, its outward patterns—that hierarchy of "male" domination and "female" submission, that solar system in which nurturers orbit around a shining, central male genius—seem obsolete, even cannibalistic. To avoid recognizing them, some even try to womanize Stein, to call her the mother or "the grandmother" of experimentation and nonconformity.[50]

Despite their idiosyncratic marriage, they also exemplify a crucial fact of their period, and of ours: Women often do their best work in the intimate company of other women. Those independent women who wish to enlarge their field of interests and activities have persistently been happy in and benefited from ". . . the many networks, both contemporary and historical, of egalitarian and nurturing friendships among creative and publicly active women."[51] Probably Stein and Toklas would have been less celebrated, and thought more dangerous, if they had been more overtly egalititarian,[52] if Toklas had stood less often in the background of their portrait. Yet within their set of rules, they did permit that portrait to be shown, and, so doing, announced the value of a women's we-ness.

They share a gravesite in the Père Lachaise cemetery in Paris. Colette is there, and Chopin, and Paul Eluard. Near the brick wall where members of the Paris Commune were shot at dawn in 1871 are memorials in honor of members of the French Resistance and of victims of the Holocaust. Cedars, willows, and rhododendrons guard the stones and cenotaphs. Stein's name is on one side of a block of granite, Toklas's on the other. People bring flowers, and sometimes they scatter glass beads in tribute too. Stein and Toklas have what they wanted. They are buried together, and now we write—about them, and the mind of Gertrude Stein.

NOTES

1. "Gertrice/Altrude" appears in a Stein manuscript. I am indebted for the reference to Wendy Steiner, *Exact Resemblance to Exact Resemblance: The Literary Portraiture of Gertrude Stein* (New Haven: Yale University Press, 1978), p. 187. I have anticipated this essay, and my debts, in some of my previous work: "The Mind, the Body, and Gertrude Stein," *Critical Inquiry* 3 (Spring 1977), 489–506; and "Toklas, Alice B.," in *Notable American Women: The Modern Period*, ed. Barbara Sicherman and Carol Hurd Green (Cambridge: Harvard University Press, 1980), pp. 693–94.

2. Gertrude Stein, "Portraits and Repetition," in *Lectures in America* (Boston: Beacon Press, 1967), p. 166.

3. See, for example the Introduction by Mabel Weeks, who had known Gertrude and Leo since they were students, in Leo Stein, *Journey into the Self, Being the Letters, Papers and Journals of Leo Stein*, ed. Edmund Fuller, intro. Van Wyck Brooks (New York: Crown, 1950).

4. Richard Kostelanetz, Introduction, *The Yale Gertrude Stein* (New Haven: Yale University Press, 1980), p. xxx. Kostelanetz, like a growing number of critics, defies my generalization. Their forerunner is Donald Sutherland, *Gertrude Stein: A Biography of Her Work* (New Haven: Yale University Press, 1951).

5. Virgil Thomson, *Virgil Thomson* (New York: Knopf, 1967), p. 247.

6. Gertrude Stein, *Everybody's Autobiography* (New York: Vintage, 1973), pp. 132–33. Hereafter I shall refer to this edition as *EA* and cite quotations in my text.

7. William H. Gass, "Gertrude Stein and the Geography of the Sentence," in *The World Within the Word* (New York: Knopf, 1978), p. 67.

8. Edward Burns, ed., *Staying on Alone: Letters of Alice B. Toklas*, (New York: Vintage, 1975), p. 345.

9. Thomson, *Virgil Thomson*, p. 170.

10. James Mellow, *Charmed Circle: Gertrude Stein and Company* (New York: Praeger, 1974), pp. 476–77.

11. Alice B. Toklas, *What is Remembered* (London: Michael Joseph, 1963), p. 26.

12. Leo Stein, *Journey*, p. 298.

13. Virgil Thomson, "Secrets of Gertrude Stein," *New York Review of Books* 16 (April 8, 1971), 4.

14. Leo Stein, *Journey*, p. 52.

15. Janet Scudder, *Modeling My Life* (New York: Harcourt, Brace, 1925), pp. 234–5. Scudder's prose, like her sculpture, is clean, charming, and unoriginal.

16. A conscientious bibliographer says that she found no such references before 1944. See Maureen R. Liston, *Gertrude Stein: An Annotated Critical Bibliography* (Kent, Ohio: Kent State University Press, 1979), p. 48.

17. Ernest Hemingway, *A Moveable Feast* (New York: Scribner, 1964).

18. They include not only Gass and Thomson, but Richard Bridgman, *Gertrude Stein in Pieces* (New York: Oxford University Press, 1970); Linda Simon, *The Biography of Alice B. Toklas* (Garden City, N.Y.: Doubleday, 1977); Elizabeth Fifer, "Is Flesh Advisable? The Interior Theater of Gertrude Stein," *Signs* 4 (1979), 472–83.

19. Hemingway, *A Moveable Feast*, p. 20.

20. Gass, "Gertrude Stein and the Geography of the Sentence," pp. 99–100. The passage follows a *tour de force* reading of the sexual themes in "A Box" from *Tender Buttons*.

21. Samuel M. Steward, *Dear Sammy: Letters from Gertrude Stein and Alice B. Toklas* (Boston: Houghton Mifflin, 1977), p. 55–56. The full conversation, if it happened, is a wonderful example of Stein's getting information out of someone, in this case about Steward's own sexuality, and about what mutual friends have said to him about Toklas and her. For another young man's affectionate memoires about Stein and Toklas, see W. G. Rogers, *When This You See Remember Me: Gertrude Stein in Person* (New York: Avon, 1973).

22. Cynthia Secor, "*Ida*, Great American Novel," *Twentieth Century Literature* 24 (1978), 99. See, too, Cynthia Secor, "Alice and Gertrude," *Female Studies VI* (Old Westbury, N.Y.: Feminist Press, 1972), pp. 50–52.

23. Nancy Blake, "Here and Now with Gertrude Stein," *Delta*, No. 10 (May 1980), 6–7.

24. Kostelanetz, Introduction, *Yale Gertrude Stein*, p. xvii.

25. Scholars disagree about the degree to which Toklas's editing became writing. For example, Steiner, *Exact Resemblance*, p. 187, takes issues with Bridgman's assessment of Toklas's contribution to *The Autobiography of Alice B. Toklas*, which, as Stein's "secretary," she ostensibly wrote. Sociologists, psychologists, and literary critics can have fun with this series of fictions. I believe that Toklas's typing, appraising, and editing often became a mild rewriting, but to call Toklas the writer, rather than the frame that kept the writer within bounds, would be excessive. For two good, recent analyses of *The Autobiography*, see Paul K. Alkon, "Visual Rhetoric in *The Autobiography of Alice B. Toklas*," *Critical Inquiry* 1 (1975), 849–81; and Neil Schmitz, "Portrait, Patriarchy, Mythos: The Revenge of Gertrude Stein, *Salmagundi* 40 (1978), 68–91.

26. Bravig Imbs, *Confessions of Another Young Man* (New York: Henkle-Yewdale House, 1936), p. 181. Imbs, one of the young men who courted Stein/Toklas and with whom they broke, ends his autobiography snidely. For example, falling on tired old insults, he calls the two "old maids." However, skilled infighters in the verbal wars of Parisian Bohemia, Stein/Toklas gave him no quarter. For example, Stein tells Steward that Imbs was " . . . as dull as Gissing, thoroughly and perfectly. Too bad. He tried to buy a castle and he failed even in that" (*Dear Sammy*, p. 12).

27. Sylvia Beach, *Shakespeare and Company* (New York: Harcourt, Brace, 1959), p. 31.

28. Hemingway, *A Moveable Feast*, p. 31.

29. Gertrude Stein, *Geography and Plays*, with a Foreword by Sherwood Anderson (New York: Something Else Press, 1968), p. 302.

30. Thomson, *Virgil Thomson*, p. 171.

31. Ibid., pp. 176–77.

32. Karen Horney, "The Overvaluation of Love," in Harold Kelman, ed., *Feminine Psychology* (New York: Norton, 1967), pp. 201–202.

33. Gertrude Stein, "The Situation in American Writing," *Partisan Review* 6, 4 (Summer 1939), 41.

34. Elizabeth Sprigge, *Gertrude Stein: Her Life and Work* (London: Hamish Hamilton, 1957), p. 216.

35. Genêt (Janet Flanner), "Letter from Paris," *The New Yorker* 38 (December 29, 1962), 67.

36. Mellow, *Charmed Circle*, p. 149.

37. Critics have called Stein's writing childish. Even in a sympathetic review, F. S. Flint says, "Miss Stein's essences are a trifle peculiar, the intuitions of a gifted child setting out to write history merely from the sound of names." "Cambridge Theatricals," *Partisan Review* 23 (1956), 205. I am making a different point, i.e., about the recreation of a psychological state that Stein and Toklas liked. Possibly, Stein was too indulged, and got away with too much. Certainly, during World War II, when things were very hard for the two elderly Jewish–American women living in France, she lost weight and gave her writing new vigor. However, I would not call her texts "childish." They are both repetitive and spontaneous, but because we associate these qualities with children, we cannot logically go on to say that Stein's work is childish. If we do, it becomes a form of guilt by association.

38. See, with care, Imbs, *Confessions*, pp. 288–89.

39. Gertrude Stein's, *Geography and Plays*, p. 16. Mellow, *Charmed Circle*, p. 130, writes that "Ada" shows that Stein believed she had "a benevolent effect . . . upon Alice's previously unsettled emotional life." Slyly, in *Geography and Plays*, "Miss Furr and Miss Skeene," a portrait about a lesbian couple that separates, follows "Ada," the portrait of the couple that trembles and stays together.

40. See the critics listed in note 18. Some of the interpretations might be even better if they were more aware of the technicalities of lesbian sexuality. For example, hands, fingers, and the tongue, as well as things, can be vaginally inserted.

41. See Steiner, *Exact Resemblance*, p. 186.

42. Mellow, *Charmed Circle*, p. 42.

43. Thomson, *Virgil Thomson*, p. 179. Thomson, in "Secrets of Gertrude Stein," p. 4, calls the Stein/Toklas home life "genuinely beatific."

44. Steward, *Dear Sammy*, p. 9

45. Genêt (Janet Flanner), "Letter from Paris," *The New Yorker*, 43 (March 25, 1967), 174.

46. Genêt (Janet Flanner), "Letter from Paris," *The New Yorker* 22 (August 10, 1946), 42. That the remark is also a metaphor for sexuality was doubtless unconscious.

47. Genêt, "Letter from Paris," (March 25, 1967), p. 174.

48. Horney, "The Overvaluation of Love," p. 182.

49. Hemingway, *A Moveable Feast*, p. 117.

50. Steward, *Dear Sammy,* p. 25.

51. Blanche Wiesen Cook, "'Women Alone Stir My Imagination': Lesbianism and the Cultural Tradition," *Signs* 4 (1979), 719.

52. Ibid., p. 730. For an interesting interpretation of the enigmatic quality of their joint photographs, see Erling Larsen, "I Know, Pablo, I Know," *Carleton Miscellany* 16 (Fall/Winter 1976–77), 159–81. For another sign of the Stein/Toklas entrance into popular myth, see a raunchy, witty comic book, T. Hachtman, *Gertrude's Follies* (New York: St. Martin's, 1980), no pagination. Subtitled "An Irreverent Look at the Life and Times of Gertrude Stein and Her Faithful Companion, Alice B. Toklas," the book collects strips that previously appeared in the *Soho Weekly News.*

Mothers Real and Imagined

Paule Marshall.
Courtesy of Rhoda
Nathans

Alice Walker. Photo
© 1982 L. A. Hyder

I Sign My
Mother's Name

ALICE WALKER,
DOROTHY WEST,
PAULE MARSHALL

Mary Helen Washington

Dorothy West.
Courtesy of Alison
Shaw

⌒○Alice Walker, *born in 1944 in Eatonton, Georgia, was the youngest of eight children of a sharecropper and a domestic. Scholarships enabled her to attend Spelman College and Sarah Lawrence. While at Sarah Lawrence, she slipped a sheaf of her poems under the door of the poet Muriel Rukeyser. Rukeyser gave them to her editor at Harcourt Brace Jovanovich, who published Walker's first book of poetry. Walker went to Mississippi to work in the civil rights movement of the 1960s, and subsequently has lived in Brooklyn and San Francisco. She has published three books of poetry* (Once [*1970*], Revolutionary Petunias [*1973*], *and* Good Night Willie Lee, I'll See You in the Morning [*1979*], *three novels* (The Third Life of Grange Copeland [*1970*], Meridian [*1976*], *and* The Color Purple [*1982*]), *and two books of short stories* (In Love and Trouble [*1974*] *and* You Can't Keep a Good Woman Down [*1981*]). *A contributing editor at* Ms. *magazine, she is also well known for her essays. In 1983 she was nationally recognized with both the National Book Award and the Pulitzer Prize for her novel* The Color Purple.

Dorothy West, *born in 1912 in Boston, attended Girls' Latin School and Boston University. She went to New York in the early 1930s to study at the Columbia School of Journalism, where she participated in the artistic and cultural ferment that came to be known as the Harlem Renaissance. In 1934 she founded* Challenge, *one of the first literary journals to merge both political and aesthetic concerns. Her novel,* The Living Is Easy, *was published in 1948. For the past thirty-five years, West has lived on Martha's Vineyard, where she writes a regular column for the* Vineyard Gazette.

Paule Marshall, *whose parents emigrated from Barbados during World War I, was born in Brooklyn, New York, in 1929. After graduating Phi Beta Kappa from Brooklyn College, she worked as a magazine researcher, a librarian, and eventually as a writer. She has published three novels* (Brown Girl, Brownstone [*1959*], The Chosen Place, the Timeless People [*1971*], *and* Praisesong for the Widow [*1982*]) *and a book of short stories* (Soul Clap Hands and Sing [*1961*]). *During the 1950s and 1960s, Marshall was associated with American Youth for Democracy and also with Artists for Freedom, a militant black movement formed after the bombing of a Birmingham church that killed four little black girls. Although she was a successful writer in the 1960s, Marshall came into her own in the 1970s, the decade of feminism.*

And so our mothers and grandmothers have, more often than not anonymously, handed on the creative spark, the seed of the flower they themselves never hoped to see: or like a sealed letter they could not plainly read.

—Alice Walker, "In Search of
Our Mothers' Gardens"[1]

I ain't good lookin' and ain't got waist-long hair
I say I ain't good lookin' and I ain't got waist-long hair
But my mama gave me something that'll take me anywhere.

—Traditional blues song[2]

⌒⌒Alice Walker grew up in rural Georgia in the late 1940s, a daughter of Southern sharecroppers; Dorothy West was born and bred among Boston's black middle class in the first decades of this century; Paule Marshall, born in 1929, grew up in Brooklyn, the daughter of Barbadian emigrants. All three of these writers have made special claims about the roles their mothers played in the development of their creativity. In fact, the bond with their mothers is such a fundamental and powerful source of their art that the term "mothering the mind" might have been coined specifically to define their experiences as writers. Walker, West, and Marshall found in their relationships with their mothers the key to the release of their creative powers—"those momentary and transient extravagances of the imagination," Freud called them—which allow the artist to select images and symbols to impose her inner visions on the world. With so many active and brutal restrictions against female creativity, particularly against the creativity of black women, it is remarkable that these black mothers—denied power in nearly every realm of their lives—arrogated to themselves and their daughters the power to create through language, to define themselves by the written word, to become witnesses to the special sensibility of black women.

Alice Walker's essay "In Search of Our Mothers' Gardens: The Creativity of Black Women in the South" was my first confirmation of how crucial a nurturing female community has been for the development of black women writers.[3] How, she wonders in this landmark essay, was the creativity of black women kept alive in the centuries when the freedom to write or paint or sculpt did not exist, when a highly gifted black girl would have been thwarted and hindered by chains, guns, the lash, the ownership of one's body by someone else, by submission to an alien religion, not to mention twenty-four-hour back-breaking work?[4] And her wondering brings Walker to her own myths:

> It is my mother—and all our mothers who were not famous—that I went in search of, the secret of what has fed that muzzled and often multilated, but vibrant, creative spirit that the Black woman has inherited, and that pops out in wild and unlikely places to this day.[5]

Her mother, Walker remembers, was an artist who passed on orally the stories of her life, and not only the stories themselves but a respect and care for the creative spirit that nurtured her own creativity as she was growing up. There was a special quality in her relationship with her mother that gave Walker the "permission" to be a writer, a sense that, farmer's daughter or not, she was a poet and writer. Even though her mother worked out of the house all day—in other women's kitchens— leaving her the lone girl in a family of men (her sisters were grown and gone by that time), her mother never demanded that she take on the household chores; nor did she make Alice feel that she would be a disappointment if she did not take on those chores:

> I did those things out of love not because I had to. I could go into my room and shut the door and lie on the bed and read, knowing I would never be interrupted. No matter what was needed there was no word about making me leave a book. It was not just the "permission" to read. My mother trusted me implicitly and completely. She never questioned me about any relationships with boys. She trusted my ability to go out into the world and learn about the world. I suppose because I was the last child there was a special rapport between us and I was permitted a lot more freedom. Once when I was eight or nine she was about to whip my brothers and me for something and when she finished whipping the others and got to me, she turned around and dropped the switch and said "You know, Alice, I don't have to whip you, I can talk to you."[6]

Walker is describing the source of her own trust in herself, an essential quality for any artist. She never doubted her powers of judgment because her mother assumed that they were sound; she never questioned her right to follow her intellectual bent, because her mother implicitly entitled her to it. It was not so much that her mother created a space within which Walker could work; but she reinforced Walker's sense of her absolute right to her own thoughts and feelings.

Many contemporary black women writers report this same experience of being singled out, of being given at an early age a sense of specialness that was encouraging and prophetic. Gwendolyn Brooks told me once at a reading that when she first showed her poems to her mother, Mrs. Brooks proclaimed that her daughter was going to be the lady Paul Laurence Dunbar. Toni Cade Bambara recalls with some amazement that her mother was so respectful of her young daughter's preoccupation with words that when she came across her on the floor with a book she would mop around her: "She gave me 'permission' to wonder, to dawdle, to daydream."[7]

Walker's mother gave her three gifts when she was in high school which later came to take on an important symbolic value for her. They were things her mother never owned herself, items she bought on lay-away when she was earning less than twenty dollars a week. When Walker was fifteen or sixteen, her mother gave her a sewing machine for her birthday so she could learn to make her own clothes. "I even made my own prom dress, such as it was, something chartreuse net, I think. But the message about independence and self-sufficiency was made clear."[8] The second gift was a suitcase, a high school graduation gift:

> . . . As nice a one as anyone in Eatonton had ever had. That suitcase gave me permission to travel and part of the joy in going very far from home was the message of that suitcase. Just a year later I was in Russia and Eastern Europe.[9]

The third gift was a typewriter, a gift Walker had forgotten and remembered in the course of these reminiscences:

> O yes, she bought me a typewriter when I was in high school. How did my mama ever get that typewriter? She must have ordered it from Sears. A typewriter and a little typewriter table. She did all this on less than $20.00 a week. If that wasn't saying, "Go write your ass off," I don't know what you need.[10]

A sewing machine, a suitcase, and a typewriter: These were gifts and messages that were to carry Walker far beyond her mother's own experiences. That distance between her mother's experiences and her own is significant, for many of Walker's stories are about women who survive and endure but who do not have the power to articulate the meanings of their lives. There is the mute Roselily, a bride who thinks of herself at her wedding as a trapped animal; the unlettered Mrs. Jerome Washington, who loves "her sweet Jerome" even though he uses her for her money; the mother in "Everyday Use," who dreams of having a quick and witty tongue but who in real life cannot even look a strange white man in the eye.[11] The mother in "A Sudden Trip Home in the Spring" stood "stout against the years," but it is the daughter, "versed in many languages," who speaks for her.[12]

In a poem called simply "Women," Walker describes the women of her mother's generation as "headragged generals" who led the armies of the next generation across the mined fields of oppression and exploitation into a place of discovery. In this poem she emphasizes the mysterious ability of these women to pass on to their children something they themselves neither possessed nor understood:

> To discover books
> Desks
> A place for us
> How they knew what we
> *Must* know
> Without knowing a page
> Of it
> Themselves.[13]

There is more than simply the transference of the authority and power to write in Walker's relationship with her mother. Her mother *was* an artist, a woman whose creativity with flowers earned her fame in several counties:

And I remember people coming to my mother's yard to be given cuttings from her flowers: I hear again the praise showered on her because whatever rocky soil she landed on, she turned into a garden. A garden so brilliant with colors, so original in its design, so magnificent with life and creativity, that to this day people drive by our house in Georgia—perfect strangers and imperfect strangers—and ask to stand or walk among my mother's art.[14]

Watching her mother in this garden, Walker says she saw her mother "involved in work her soul must have," "ordering the universe in the image of her personal conception of beauty." When Carol Christ speaks of the meaning of models in our lives, she makes an important distinction between knowing something intellectually and knowing it in the visceral, emotional way that creates change. "Not remembering transcendent experiences is a common human problem, but it is intensified for women who have no stories, models, or guides to remind them of what they know."[15] I think that with the aid of these oral testimonies about their mothers as artists, black women writers are beginning to piece together the story of a viable female culture, one in which there is generational continuity, in which one's mother serves as the female precursor who passes on the authority of authorship to her daughter and provides a model for the black woman's literary presence in this society.[16]

Women, we have been told, have trouble conceiving life as a whole, are unable to shape it according to its own inner logic, without relating it to a man. Women, it is also said, fail to achieve generational harmony because traditionally the mother-daughter relationship has been one of hostility, and the psychic harmony men learn as they progress toward reconciliation with their fathers is impossible for women because "no such model exists for female life."[17] But many black women writers have testified to the existence of this sort of generational continuity between themselves and their mothers, and they write that continuity into their texts. Gayl Jones says the women she descended from have a special significance for her writing: "The generations of women are there because of something I needed to clarify in my own life."[18] In her novel *Corregidora*, Ursa is told by her grandmother and her mother "to make generations," to pass down the story of slavery and its degradations from one generation to the next so it will never be forgotten:[19]

> Because they didn't want to leave no evidence of what they done—so it couldn't be held against them . . . you got to leave evidence too. And your children got to leave evidence, we got to have evidence to hold up. That's why they burned all the papers, so there wouldn't be no evidence to hold up against them.[20]

The mother-daughter relationship is not just a personal dyad, a psychic bond between the two. It is part of the tradition of the community. Ursa's mother wants her to have babies to pass on the tradition, but Ursa remains childless. The telling of her ancestors' stories must be the evidence she passes on. Alice Walker's mother was not just a model for her of artist and creator. She too had "evidence" of the black past that had to be transmitted. The need to record her mother's life, to make it fully articulate, was the motivating force behind her writing:

> Through years of listening to my mother's stories of her life, I have absorbed not only the stories themselves, but something of the manner in which she spoke, something of the urgency that involves the knowledge that her stories—like her life—must be recorded.[21]

In assuming the voices of their mothers, these writers assure that character, culture, and creativity are interlocking systems in their works. This oneness with the community which these writers express is profoundly connected to creativity. No black writer has been able to reveal the black experience in all its range and complexity without that sense of unity— of oneness with his or her people. For black women writers, the mother is often the key to that unity. It is Barbara Christian's contention that black women writers are "immersed into their communities and their communities' ways of making meaning through their mothers," and their novels become "the literary counterparts of their communities' oral traditions."[22]

One of Walker's stories, "The Revenge of Hannah Kemhuff," based on an incident that happened to her mother during the Depression,[23] shows how her mother's experience is transformed into "a metaphor for human existence."[24] Her mother went into town to the Red Cross for food and flour, which were almost impossible for poor sharecroppers to get. Dressed in her best, though worn clothes, her mother presented her voucher for flour and was immediately and angrily dismissed by the white woman who was distributing the food: "'Anybody dressed up as good as you don't need to come here begging for food. . . . The *gall* of niggers coming in here dressed better than me!'" In her mother's mind the story is not finished when she walked away humiliated, pulling three small children with her, nor is it finished that winter she spent swapping food so they could get by. The story ends thirty years later, when Mrs. Walker's eight children are grown and she herself is still hale and hearty, "and that old woman that turned me off so short got down so bad in the end that she was walking on *two* sticks and here I am with hardly a sick day in my life."[25] In a later essay, "Saving the Life That Is Your Own: The Importance of Models in the Artist's Life," Walker describes how after hearing the story for the fiftieth time she came to see the possibilities of that story for fiction. It was her mother's investment in the story, and her tone of voice that interested Walker:

> My mother always told this story with a most curious expression on her face. She automatically raised her head higher than ever—it was always high—and there was a look of righteousness, a kind of holy heat coming from her eyes. . . . To her this was clearly the working of God, who, as in the old spiritual, "may not come when you want him, but he's right on time."[26]

Out of this incident grew a story that incorporates Zora Hurston's voodoo experiences as well as the real-life incident from her mother's life.[27] As an apprentice to an old black rootworker named Tante Rosie, the narrator in "Hannah Kemhuff," like Alice Walker, is the guardian of this folktale, the griot who remembers and saves her memories and shapes the tale. There are some variations in the tale her mother passed on to her. Impatient with a Christian justice that takes twenty-five years to bear fruit, and eager to render more realistically the sense of power that righteousness gave her mother, Walker substitutes voodoo rites from Hurston's *Mules and Men* for her mother's Christian consciousness. Hannah Kemhuff, who is humiliated in the food line by the young white woman, seeks out the old rootworker, Tante Rosie, and orders revenge on Mrs. Holley. In her fear of the spell Hannah is working, the white woman, Mrs. Holley, unwittingly and ironically fulfills the curse of Hannah Kemhuff. She dies in a horrible state, collecting her own hair and her own feces in order to prevent the old rootworker from using them to destroy her.

The look of righteousness, the holy heat from her mother's eyes, and the sense of retribution are all evident in this tale. A black ethos is shown in triumph over the destructiveness of the white world. But there is something still more important about the way Walker's mother influenced the tale: Women order and control the universe in this story. Women's rituals and women's folklore are the central elements of the tale, and in it a woman's history and a woman's sense of community are revealed. The community is seen, as women see it, from within, where its inner working, its logic, its rituals, make up a world, like Zora Hurston's Eatonville, that is complete in itself. Walker makes this final comment about the meaning of passing on her mother's history:

> In that story I gathered up the historical and psychological threads of life some of my ancestors lived, and in the writing of it I felt joy and strength and my own continuity. I had that wonderful feeling writers get sometimes, not very often, of being *with* a great many people, ancient spirits, all very happy to see me consulting and acknowledging them, and eager to let me know, through the joy of their presence, that indeed, I am not alone.[28]

On the island of Martha's Vineyard in February of 1980, I interviewed Dorothy West, who provided the most immediate and dramatic account of a woman discovering her voice through the mediation of a female power—her mother. Somewhere around 1926, when West was not yet twenty years old, she went to New York and became a part of the group of younger Harlem Renaissance writers which consisted of Wallace Thurman, Zora Hurston, Aaron Douglas, Augusta Savage, and Langston Hughes. West describes herself in the group as a quiet and shy spectator, a writer without a voice:

> I went to the Harlem Renaissance and never said a word. I was young and a girl so they never asked me to say anything. I didn't know I had anything to say. I was just a little girl from Boston, a place of dull people with funny accents.[29]

The "group" went to Wallace Thurman's loft regularly on Sunday nights, but one Sunday, instead of joining them, West went to visit a family of very proper black Bostonians who managed to do everything right. They had the correct manners, the proper dress and decorum; they even stood around the piano singing after dinner, trying to project the "proper" image of the happy family. In this one incident, a powerful transformation in West's sensibility began, and she discovered the beginnings of her own creative voice by remembering her mother's voice:

> Our family was much more colorful and much less proper, and at one point in the midst of all this proper behavior I saw my mother's disembodied face laughing at me for being with these people—these middle class, proper folks. They were my class but not my people. I rushed out of there and went straight to Wally's loft, hoping I wouldn't be too late. I could have gone home, but I couldn't. I had to be with them. And I went in and began to tell them that story, making fun of those proper people *just as my mother would. All my mother's blood came out in me. I was my mother talking.* All of the things I thought I admired and there I was making fun of them. *I became me.* I thought I was a proper Bostonian until I met some. It was the first time I had something to say.[30]

West is released from silence (both from without and within) by the example of her mother's power and her mother's voice. In her identification with her mother's sensibility—her ironic view of pretentious blacks, her ability to satirize their foibles, her magnificent storytelling gift—West's creative imagination comes alive. What is also interesting about this transformation is the recognition (which occurs simultaneously) that she does not have to reject her own culture to be a writer. Thus cultural integrity and creative freedom, which are vitally interrelated, come together in the moment she experiences the power of self-articulation.

Freedom in West's account is also associated with a break from male power. When she identifies with her mother's voice, she rejects the dominance of the male clique of the Harlem Renaissance, who had reduced her to a mere girl with nothing of importance to say. That ironic tone she adopted from her mother is there in her first novel, *The Living Is Easy*, which she published in 1948, almost twenty years after her experiences with the Harlem literati. In this novel she satirizes the pretensions of the Boston black elite, especially their desire not to be associated with ordinary black people, with the same satiric humor of her mother:

> Though they scorned the Jew, they were secretly pleased when they could pass for one. Though they were contemptuous of the Latins, they were proud when they looked European. They were not too dismayed by a darkish skin if it was counterbalanced by a straight nose and straight hair that established an Indian origin. There was nothing that disturbed them more than knowing that no one would take them for anything but colored.[31]

There is another side of Rachel West's influence that is not so positive. According to West, her light-skinned, beautiful mother was never quite able to accept having a plain, dark-skinned child like Dorothy. She was as class-conscious and race-conscious as the main character of *The Living Is Easy,* Cleo Jericho Judson, and she tried to rear Dorothy in the same mold. Her mother's domineering ways rankled West so much that in a fit of anger she once complained about her to her father, who quietly and cryptically said, clearly indicating that he wanted to hear no more: "*I* understand your mother." West was not admitted to that inner circle.

West tried to deal with her mother in her first novel. Cleo is patterned after Rachel West. The father, Bart Judson, the Black Banana King of Boston, is modeled after West's father, and in West's retelling of their story, it is their strange little dark-skinned daughter Judy who triumphs over a villainous and unregenerate mother. The novel is mother-obsessed. Trying to recreate her dead mother's life, Cleo lies and connives until all three of her sisters leave their husbands and bring their children to live with her, Bart, and Judy in a large house in Boston. Then she swindles her husband out of money in order to support the extended family she has concocted. In that one act, Cleo manages to people her entire house with mothers, including her own mother, in whose memory all of this has been done.

But these mothers do not illuminate the text. They are kewpie dolls at a carnival, sitting ducks, waiting passively to be shot down by their own willingness to play the parts of victims. Once these mothers are all assembled, West begins to mete out the punishments due them for having left their husbands. Each marriage is destroyed in some tragic way, the clear implication being that none of these tragedies would have occurred had these women been beside their struggling mates. Cleo is the real villain, but her villainy is so exaggerated that she becomes merely grotesque. Mean and duplicitous, she continues to steal from her husband as he tries to support her family while his business is failing. She too is punished when she finally realizes, when he is about to leave her, how much her husband means to her:

> . . . in him was a vital power from which she was renewing her own. His presence was calming her turbulence, restoring her courage. . . . If he left her alone, some part of herself that had fastened itself to him with tentacles would be torn from her.[32]

The child Judy inhabits the background of this text as a foil to Cleo. Whereas Cleo tolerates and uses Bart, Judy genuinely loves her father; she talks to the people Cleo snubs; she forms an alliance with Tim, the only male cousin in this house of women. A "strength and stability beneath Judy's shy exterior" make her cousins come to depend on her in their effort to resist Cleo's domination. Judy becomes "the fountainhead of their search for truth,"[33] resisting Cleo and allowing us to feel that the hope for the future will be this good little girl who usurps the power of the bad mother and replaces her as the head of a little flock. She has a miniature patriarch for her partner in her cousin Tim.

And yet the novel makes us question the very male authority it comes to embrace at the end. Cleo's manufactured extended family of women is a world in which women are autonomous, and the female voice within that world, as in Toni Morrison's *Sula,* is confident and bold, shaping its own myths and realities. When the women gather together upstairs around a pot-bellied stove to listen to Cleo's tall tales, she holds them spellbound with her outrageous, humorous stories. Aching with laughter, no one wants to leave until Cleo is finished:

> Was it her voice? Did they like to listen to her talk just to hear the music sounds she made? Was it because she was so full of life that she made things move inside you, tears or laughter or anger, and when she went out of a room something like something alive left with her.[34]

We understand how little that voice is appreciated outside the female community. Women in Cleo's class have no value except as their husband's showpieces. In the world of men, even the powerful Cleo is silenced:

> When men spoke, she knew that their worlds were larger than hers, their interests broader. She could not bear knowing that there were many things she didn't know; that a man could introduce a subject and she would have to be silent.[35]

Cleo tries to exert her will against a world of male prerogative, but unlike her creator, she finds no outlet for her wild and boundless energy. The relationship between mother and daughter in West's novel is almost entirely negative. Cleo is powerful but she is villainous. She is left alone and frightened by the destruction she has caused. Her daughter and the extended family she has manipulated are, by the end of the novel, "sufficient to each other." The mother is deposed. Again, though, there is the connection between the mother and the community. Like Cleo, the black community imagined in this novel is desperate for status, concerned about "which parties and churches to attend and which to avoid."[36] They are emerging black professionals who pride themselves on the distance they can create between themselves and poor blacks. The mother is a metaphor for the community, and Judy's rejection of Cleo is parallel to West's rejection of that insular and narrow community of elitist blacks.

Paule Marshall also had a difficult experience with her mother, but she used that relationship in her novels to move her characters to a personal freedom necessary for the greater political freedom she envisions for them. From her mother and the Barbadian–American community in Brooklyn, Paule Marshall inherited an entire cultural and linguistic vocabulary, one that combines idioms and myths from Afro–American, Afro–Caribbean, and African cultures. Marshall's very special relationship with the mother who embodied those cultures has resulted in a unique example of "mothering the mind" of a creative artist. Marshall says that her strongest and most truthful writing is a celebration of the art she learned from her mother: "She laid the foundations of my aesthetic, that is the themes and techniques which characterize my work."[37]

In a 1973 essay, "Shaping the World of My Art," and in a recent *New York Times* article,[38] Marshall has explained the ways her creativity was nurtured by her mother and the other women in the Barbadian–American community. Like Alice Walker's mother, these storytelling women, themselves artists, provided a model of woman as artist, thereby giving Marshall the freedom to become one. They left the houses where they worked as servants and gathered in her mother's kitchen after work to talk—about "this white-man country," about economics, psychology, sociology. These poor peasant women, recent emigrants from Barbados in the 1920s, recounted many of the tales found in her first novel, *Brown Girl, Brownstones*. Their angry recollections of poverty and colonial exploitation in Barbados, as well as the racism they encountered here, were the content of their "exhaustive and vivid discussions." Paule sat unnoticed in a corner, listening, absorbing the insight and irony they brought to words, and above all "their poet's skill":

> . . . All that free-wheeling talk together with the sometimes bawdy jokes and the laughter which often swept the kitchen, was, at its deepest level, an affirmation of their own worth; it said that they could not be either demeaned or defeated by the daily trip out to Flatbush. It declared that they had retained and always would a strong sense of their special and unique Black identity.[39]

In Marshall's novel, these women become a kind of Greek chorus observing the tragic fate of Silla Boyce, her husband, Deighton, and their daughter Selina, through whose consciousness the narrative is told. Like the young Paule, Selina sits in corners of the house, observing "the mother and the others, for they were alike—those watchful, wrathful women whose eyes seared and searched and laid bare, whose tongues lashed the world in unremitting distrust."[40]

Language for these women of Marshall's youth became both refuge and weapon, a form of self-expression as well as a means to interpret and control their lives: " '. . . In this white-man world you got to take yuh mouth and make a gun.' "[41] As these women sat in her mother's kitchen each afternoon, narrating their lives and memories, they not only showed women in the powerful act of storytelling, they formed a peculiarly female kind of folklore: "Then lemme tell you and listen and believe . . . this Affie was running with my wuthless uncle, and when his wife, my dear aunt Dorie found out she swear she was gon work obeah and kill Affie Cumberbatch dead-dead."[42] Then follows a story of the wife Dorie working obeah and causing Affie's much-deserved death. They had words for pregnancy; the expectant mother was "in the way" or "tumbling big." A woman who was too free with her sexual favors was known as a "thoroughfare," or she might be called "a free-bee," which was Marshall's favorite of the two:

> I liked the magic it conjured up of a woman scandalous perhaps but independent, who flitted from one flower to another in a garden of male beauties, sampling their nectar, taking her pleasure at will, the roles reversed.[43]

The way Marshall handles sex in her novels reflects this same spirit of female independence. Selina is an active, aggressive agent in her first love affair. Selina's mother's passion is even more powerful and more urgent than her adulterous husband's. Marshall conceives of the beautiful woman as an active force, not a passive object. Silla is described as "handsome," a woman who does not even glance in the mirror for reassurance of her beauty, a beauty expressed in gestures that she and her foremothers used to defy passivity:

> They seemed to use this beauty not to attract but to stave off all that might lessen their strength. When a man looked at them he did not immediately feel the stir in his groin but uneasiness first and then the challenge to prove himself between those thighs, to rise from them when he was spent and see respect and not contempt in their faces.[44]

The large, brooding figure of "the mother," Silla Boyce, strides through this novel as she does through Brooklyn's Fulton Park on her way home from work, so powerful that the child Selina imagines the sun giving way to her force. Selina calls her "the mother," not "my mother," reinforcing this sense of Silla's dominance and power. She is the main-stay of the Boyce family and the preeminent member of the Bajan community, a pioneer who came to America as a girl to escape the dead-end life of poverty in the islands. It is the mother's voice we hear throughout the novel, denouncing the institutions that subordinate her race. On every issue confronting their lives, Silla imposes her own meaning, affirming for herself and the others the role of language in the survival of oppressed people.

Marshall says that Silla's indomitable character is modeled after her own mother, from whom she learned that ancient African tradition of transmitting the culture, history, and wisdom of a race through oral speech:

> Her imaginative and poetic approach to language was as natural as breathing, and I sensed that her power came from her manipulation of language. I couldn't hold forth on my feet, because I had absorbed their [the Bajan women's] ability to work magic with language, I tried to duplicate it in standard English. I wanted to emulate my mother's powerful ability to handle language and to do one better—with the hope that this would please her.[45]

The dynamic of that early relationship with her mother has profoundly affected the style and themes of Marshall's work. Her own struggle to be in her mother's presence her own person, to break away from her domination, to match the mother's power with words is re-created in *Brown Girl, Brownstones* in Selina's seven-year battle with Silla. As important as this relationship was to Marshall's development as a writer, it was, in many ways, problematic and negative:

> The influence was absolutely fundamental and crucial but it came in a negative way. My mother never directly encouraged me to write. What I absorbed from her was more a reaction to her negativity. It was her saying to me when I was in junior high school after I'd won all the medals, saying to me out of her own defeat and failure, that I was a failure. No, the influence was not positive, it was full of problems, stress, antagonisms. My mother was well aware that it was a power struggle, that I was seeking to replace her. She called me a "force-ripe woman"; "two head bulls" she would say "can't reign in a flock"; or "Here you've come to read the burial service over me"; "Look how I done brought something in the world to whip me." . . . Because of all my grand ambitions she used to call me "poor-great." She wanted me to get a job as a secretary, not go to college. She wanted to get along in a kind of minimal way and she disapproved of all my ambitions. She was always telling me I looked as if I were living my old days first.[46]

Writing became for Marshall a way of imitating her mother and of throwing off her domination. She hoped her success as a writer would please her mother so that she would have to retract her verdict of failure. Success with words would also signal that eventually she would reign as "head bull" in the flock.

The relationship between Silla and Selina Boyce is so full of mystery, passion, and conflict that it may well be the most complex treatment of the mother-daughter bond in contemporary American literature. Marshall writes the mother figure into the entire novel, resisting the temptation to make the daughter's life preeminent, to make the daughter's victory contingent on the rejection of the mother's world or on her elimination from the narrative. Silla and Selina are so embedded in each other's lives that Selina can only come to know herself by acknowledging that connection and by respecting that part of herself which is like her mother.

As a child of eleven, Selina thinks of the mother as an Atlas, keeping her world from collapsing: "Wasn't the mother, despite all, its only prop?"[47] Though her father also works to support Selina and her sister, he is never able to provide the same sense of security as the mother. He is wasteful with money, an impractical dreamer, a lover of fine clothes, women, and "spreeing." In reaction to Deighton's improvidence, his inability to turn his life into a fight for "the dollar," Silla becomes a tough, formidable force, using all of her strength to get ahead, to buy a house. Frightened and angered by the memories of childhood poverty in Barbados, "'working harder than a man at the age of ten,'" Silla is determined to make a better way for her family in America, "'even if I got to see my soul fall howling into hell.'"[48]

As respectful as she is of her mother's "god-like" power, as much as she says she fears it, Selina is never shown in the novel as a timid, frightened girl. Silla gives Selina permission to rebel against her, just as she rebelled against her own mother. From the beginning of the novel, Silla admires and is awed by Selina's fierce little spirit, and while she seems to dominate her, she subtly encourages Selina to resist her. When Selina is begging to be allowed to go to Prospect Park on the trolley without her older sister, Silla says to her "without annoyance": "'Pestilence . . . here it tis the world is almost in war and all you thinking 'bout is patrolling the streets.'"[49] Selina continues to plead for her chance to go out into the world, and her mother gives in with these words: "'What you need Ina for any more? You's more woman now than she'll ever be, soul. G'long.'"[50] Silla uses the word "woman" as both accusation and acknowledgment of Selina's right to self-assertion. When Selina comes one night to the factory where Silla works, trying to stop her mother from selling her father's land, Silla lashes out in a tirade that once again is a subtle form of respect for Selina's emerging autonomy: "You's too own-way. You's too womanish. . . . I wun dare strike you now 'cause I'd forget my strength and kill you. . . . Yuh's just like my mother. A woman that did think the world put here for she."[51]

The recognition of Selina's old ways and her resemblance to Silla's mother is further testimony to Silla's respect for her daughter, as though she sees in Selina something that precedes her and is wiser than she. Marshall allows both mother and daughter the power to imagine the other, in the past as well as in the present. Selina looks at the photograph of the mother on the dining-room table and, seeing Silla as a girlish, shy beauty with a 1920s headband around her forehead, wonders if this could be her mother. She thinks of her mother back in Barbados, a girl of ten hurrying to work in the dark mornings with a basket of fruit on her head, afraid of dawn ghosts. She hears the tales of her mother dancing in Bimshire until she falls out on the grass.

The freedom and independence and wildness of spirit she sees in her mother give Selina access to a larger psychic world than girls are generally allowed—in fiction and outside of it. At a party given by Selina's best friend, Beryl, when they are both seventeen, Selina is the only one of the girls who is not dominated by her parents. The girls at this soirée are lifeless and dull and imitative, not daring to question their fathers' plans for their lives. Beryl will become a lawyer, she says, because her father needs her to help control the tenants in his property. The child who has done battle with the fierce Silla, the "womanish" child, is the only one there who is her own person; and it is the rebellion against her mother that has nurtured this self-ownership. Ironically, though she loves her father dearly, Selina never challenges him. When Deighton is angry with Selina and shuts her out of his room, Selina feels hurt—just as women often do in romantic affairs—not because her rightful anger has been denied, but because she fears the loss of intimacy. Silla, on the other hand, snatches Selina to her when she is angry, expressing in that motion a sense of a worthy foe. In one scene Selina springs at her mother, shouting for Silla to stop comparing her to the frail little brother who died in infancy, so stunning her mother with her ten-year-old audacity that all Silla can do is stare at the small back, "as unassailable as her own," and whisper in helpless pride, " 'Look how I has gone and brought something into this world to whip me.' "[52]

Marshall insists that the mother-daughter bond, important as it is for revealing character, for allowing women to be the central characters in their lives, the activists, the centers of power, has a significance for black women far greater than their individual lives. She repeats the theme that recurs throughout black literature: "Selfhood must be conceived in political terms":[53]

> The element of struggle has deeply affected my writing because it reflects my own struggle to be in her presence my own person, and that struggle—that need to break away, to move away from domination, to prove your own worth—is connected to the larger struggle of black people.[54]

Before Selina can truly become reconciled with her mother she has to come up against that hostile, racist world her mother has dealt with all her life: "'Girl do you know what it tis out there? How those white people does do yuh?'"[55] Selina does not know the reality of that world "out there" until she enters City College and has her first taste of its abuse. Then she finally understands the mother, that ancient African woman whom the entire Western world has humiliated and despised, and she proclaims her allegiance with her mother and with all the oppressed people she represents:

> And she was one with them: the mother and the Bajan women, who had lived each day what she had come to know. How had the mother endured, she who had not chosen death by water? . . . How had the mother contained her swift rage?[56]

Selfhood is not defined negatively as separateness from others,[57] nor is it defined narrowly by the individual dyad—the child and its mother—but on the larger scale as the ability to recognize one's continuity with the larger community. Selina does not remain, like Silla, uncritical of that community. In refusing to follow the neat, codified life devoted to money, power, and ownership, Selina symbolizes the community's need to reorder itself. Paradoxically, she must disrupt the community's destructive and constricting circle while preserving the power of its rugged endurance in a hostile white world. That task parallels the one she must also perform with the mother—separating from her while acknowledging that part of herself which is truly her mother's child.

In the quest for traditions to illuminate the meanings of the mother-daughter bond, white feminist writers often turn to Western myths—the myth of Demeter and Persephone as an example of generational continuity between women, variations of the Medusa myth as the terrible but powerful mother, mothers and stepmothers in fairy tales who predict an archetypal mother-daughter hostility. That bias toward Western white models ignores African mythology as a source of black maternal imagery. Without sufficient knowledge of African myths, I cannot trace Marshall's symbols back to their ultimate African sources, but there is enough evidence to suggest that the image of the Afro–American slave mother is one of the sources for the characterization of Silla Boyce. Everything about Silla's portrait suggests the slave mother—her standing on the corner waiting for suburban housewives to offer her a day's work; the emphasis on her body as an instrument she uses to protect her children; her working out all day and then returning home to make Barbadian delicacies for her family; her manlike strength. In the one well-known narrative by a slave woman, Linda Brent's *Incidents in the Life of a Slave Girl*,[58] the mother-child bond is central to the entire text. Unlike the male slave narrators, who were often willing to cut familial bonds to escape slavery, Brent will not take an opportunity to escape to the North because she refuses to leave her children in bondage. Like that slave woman, Silla remains behind with the children while Deighton devises a number of escapes from the bondage of his life.

The historical mythology of the slave mother as a way of envisioning and defining motherhood maintains the importance of understanding motherhood in its political context. It challenges the fiction of mother-daughter hostility and the traditional ways of seeing mothers as powerless in the world of men. Clearly, Paule Marshall's mother nurtured her creativity in this tradition. In Marshall's later novels, *The Chosen Place, The Timeless People,* and *Praisesong for the Widow,* the mother-daughter relationship is not treated directly; she writes about two women—Merle Kinbona and Avey Johnson—in larger social and political contexts. However, the themes generated by that early relationship are still present: the concern with oppressed people engaging their history, facing up to colonial oppression, moving to control their own lives, and refusing to be dominated by the materialism of the Western world. "The basic pattern is still there, but translated into a larger kind of concern."[59]

The evidence from black women writers shows a distinctive tradition in their literary history. So many black women have named their mothers as their literary precursors that much of contemporary writing by black women has to be seen as a response to this oral history. These oral stories are one of the sources for twentieth-century black women's literature. They clearly tell us some important things about the black women's literary tradition. It is not marked by a "dread of the patriarchal authority of art," nor by "culturally conditioned timidity about self-dramatization," nor by any sense of female inferiorization. Those qualities, which Gubar and Gilbert[60] posit as part of the white woman writer's fear and isolation, do not explain black women writers' sense of authorship and authority over their stories.

In their search for self and form, black women writers as diverse as Dorothy West and Alice Walker and Paule Marshall have found in their mothers' legacies the key to the release of their creative powers. I think that, as either conscious myth or literal reality, the connection between the mother and daughter and the daughter's decision to be a writer are essentially interrelated. Maybe it is the educated daughters' need to open the "sealed letter" their mothers "could not plainly read,"[61] to have their mothers' signatures made clear in their work, to preserve their language, their memories, their myths. Certainly there is a connection between the black woman writer's sense of herself as part of a link in generations of women, and her decision to write. One thing these three writers have already convinced me of is that the long chain of presences that inhabit the literature of black women does not convey inferiority, or submissive femininity, or intellectual powerlessness: What these mothers passed on would take you anywhere in the world you wanted to go.

NOTES

1. Alice Walker, "In Search of Our Mothers' Gardens: The Creativity of the Black Woman in the South," *Ms.*, May 1974, pp. 64–70, 105.

2. Rosetta Reitz says this verse was often inserted into songs by blues singers and is considered a traditional verse.

3. When a black woman, Jarena Lee, felt the call to preach in the early 1800s, it was considered improper for a woman to preach in the African Methodist Episcopal Church, and it was only her radical interpretation of Scriptures, her unshakable conviction of her own calling, and eight years of appeal that broke through that male barrier. Orators in the black community have been men, and up until the 1970s most celebrated black writers were men. Thus when we come across these unusual cases of black women, for the most part uneducated formally, asserting their daughters' right to authorship, we are on the trail that may lead to a lost or hidden oral tradition.

I take the idea of women writers needing a female precursor to establish their authority from Susan Gubar and Sandra Gilbert's *The Madwoman in the Attic: The Woman Writer and the Nineteenth-Century Literary Imagination* (New Haven and London: Yale University Press, 1979), which argues that women need such an example in order to revolt against the patriarchal models that trap them within male-defined texts. In a sense these black women writers create their own precursors by naming their mothers as models for their literary activity.

4. Walker, "In Search of Our Mothers' Garden," p. 66.

5. Ibid., p. 70.

6. Mary Helen Washington, "Her Mother's Gifts," *Ms.*, June 1982, p. 38.

7. Claudia Tate, *Black Women Writers at Work* (unpub. ms.), p. 75.

8. Washington, "Her Mother's Gifts," p. 38.

9. Ibid.

10. Ibid.

11. "Roselily," "Her Sweet Jerome," and "Everyday Use" are from Alice Walker's *In Love and Trouble* (New York: Harcourt Brace Jovanovich, 1973), pp. 3–9, 24–34, 47–59.

12. Alice Walker, "A Sudden Trip Home in the Spring," in Mary Helen Washington, ed., *Black-Eyed Susans: Classic Stories by and about Black Women* (New York: Doubleday, 1975), pp. 141–54.

13. Walker, "In Search of Our Mothers' Gardens," p. 105.

14. Ibid.

15. Carol P. Christ, *Diving Deep and Surfacing* (Boston: Beacon Press, 1980), p. 56.

16. Gubar and Gilbert, *Madwoman in the Attic,* p. 49.

17. Much of this nonsense about women's lives appeared in an article by Mary Carruthers entitled "Imagining Women: Notes Toward a Feminist Poetic," in *Massachusetts Review* 20 (1979), 281–307, which is another painful example of how white feminist writers cannot imagine the lives of black women.

18. Michael Harper, "Interview with Gayl Jones," *Massachusetts Review* 18 (1977), 713.

19. Gayl Jones, *Corregidora* (New York: Random House, 1975).

20. Ibid., p. 14.

21. Walker, "In Search of Our Mothers' Gardens," p. 70.

22. Barbara Christian, *Black Women Novelists: The Development of a Tradition; 1892–1976* (Westport, Connecticut: Greenwood Press, 1980), p. 239.

23. Alice Walker, "The Black Writer and the Southern Experience," *New South: A Quarterly Review of Southern Affairs* 25 (Fall 1970), 23–26.

24. Christian, *Black Women Novelists,* p. 240.

25. Walker, "The Black Writer and the Southern Experience," p. 24.

26. Alice Walker, "Saving the Life That Is Your Own: The Importance of Models in the Artist's Life," Women's Center Reid Lectureship, Barnard College, 1976, p. 8.

27. Alice Walker, "The Revenge of Hannah Kemhuff," in *In Love and Trouble,* pp. 60–80.

28. Walker, "Saving the Life That Is Your Own," p. 12.

29. Mary Helen Washington, "These Self-Invented Women: A Theoretical Framework for a Literary History of Black Women," Bunting Institute Working Paper, Radcliffe College, 1980, p. 8.

30. Ibid., p. 9.

31. Dorothy West, *The Living Is Easy* (Old Westbury, N.Y.: Feminist Press, 1982), p. 105.

32. Ibid., p. 273.

33. Ibid., p. 210.

34. Ibid., p. 202.

35. Ibid., p. 140.

36. Adelaide Cromwell Gulliver, Afterword to West, *The Living Is Easy.*

37. Paule Marshall, "Shaping the World of My Art," *New Letters* 40 (Autumn 1973), 105.

38. Paule Marshall, "From in the Kitchen," *New York Times Book Review,* January 9, 1983, pp. 3, 34–35.

39. Marshall, "Shaping the World of My Art," p. 104.

40. Paule Marshall, *Brown Girl, Brownstones* (Old Westbury, N.Y.: Feminist Press, 1982), pp. 10–11.

41. Ibid., p. 70.

42. Marshall, "Shaping the World of My Art," p. 100.

43. Marshall in *The New York Times Book Review,* January 9, 1983, p. 34.

44. Marshall, *Brown Girl, Brownstones,* p. 135.

45. Mary Helen Washington, "Interview with Paule Marshall," October 24, 1981 (unpublished).

46. Ibid., p. 1.

47. Marshall, *Brown Girl, Brownstones,* p. 46.

48. Ibid., p. 75.

49. Ibid., p. 53.

50. Ibid.

51. Ibid., p. 102.

52. Ibid., p. 47.

53. Stephen Butterfield, *Black Autobiography in America* (Amherst: University of Massachusetts Press, 1974), p. 109.

54. Washington, "Interview with Paule Marshall," p. 1.

55. Marshall, *Brown Girl, Brownstones,* p. 306.

56. Ibid., pp. 292–93.

57. Marianne Hirsch, "Mothers and Daughters," *Signs* 7 (1981), 207. Hirsch is summarizing the perspective on selfhood in Jessie Benjamin's article, "Rational Violence and Erotic Domination."

58. Linda Brent, *Incidents in the Life of a Slave Girl* (New York and London: Harcourt Brace Jovanovich, 1973).

59. Washington, "Interview with Paule Marshall," p. 3.

60. Gilbert and Gubar, *Madwoman in the Attic.*

61. Walker, "In Search of Our Mothers' Gardens," p. 70.

Colette in 1935.
Photo by
George Platt
Lynes

The Magic Spinning Wheel
STRAW TO GOLD—
COLETTE, WILLY, AND SIDO

Jane Lilienfeld

Colette and Missy. Courtesy of the
Bibliothèque Nationale

Gabrielle Sidonie Colette (1873–1954) was the second and last child of Adèle-Eugénie Sidonie Landoy's second marriage, to Jules-Joseph Colette. Her mother, a charming woman of great privacy and unavailability, exerted an influence so overwhelming that Colette repressed consciousness of it until well into her thirties. In 1893 she married Henri Gauthiers-Villars, who brought her from provincial life to the demimondaine life of Paris in the 1890s. "Willy" issued her Claudine *novels under his name. In 1906 Colette and Willy mutually dissolved their partnership, and until 1911 she made her living as a vaudevillian and mime in traveling road shows and as a journalist. She accepted further emotional and material support from "Missy," the Marquise de Belboeuf, niece of Napoleon III and great grand-daughter of the Empress Josephine. In 1911 Colette began living with Henry Bertrand Léon-Robert, Baron de Jouvenel des Ursins, a wealthy political journalist. His World War I duties became hers as she reported French life under siege. Two years after De Jouvenel ended their marriage legally in 1923, she joined her life to that of Maurice Goudeket, who enjoyed with her the opening of a cosmetic business, international travel, and owning several homes in France. After World War II ended, a chance fall eventually led to paralysis, but the famous and the obscure made pilgrimages to Colette in her rue de Beaujolais Paris apartment.*

Colette was established as a serious writer with the appearance of Chéri *in 1920. That year she was elected as a Chevalier de la Légion d'Honneur, and, in 1936, to the Belgian literary academy, an unheard-of recognition for most women writers. When she died she received a state funeral (after an enormous ruckus because of her sex and her atheism). She left fifty volumes at her death, and by 1975, eleven more had appeared posthumously.*

The absence at the back of desire creates a void, a white page, a space. In that space one places many things—what one needs to see, usually, if one can imagine what that is. For Colette, that space became a series of closely written, canceled pages[1] on which she learned to project what she saw—"*regarde,*"[2] after all, being her mode of being. This essay confronts the question of who presented Colette with this absence, this space of writing; who presented her with the material to fill it, to paint it in with printer's ink.

At the back of the east wind, according to mythographers, charters of cultural blank pages, stand fairy tales.[3] But the exact way fairy tales arise out of the myth, from out of the watery bed of the unconscious, has never been traced completely, although feminist theorists explain that fairy tales do not just imbue women's pages, but shape their gestures as well. Colette's mode of *regarde,* of seeing as being, of seeing as the mode of writing, was a mode of absorption and complete openness, and yet took place, according to Colette, in a land of fairy tales.

The first fairy tale was the story of Eden. Colette grew up in Saint-Sauveur in Puisaye, France, a village so remote that even today only one coach visits it per day.[4] In an ugly house squat on the street lived Sido, her mother, a bewitching woman. She had been first the wife of Le Sauvage, and by him had two children: Juliette, who later committed suicide over an inability to leave her mother for heterosexuality, as Colette makes clear in *My Mother's House,*[5] and Achille, who loved her so that he died very soon after her.[6] Sido next allowed herself to be loved by Jules-Joseph Colette, with great spaces of reserve, and produced in that marriage Léo and then her youngest child, Gabrielle Sidonie Colette.

Léo and Colette were—if possible—as attached to their mother's garden as to Sido herself. Leo once, years after his manhood, long after they had lost the house (bequeathed to Sido by Le Sauvage) because of Jules-Joseph's inability to manage his wife's money, revisited the garden. He complained that the gate had been oiled; Eden was ruined for him by that change. For Colette, Eden was embowered by her mother's nature:[7]

In her garden my mother had a habit of addressing to the four cardinal points not only direct remarks and replies that sounded, when heard from our sitting-room, like brief inspired soliloquies, but the actual manifestations of her courtesy, which generally took the form of plants and flowers. . . . "Is that you I hear, Cèbe?" my mother would call. "Have you seen my cat?"[8]

Clearly, Sido was a witch. She could make anything bloom, seduced the curé with her cuttings—even though she brought her dog to mass and hid novels in her psalter to read during services—and "had a curious habit of lifting roses by the chin to look them full in the face."[9] Colors flowed from her, odors, life itself, a river of fecundity. Sorceress-like, Sido had made imprisonment look like freedom.

Colette had watched this witchery since her earliest youth. Only when sent back into herself for the way out of her prison did she realize the discipline behind her mother's look of freedom. For she had been misled by her mother's force of character, wrestling freedom out of capture, to think that with marriage she would inherit the keys to her mother's garden. But those scissors, clippers, pruners, and thick gloves—what Colette called her mother's "weapons"—were not the accoutrements of life with a city-bred man, and the freedoms of Puisaye did not exist in Paris of the demi-monde during the 1890s. The sky, fresh air, sunshine, solitude, open space, streams, and seasonal changes were replaced by ". . . a book, hundreds of books, low, airless rooms, sweets instead of meat, an oil lamp instead of sunshine. . . ."[10] It was only after she married and lost her innocent participation in her mother's nature that she came to realize that her mother too had been subject to economic and sexual oppression,[11] and that Sido's freedom was an inner state maintained in spite of marriage rather than granted by it.

A myth as old as Greece grows out of a garden of wild flowers. One day on a hillside, gathering spring flowers, Persephone, daughter of Mother Earth, is surprised by joy or by violent rape—depending on your point of view—as the garden heaves open to reveal Dis, King of the Underworld, who abducts the lovely girl to his domain, where she sups with him on six pomegranate seeds, and so remains condemned to an uneasy heterosexuality her whole life: six months with Mother, six months with Lover, the seasons changing according to which sex was winning the power struggle.

This is the first of the two tales out of which Colette wove her magic spinning-wheel tale. She placed the enclosed garden of Saint-Sauveur in Puisaye in a dirty, crowded, locked room presided over by Dis, her first husband of three, Willy, handed him the key, and then pretended he was Rumpelstiltskin and she the distressed maiden. As my mother told the second story to me long ago, it is a tale of a young girl, crying and disheveled, sitting in a loft of straw, sobbing. To her comes an ugly dwarf. "Why are you crying?" he asks. "I am crying because unless I can spin this straw into gold by daylight, I cannot marry the prince, and if I cannot marry the prince, I will surely die." In some versions, she actually is threatened by beheading. And so Rumpelstiltskin spins the straw into gold on one condition: that he get the girl's firstborn child. The disheveled girl agrees. She gets the prince, and only later realizes that the price is too high.

Colette met Willy during the four years of transition on "the marriage market," staying with her brother Achille "not far away at Chatillon-Sur-Loing, now Chatillon-Coligny."[12] During that time, riding with Achille on his horse-drawn rounds at his doctoring, "she often helped [Achille] dress wounds and in the afternoon she would accompany him . . . holding the reins while he visited his patients in their isolated farmhouses and cottages."[13] Much like Renaud in *The Claudines,*[14] Willy came to that house because of the scientific interests of the man of the house. He had an introduction because his father, Albert Gauthier-Villars, founder of the prestigious press, had been a wartime comrade of Colette's father, Jules-Joseph Colette. His real name was Henri, but Sido dubbed him "Monsieur Willy." Even then he was puffed up by the excessive indulgence permitted by the spirit of the 1890s, when he met the braided, silent, slant-eyed schoolgirl. As in the old story, the beast met the innocent.

What Colette said of their wedding night, two years after an engagement during which she "learned to write" by penning letters to Willy,[15] had two parts. The first part was that she did not remember her mother's face on the morning after she lost her virginity, until many years later, and then her mother's unmasked visage as she stirred her morning chocolate was of the grief of the ages.

> The white train of my dress draped over one arm, I went down, alone, into the garden. . . . I could hear the clatter of the knives and forks that were being laid on the big table. The long evening was falling without modifying the unseasonable heat. With eyes and voice I sought for Sido who gave no sign. Ever since morning she had avoided me as if I were the plague . . . [on the carriage journey to Paris] I suffered from thirst, and my heart was swollen with pain over a mental impression that remained with me. My mother had stayed up all night and at daybreak was still wearing her grand outfit of black faille and jet. Standing at the blue-and-white tiled stove in the little kitchen, Sido was pensively stirring the morning chocolate, her features, unguarded, betraying a look of terrible sadness. . . .[16]

Colette, who in later years adopted the appetites of Willy, was at that time a slim, lithe teenager, disgusted by Willy's excessive flesh. She also recalled the actual physical loss of her virginity:

> Fear does not live easily in young people when they are healthy with spirit. Even a martyred child . . . does not fear her tormentors all the time

for these have their hours of compassion and laughter. Perhaps even the mouse has the freedom from the cat's paw, when that paw is soft.

Among unsung courage, young girls' bravery is noteworthy. But without it, one would see fewer marriages. One would see still less of these escapades which forget all, even her hand in the velvet paw, giving her mouth toward the convulsive glutton of an exasperated mouth, she [who] watches peacefully, passively, on the wall, the enormous shadow of the Unknown Male,—it is sexual curiosity which throws her these curve-balls of counsel, so overwhelming. In a few hours, an unscrupulous man makes, of an innocent girl, a prodigy of Libertinage, who deals with not one iota of disgust. Disgust is not ever an obstacle. It comes later, like integrity. I wrote at another time, "Dignity is lacking in men." I should better have written that "disgust is not a feminine delicacy."[17]

Sido had prognosticated her daughter's macabre abduction and, to save her, had carried her during the night down the back passage, to another room in the rambling house of the garden of Saint-Sauveur.[18] Quite literally, one night before her marriage, Colette had awakened to find herself kidnapped by her own mother, anxious about the loss of her daughter to a "stranger."

Like Persephone in the Underworld, Colette pined away in her new location. The doctor told Sido that he could do no more to save her daughter from her mysterious illness. Past caring, desiring death, Colette lay first in Willy's dusty, airless, sunless flat in Paris. Her mother came and tended her. Willy lived outside this in the next apartment. Captured by innocence, he had seduced and then lost interest in the debauched girl, who had come to hunger for his phallus. Sido nursed Colette in the second apartment at rue Jacob: "I dreaded more than anything that hour when she tucked me in, when we were alone, after the day was over, when she would ask me without saying a word." After Sido's death, Colette said it all, although she never explained why she wanted to die. But Sido had predicted it, and she came to lead Colette out of the Land of Dis to Demeter's fields.[19]

Along with Sido, Marcel Schwab and Paul Masson climbed the stairs to the fourth floor in those years. Every day they came and sat in her room. They encouraged her to forget and directed her attention to life, by their physical presences.[20] Gradually she became limber and went outside. Gradually she revived, but her heart was frozen within her.

A chance, anonymous letter led her to an establishment where Charlotte Kinceler and Willy sat together at a table over his open account books—a scene the equivalent, for others, of finding one's husband *flagrante delicto*. Charlotte grasped a scissors. Colette looked.

"*Regarde.*" What she saw she spoke of guardedly, in pieces, lines at a time, in various of her books. Willy had betrayed her by taking her virginity, the only possession of hers he had desired, the only possession she, dowerless, had meagerly to give. But mere betrayal had nothing to do with the coating of complexity Colette later gave the look that passed between her and Kinceler, a suicide at twenty-six. Colette knew in that moment that she and Charlotte were lovers too, enemies and lovers, as were she and Willy. Or rather, she was his enemy and his lover; he was her indifferent husband.[21]

She had one other asset for him. With a genius for plagiarism, Willy lived off the writings of others. He would produce ideas for stories, but would hire various starving hacks to write from his notes. No hack knew that another hack was working on part of the piece; Willy paid them little and used them all. The only thing we know he wrote was the brilliant early column of musical criticism that made him famous when he first launched himself into this life of stolen ink. "Money's short," he said to Colette one day in 1894 or 1895. "You ought to put down what you remember of your board-school days. Don't be shy of the spicy bits. I might make something of it."[22] And so again the shadow on the wall led her. He beckoned with a pen. Obediently she took a ruled notebook and wrote, neatly from side to side, making sure not to infringe the margins. At first when Willy read Colette's holograph of *The Claudines,* he dismissed it. "I was wrong. It's no use at all." He threw it aside. She noted: "Relieved, I returned to the divan, to my cat, my books, my new friends. . . ."[23] Years later, rifling his drawers, money-hungry, he came upon the notebooks again. As he read, he realized intensely their salability. By now, the story having been told by so many, we cannot know what he saw in the drafts with tightly controlled margins of *The Claudines.* He urged Colette to leaven up the lesbianism, then the rage of the 1890s, as were all so-called perversions;[24] "'My God!' he muttered. 'I am the bloodiest fool.' He swept up the scattered copy books just as they were, grabbed his flat-brimmed top hat and bolted to his publisher's. And that is how I became a writer."[25]

As he had stolen her dowerless virginity, so he stole her writing. *Claudine à l'Ecole* by Willy appeared in 1900. It sold fifty thousand copies "almost at once."[26] Willy was a famous writer. Together or separately, he and Colette wrote, or he edited and she wrote, or he suggested and she amended, or they collaborated on, two more books—*Claudine in Paris* and *Claudine Married.* Then, after she had left him, came *Claudine and Annie.* Claudine dolls, shoes, a play appeared. The Claudines were staged, with Polaire as Claudine. "I am Claudine," declared Polaire.[27] Willy, never one to refuse a perversion, cut Colette's hair, dressed her and Polaire as twins, and took them all over the Parisian demi-monde, where, of course, he hoped sales of the books would be raised by salacious speculations about who slept with whom.

Colette lived with Willy for thirteen years, from 1893 to 1906. His shadow on the wall became in one sense something she looked for, for always her writing space was enclosed, cornered, white, bare. Yvonne Mitchell selected a telling passage from Maurice de Goudeket's memoirs, of the narrowing walls of Colette's writing room: "She wrote at a small Provençal desk, which she had placed in an angle of the room, so that the two walls isolated her like blinkers: a voluntary prisoner."[28] This enclosure helped to create a space for writing, the blank page of the creative mind, the self that sinks far down and can go anywhere. She came to think of her writing as the ransom she paid to Willy because he had captured her, the blackmail he extorted as her jailer.

> A prison is indeed one of the best workshops. I know what I am talking about: a real prison, the sound of the key turning in the lock and four hours claustration before I was free again. "Show your credentials!" What I had to show were so many well-filled pages.[29]

When she finally did so, they had no paw print of a *patte valué*. They bore the sign of her mother's hand. Ironically, the restriction released her imagination and made available again to her the freedom of Sido's walled garden. Writing in a safely enclosed space was like being granted permission by Sido to explore the world.

> . . . For even then I so loved the dawn that my mother granted it to me as a reward. . . . It was on that road and at that hour that I first became aware of my own self, experienced an inexpressible state of grace, and felt one with the first breath of air that stirred, the first bird, the sun so newly born that it still looked not quite round . . .[30]

Because Willy captured Colette only to lead her to a life she rejected, she could return to her mother's country and her mother's space. Like a Persephone stolen from Demeter's side, she recreated the enclosed garden of Saint-Sauveur in Puisaye in the dirty, crowded, locked room where Willy reigned. Her genius is not in the thin fictionalizations of male figures, who her critics generally feel are not fully realized, but in the world of woman's narrative, in dailiness and sensuality, the smell of bread rising in the house and light on the mosaics of the fireplace.

Adrienne Rich calls attention to the subterfuge of women's writing in *Lies, Secrets, and Silence*. Willy first taught Colette to lie through the opaque medium of traditional fiction. He taught her to speak so that he could sell her pages. The desire in *Claudine at School* of one woman for another, so risqué, so true in the 1890s as the lesbian subculture seethed in Montmartre, had been lived in innocence by Colette in Puisaye. Willy suggested complicating this simplicity by lasciviousness. The book sold; Willy had taught her what she needed to set her into the locked room. Her own courageous heart taught her the rest.

A young writer once went to visit Colette. He went up to her building in the elevator with a middle-aged, portly gentleman. They arrived at the apartment and spent the evening talking; he noticed the gentleman was a bit uncomfortable, and the evening ended. This "gentleman" was the Marquise de Belboeuf, the woman who nursed Colette back to health after Willy. Missy, as she was called, spent six years with Colette, 1906–1911. She wore transvestite clothing, as did most of the lesbian community in Paris at that time.[31] In fact, she was very worried that her feet were too small for the masculine shoes that she desired, and she stuffed the large pointy shoes she bought with paper to fill them out.

There is a picture of them on the lawn of their country house, with Colette practicing for her vagabondage on the parallel bars while Missy looks on.[32] Colette has described Missy's watching face in another context; that face broods over her in a piece in *Les Vrilles de la Vigne* called "Nuit Blanche." Restless in bed, two lovers lie awake, desiring one another. There is no fulfillment as the dawn rises with their need. When the face of the longing lover bends over the face of the other, resistant lover, the pronouns for the first time reveal that both people in bed are women:

> . . . for I know quite well that you will then tighten your arms about me and that, if the cradling of your arms is not enough to soothe me, your kiss will become more clinging, your hands more amorous, and that you will accord me the sensual satisfaction that is the surcease of love, like a sovereign exorcism that will drive out of me the demons of fever, anger, restlessness . . . you will accord me sensual pleasure, bending over me voluptuously, maternally, you who seek in your impassioned loved one the child you never had.[33]

The life lived in secret at the end of the 1890s by the lesbian community took shape in what Colette called the best book she had ever written, *The Pure and the Impure*.[34] Colette's use of the words "pure" and "impure" is in itself remarkable, for as Elaine Marks remarked, the point of her writing is the word *regarde*. Colette did not *regarde* with judgment; she simply looked. And yet the tone toward the bending moon-faced lover is judgmental. The one she bends toward is needy, like a "fractious child," as the central intelligence of *To the Lighthouse* says of Mr. Ramsay.

The difficulty of having a mature, equal relationship had not been re-solved either by marrying Willy or by being Missy's mistress. *The Pure and the Impure* shows the problem by displacement in Colette's descrip-tion of the most notorious and celebrated love affair of the turn of the century—the relationship of Natalie Barney and Renée Vivien. The de-piction of Renée Vivien's madness (her real name was Pauline Tarn) and the secret woman who was her master, in *The Pure and the Impure*,[35] is in some sense a disguise for the only emotion Colette ever considered impure in herself: her sexual love for women. *The Pure and the Impure* disguises and lies about sexual love, an interesting fact when one realizes that Colette's reputation rests on her simplicity, openness, and honesty. What she could not say, and what was impure, is shown in the word "maternally" about the face of the bending lover, in the passage quoted above.

The incest taboo best known in our culture is that between mother and son. But Nancy Chodorow and Adrienne Rich have noted the point of the hidden incest taboo of this culture: Daughters do not have inter-course with mothers.[36] And yet in this passage Colette does. When she came to write about it later in disguise, she chose to call the book her best and to title it *The Pure and the Impure*, because Monsieur Willy's teaching needed to be refashioned.

Missy's love for Colette was maternal. Sue Silvermaire's insight, quoted in *Of Woman Born*, enunciates the implicit meaning in the mater-nal curve of Missy hovering over Colette: "When I kiss and stroke and enter my lover, I am also a child re-entering my mother."[37] Into that space one plunges; from it one emerges; within it one is both mother and daughter. Thus Missy's "maternal" tenderness appears in her face in the picture, as she broods with concern while Colette arches over the parallel bars. Her maternality showed in her taking the stage as Yssim in Colette's mime. It can be seen in her willingness to put Henriot in Co-lette's bed instead of herself, if that would please her lover and keep her longer. True to one ideology of motherhood, Missy put Colette's needs before her own—and with the usual reward. Sido was praised; Missy was abandoned. Colette did not love Missy, as the quoted passage makes clear, but she needed a refuge. Missy's maternal care sheltered her until she was ready to reenter the world of heterosexuality.

Colette's relationship with Henri de Jouvenel was, of course, not permanent, and was possibly more damaging than that with Monsieur Willy. He mocked her: "But is it impossible for you to write a book that isn't about love, adultery, semi-incestuous relations? About those other things in life?"[38] He was not willing to be scrutinized by her, just as

M. Willy had avoided her gaze. The marriage produced a great deal of journalism and a daughter—Belgazou—conceived at the time Sido died.

Sido was involved in this marriage, of course, as she had been in that of Monsieur Willy. She made a number of very sensible remarks to Colette about Henri de Jouvenel. She remarked that journalism was not good for her daughter; she pointed out to her that a steady newspaper column kept one away from one's novels. She also had no illusions about the inequity of the relationship, and she knew that as the years progressed and Jouvenel got more and more restless, Colette would suffer again. Sido had not suffered in either marriage, and she morally disapproved of suffering over men. She found nothing Colette ever did inexcusable, because she loved Colette unconditionally. But it worried her a great deal to see that Colette was not happy with this man who became less available the more Colette desired him. In those years it was longing that Colette wrote about best, and it was longing that made her famous.

In 1920 Colette became the most famous writer in Paris, with the appearance of the novel *Chéri*, a novel about a mother-son relationship, a disguised form of Colette's mother-daughter incest theme. Chéri is the pampered son of a courtesan, to whose best friend he loses his virginity, and with whom he falls in love. The prose is magnificent, the unblinking *regardes* are stunning, and the novel was applauded by Gide and Proust, the male writers Colette most admired. Just as Monsieur Willy had locked her in a room with her margined, lined notebook, so the absence of Henri de Jouvenel and the ever-enlarging space of unfulfilled and unattainable desire that his absence produced provided yet another impetus for her art, a void into which she projected what she saw, a larger room in which to pile straw to be spun into gold.

Tolstoy once said, "Happy families are all alike; every unhappy family is unhappy in its own way." Of Colette's final heterosexual relationship, with a man who played her son and her mother and her father and her best friend, there is little to be said. Colette did not write about her fulfillment with Maurice de Goudeket because she did not need to. She had written about that fulfillment with her mother.

Later in her life, Colette realized how that relationship had worked, and, being Colette, she wrote about it. She immortalized Sido first in *La Maison de Claudine—My Mother's House*—in 1922, and then in *Sido* in 1930. She wrote *Break of Day* in 1928, imagining her life as a middle-aged woman, with the sexuality and responsibilities of these years. She does not speak of Sido directly in this book, but invokes her everywhere. She who was once described in particular passages is now embedded in a fiction so encompassing that she has outgrown the confines of narrative itself.

Break of Day is interspersed with supposed letters Colette's mother wrote to her, although Michelle Sarde has now established the most famous as a fictionalization. In that letter Sido refuses a visit to see Colette at de Jouvenel's because her pink cactus is about to flower. She claims that because her life's blooming is over, she cannot afford to miss this event.[39] This letter is a direct reversal of the truth: Sido actually wrote that she wanted to come. She listed what she would be giving up to see "my daughter's dear face and hearing her voice . . . my cat Mine, who give[s] me all her trust and tenderness, a sedum which is ready to bloom and is magnificent, a gloxinia whose gaping chalice enables me to watch it seeding at my leisure . . ."[40] But Colette chose not to see Sido, and she reversed in fiction what happened in life. For her own reasons she transformed denial of the mother into denial of the daughter. When Sido died shortly after this, Colette wrote a brief note:

> Dear Hamel, Maman died the day before yesterday. I don't want to attend the funeral. I've told almost no one and I'm not wearing any outward mourning. For the time being, everything's all right. But I am tortured by the stupid notion that I won't be able to write to Mother now as I used to so often. My brother will be very unhappy. I'm still appearing in *L'Oiseau* and life goes on as usual, needless to say. However, as happens whenever I am truly grieved, I have got an attack of swelling . . . inside that is very painful.[41]

In *Break of Day* she wrote: "Hour after hour I fought my unutterable long yearning to go back to her."

Colette did go back to Sido, for she had never left her. In her embowered garden, in her virginity, in her unimagined happiness, unknown because unneeded,

> My felicity knew another and less commonplace secret: the presence of her who, instead of receding far from me through the gates of death, has revealed herself more vividly to me as I grow older. Ever since *Sido* appeared, this short form of her Christian name has starred all my memoirs. *La Naissance du Jour* gave me the chance to glorify her letters and boast of them. In *L'Etoile Vesper* it is to her I sometimes turn for a youthful touch—though my laugh, now that I am in my seventies, is not so gay as Sido's humour was when she mocked at the little tombstones of burnished lead and beads, and their rural epitaphs. . . . I have come late to this task. But where could I find a better one for my last?[42]

The pen came from Willy's manipulations—perhaps. And yet, in "inspired soliloquies" in the embowered garden, Colette heard her mother fictionalize all the verities of day and night. Rumpelstiltskin could not have spun that straw, nor filled the encapsulated room with it. What comes from the unconscious comes unbidden, but not unnurtured. Love tends; lust kills. Willy was an accident. Sido was necessary.

NOTES

1. The space at the back of all desire is from the French structuralist reinterpretation of Freud. For a reading of the unconscious as a verbal texture of gesture and what he so lovingly calls "absence," see J. Lacan, *Ecrits: A Selection*, trans. A. Sheridan (New York: Norton, 1977), particularly the third, fifth, and ninth essays. Lacan's enemy/lover/commentator, Jacques Derrida, speaks about the space of absence as being on the page in "Freud and the Scene of Writing," *Writing and Difference*, trans. A. Bass (Chicago: University of Chicago Press, 1978), pp. 196–278. For making me read the structuralists, I am indebted to Jean Radford of the Marxist–Feminist Literature Collective, London, England, to Michael Beard, and to the fact that Sandra Gilbert and Susan Gubar were not afraid to acknowledge their male structuralist compeers in their use of male theories in *The Madwoman in the Attic: The Woman Writer and the Nineteenth Century Literary Imagination* (New Haven: Yale University Press, 1979). The mistakes, of course, are all my own.

2. Elaine Marks, *Colette* (New Brunswick, N.J.: Rutgers University Press, 1960), p. 9.

3. I am indebted to Karen Rowe for reading a chapter of her feminist transvaluation of fairy tales in 1978, when she was a fellow of The Bunting Institute, Cambridge, Mass. See, too, C. G. Jung, "The Phenomenology of the Spirit in Fairy Tales," in *Psyche and Symbol: A Selection from the Writing of C. G. Jung*, ed. V. de Laszlo, trans. R. F. C. Hull (New York: Anchor, 1958), pp. 61–112. See as well Anne Sexton's book of poems *Transformations*, which transvalues many stories of women's victimization into their winning.

4. Margaret Crosland, *Colette: The Difficulty of Loving* (New York: Dell, 1975), p. 36.

5. Michelle Sarde, *Colette, Free and Fettered*, trans. R. Miller (New York: Morrow, 1980), p. 287.

6. Colette, *La Maison de Claudine*, trans. Una Vicenzo Troubridge and Enid McLeod, as *My Mother's House* (New York: Farrar, Straus and Giroux, 1975), p. 69.

7. Jane Lilienfeld, "Reentering Paradise: Cather, Colette, Woolf, and Their Mothers," in Cathy N. Davidson and E. M. Broner, eds., *Mothers and Daughters: The Lost Tradition* (New York: Ungar Press, 1979), pp. 160–75, discusses the ideas of mothers being nature (as viewed by lesbian daughters)—an idea Sherry Ortner and Susan Griffin have reevaluated: "Is Female to Male as

Nature Is to Culture?" in *Woman, Culture, and Society*, Michelle Zimbalist Rosaldo and Louise Lamphere, eds. (Stanford, Calif.: Stanford University Press, 1974); *Woman and Nature: The Roaring inside Her* (New York: Harper and Row, 1979). I argue that Colette's only control over Sido is over language about her—and just as Sido tames nature, Colette tames Sido by reabsorbing her into her own bodily words.

8. Colette, *My Mother's House*, pp. 157–58.

9. Ibid., p. 152.

10. Colette, *My Apprenticeship*, trans. Helen Beauclerk (New York: Farrar, Straus and Giroux, 1978), p. 23.

11. E. M. Eisinger and M. W. McCarty, eds., *Colette: The Woman, the Writer*, (Pennsylvania: Pennsylvania State University, 1981); see especially J. Whatley, "Colette and the Art of Survival," pp. 30–42; M. B. Sarde, "The First Steps in a Writer's Career," pp. 16–21.

12. Crosland, *Colette: The Difficulty of Loving*, pp. 39–40.

13. Ibid., p. 41.

14. Colette, *The Complete Claudine: Claudine at School; Claudine in Paris; Claudine Married; Claudine and Annie*, trans. A. White (New York: Farrar, Straus and Giroux, 1976). For the complexities of the story of who wrote what, who said who wrote what, and the legal tortures of who owned what, one must consult and collate all the biographies. There is no final version. New versions appear all the time. Sample Crosland, *Colette: The Difficulty of Loving*, p. 69; and Sarde, *Colette, Free and Fettered*, p. 145.

15. Crosland, *Colette: The Difficulty of Loving*, p. 47.

16. I have conflated the whole experience. See Robert Phelps, *The Earthly Paradise: An Autobiography*, various trans. (New York: Farrar, Straus and Giroux, 1966), pp. 81, 85, 87–88.

17. Colette par Colette, *La Jeunesse de "Claudine"* (Paris: Librairie Hachette, 1976), p. 373. The fictionalization is vastly different and illuminating: *Claudine Married*, pp. 370–75.

18. Colette: *My Mother's House*, pp. 26–29.

19. Colette: *My Apprenticeship*, pp. 36–37.

20. Ibid., pp. 38–43.

21. Crosland, *Colette: The Difficulty of Loving*, pp. 56–57; Colette, *My Apprenticeship*, pp. 24–25.

22. Crosland, *Colette: The Difficulty of Loving*, p. 69; Colette, *My Apprenticeship*, p. 19; for a discussion of "the spicy bits," see J. Stockinger, "The Test of Love and Nature: Colette and Lesbians," in Eisinger and McCarty, *Colette: The Woman, The Writer*, pp. 75–84.

23. Colette, *My Apprenticeship*, p. 19.

24. See Renee Vivien, *A Woman Appeared to Me*, trans. Jeannette Foster, (Weatherby Lake, Mo.: Naiad Press, 1979), pp. iii–xxxi, for an analysis of lesbianism in Paris at the turn of the century.

25. Colette, *My Apprenticeship*, p. 58.

26. Crosland, *Colette: The Difficulty of Loving*, p. 70. Sarde corrects this to forty thousand copies in two months.

27. Colette, *My Apprenticeship*, p. 77.

28. Yvonne Mitchell, *Colette: A Taste for Life* (New York: Harcourt Brace Jovanovich, 1977), p. 173.

29. Colette, *My Apprenticeship*, p. 71.

30. Ibid., p. 156.

31. Vivien, *A Woman Appeared to Me.*

32. Mitchell, *Colette: A Taste for Life,* opposite p. 85.

33. Colette, "Nuit Blanche," in Phelps, *Earthly Paradise,* pp. 167–68.

34. Colette, *The Pure and the Impure,* trans. Herma Briffault, (New York: Farrar, Straus and Giroux, 1966). See also Phelps, *Earthly Paradise,* p. xviii.

35. Colette, *The Pure and the Impure,* pp. 89–98.

36. Nancy Chodorow, *The Reproduction of Mothering: Psycho-Analysis and the Sociology of Gender,* (Berkeley: University of California Press, 1978), pp. 112, 192–96; see as well Adrienne Rich, *Of Woman Born* (New York: Norton, 1976).

37. Rich, *Of Woman Born,* pp. 232–33.

38. Phelps, *Earthly Paradise,* p. xvi.

39. Ibid., pp. 22–23.

40. Sarde, *Colette, Free and Fettered,* p. 286.

41. Ibid., pp. 286–87.

42. This short piece serves as the preface to the edition I have used of *My Mother's House* and *Sido,* and is neither dated nor attributed to any translator.

The Young Ethel Smyth. Virginia Woolf wrote that the photograph of Ethel in her coat and tie was the essence of the 1890s. Courtesy of BBC Hulton Picture Library

Julia Margaret Cameron's photograph of Virginia Woolf's mother, Julia Jackson (later Mrs. Leslie Stephen) in 1867, when she was twenty-one. Courtesy of the National Portrait Gallery, London

Virginia Woolf and Her Violin

MOTHERING, MADNESS, AND MUSIC

Jane Marcus

Dame Ethel Smyth and Virginia Woolf in the Thirties. Virginia's fragility is framed by the halo of the hat, while Dame Ethel's deafness suggests her own identification with the deaf composer Beethoven. From *Virginia Woolf: A Biography*, copyright © 1972 by Quentin Bell. Reproduced by permission of Harcourt Brace Jovanovich, Inc.

Virginia Woolf was born Virginia Stephen in London in 1882. After a long and brilliant career as the author of nine novels, the most famous of which is To the Lighthouse; *two major feminist political books,* A Room of One's Own *and* Three Guineas; *and several volumes of literary criticism; and as the successful creator of the Hogarth Press, she committed suicide in 1941. As the daughter of the Victorian man of letters Leslie Stephen, she was the inheritor of a great literary tradition, but she made her name as a feminist at odds with this tradition. The death of her mother, Julia Stephen, when Virginia was thirteen, and the tragic loss of her half-sister, Stella Duckworth, soon after, brought on breakdowns that were to continue throughout her life. At thirty she married Leonard Woolf, a Jewish intellectual. Active in Labour politics, editor of the* Nation, *and one of the framers of the League of Nations, he worked with his wife at the Hogarth Press, and both were identified with Bloomsbury pacifism, socialism, support of avant-garde art, and the ideal and ethic of friendship.*

Dame Ethel Smyth (1858–1944), the British composer who became an important mother/mentor in Virginia Woolf's life from 1930 until her death, was one of a series of such mother/mentor figures for Woolf. Dame Smyth was born into a large family of a major general in the Royal Artillery. Chiefly known for her several volumes of memoirs, especially Impressions that Remained, *she studied music in Leipzig in the 1870s in the circle of Brahms, Clara Schumann and Lily Wach, Mendelssohn's daughter. Her best-known opera is* The Wreckers, *and she also composed a brilliant* Mass in D, Der Wald, The Prison, The Boatswain's Mate, Entente Cordial, Fête Galante, *and many songs and instrumental pieces. George Henschel called her "the most remarkable and original composer in the history of music." She fought for women in music all her life and was active in the suffrage movement under Emmeline Pankhurst.*

181

When Julia Stephen praised her daughter's youthful writing, she felt ecstatic, Virginia Woolf recalled in "A Sketch of the Past": " . . . it was like being a violin and being played upon." This metaphor, with its consciousness of the mother-daughter erotic and its conception of the unawakened artist as a stringed instrument that waits for the expert hand to lift the bow, is, I think, perhaps the perfect figure to express the relationship between the woman artist and a mother/ mentor. The subject of this paper is the *mental* nurturance of the woman artist by women chosen to fill the place of the absent mother. She is the one who rescues one from silence, who tunes the trembling strings and brings forth the song. It is a romantic, Coleridgean figure of speech, but then, Virginia Woolf's great romance was with her dead mother, and one of the bonds she felt with Dame Ethel Smyth, the composer, was a shared adoration of their absent mothers. For our purposes in this essay, the violin is too small and too specifically related to Julia to resonate across the many lifelong and varied mother/mentor relationships that sustained Virginia Woolf as an artist. As Dame Ethel would say, lifting her baton, we shall have to sound a deeper note. Let us try the cello.

There was only one violin mistress in Virginia Woolf's life, a figure described often in musical terms, bringing harmony and rhythm into family life. Leslie Stephen bellowed and roared and moaned and groaned, and he didn't care for music. Escaping from the cacophony of a motherless Hyde Park Gate, Virginia Woolf matured as an artistic instrument under the bows of a series of women, mother/mentors, whom we may call the cellists in her life.

One of the remarkable things about Virginia Woolf is how willing other women were, and some dedicated men, to play cellist to her cello. And it is also notable that in these unequal friendships she was never seduced, betrayed, or abandoned. Patrons and patronesses of the arts have often been fickle, unreliable, or cruel. One thinks of the black novelist Zora Neale Hurston, whose white patroness insisted on being addressed as "godmother" and kept the artist like Cinderella, providing only one pair of shoes at a time, so that Hurston was forced to work as a domestic on and off all her life.[1] But Virginia Woolf was luckier than Zora Neale Hurston. The color of her skin and of the banknotes of her Aunt Caroline's legacy exempted her from certain kinds of suffering and from humiliating dependencies that liken the artist-patron relationship to that of the professional prostitute and her rich lovers. Woolf wrote of Harriette Wilson:

Across the broad continent of a woman's life falls the shadow of a sword. On one side all is correct, definite, orderly; the paths are strait, the trees regular, the sun shaded; escorted by gentlemen, protected by policemen, wedded and buried by clergymen, she has only to walk demurely from cradle to grave and no one will touch a hair of her head. But on the other side all is confusion. Nothing follows a regular course. The paths wind between bogs and precipices. The trees roar and rock and fall in ruin.[2]

Woolf's own experience of life on the other side of the sword, the life of an Aphra Behn, a Harriette Wilson, or a Zora Neale Hurston, was only in illness and madness, an experience, she told Ethel Smyth, that was "terrific."

She perceived very young that there were two modes of life for a Victorian girl of her class, to nurse or to be nursed, to care for invalids or to be an invalid. Her mother and her half-sister, Stella Duckworth, were deeply involved in district visiting, alleviating the ills of the poor in the tradition of ladies bountiful. Like Mrs. Ramsay in *To the Lighthouse,* Julia Stephen found scope for her desire for power (and a kind of freedom) in a conservative philanthropic exercise that was properly ladylike. As Louise De Salvo shows in her study of Virginia's 1897 diary, Virginia dreaded being dragged along on these missions of mercy.[3] Woolf has given us a fine portrait of the female philanthropist in action in the opening chapters of *The Years.* And Eleanor Pargiter sees what life on the other side of the sword is like as she compares the honest and loving experience of a daughter at her mother's deathbed among the East End Jews to her own mother's pale, cold, clean passing away. Since she had read her father's *Mausoleum Book,* Woolf knew how much he resented his wife's nursing and how much he needed it, how jealous he was of Julia's long nursing visits to her dying mother, in which patient and nurse seemed to be the only people in the world to each other.

The world of the sickroom is a little empire, and the nurse is queen. For Victorian women like Julia Stephen it was an outlet for desires for power and an arena for behavior that was not subservient to a husband. In this relationship and her relationship with her servants, she could give the orders. Her *Notes from Sick Rooms* (1883) was written with authority, for Julia was a doctor's daughter and daughter/nurse to her ailing mother for many years.[4] "I have often wondered," she writes ingenuously, "why it is considered a proof of virtue in anyone to become a nurse. The ordinary relations between the sick and the well are far easier and pleasanter than between the well and the well." Whether or not she was a little guilty about enjoying her power over the ill and the patient's dependency, relations between equals obviously did not come easily to her. She could play "princess to a patriarch," as Meredith described her relationship to Leslie Stephen, or angel in the house to her poor patients in St. Ives. Julia considered nursing an art and, interestingly enough, she remarks that "the art of being ill is no easy one to learn, but it is practised to perfection by many of the greatest sufferers." The invalid and her nurse are both *artists,* and she firmly advises the nurse to hide all troubles for the sake of the patient, even to "lie freely." One is reminded of Virginia's "lying" letters to Violet Dickinson about her brother Thoby's recovery after he had died, for Violet had been struck down by the same disease. She had learned from her mother that the nurse, the liar, and the artist are one person. And Julia is very firm and funny on the subject of crumbs in the sickbed.

But it is not to be assumed that Julia's version of the twin arts of nursing and patienthood was accepted by most members of her class. Her sister-in-law, Caroline Emelia Stephen, in *The Service of the Poor* (1871) argued that nursing was not indeed "proof of virtue" but evidence of religious and moral egotism and vanity. Nursing and social work ought to be paid professions, not forms of philanthropy subject to the whims of the rich. Julia did not care much for Caroline, the *Mausoleum Book* tells us. She had one area in which her authority was unquestioned and perhaps found it hard to hear a reformer question her motives.

One of Caroline Stephen's efforts in *The Service of the Poor* was to shift women's past burdens of caring for the poor, the sick, the insane, and prostitutes onto some other back. What ethics, she asked (and she had a lifetime of nursing her own parents to add to her authority), could claim that these people were more deserving of the sacrifice of the lives of thousands of women than the happy, rich, and good? There is nothing morally superior about those in pain, suffering, and poverty, she wrote, and therefore there is nothing morally superior about those whose lives are devoted to alleviating their ills. This is a rather shockingly rational reproof to sickbed sentimentality.

Virginia's illnesses began at her mother's death. In "On Being Ill" (1930) Woolf uses the same images she had earlier used to describe Harriette Wilson's life, life on the other side of the sword, with nature in chaos, roaring trees and precipices: ". . . what wastes and deserts of the soul a slight attack of influenza brings to view, what precipices . . . a little rise of temperature reveals, what ancient and obdurate oaks are uprooted in us by the act of sickness, how we go down into the pit of death and feel the waters of annihilation close above our heads. . . ."[5] For Virginia Woolf the art of being ill was essentially the art of letting go, as for Julia Stephen the art of nursing was the art of taking complete control.

After her mother's death, Virginia again assumed the position of the quivering violin, but no Julia came to play a tune. Stella Duckworth nursed her and fell ill herself and died. Virginia stood watch at the deathbeds of her father and her brother Thoby, at the miscarriages and lyings-in of her sister Vanessa. She rallied as an expert nurse for Vanessa when Julian Bell was killed in Spain, and later for Leonard when he was seriously ill. But one's impression is that she was the patient more often than nurse and played invalid, with Leonard as nurse, a good deal more than she wanted to.

Her "madnesses" and suicide attempts confirmed these roles. As she told Ethel Smyth, the loss of control, the spewing forth of anger at loved ones, and the hallucinations were often useful for her art. She had many examples in the family of genius related to madness, most notably her grandfather James Stephen, permanent undersecretary for the colonies, professor of modern history at Cambridge, and ecclesiastical biographer. Like Virginia, he was abstemious, fastidious, ate little, and overworked himself until he went mad. He always recovered and claimed for himself "the power of going mad" as if he had a kind of control.[6]

Nature had given his father a hair shirt, said Leslie. And he was "a living categorical imperative." He was "thin-skinned," the family phrase for madness and genius combined. Like all the Stephens after him (including Virginia Woolf), he loved the poetry of Cowper with its religious compulsion and "mad genius." In Caroline Emelia's edition of her father's letters, we can see much that Virginia inherited from the old puritan with the beautiful nose—"unremitting vigilance" and the demand that women *ought* to be beautiful, his concern with the moral significance of dress. Leslie Stephen remembers his father's tramp and his tread as he dictated to his daughter, wife, and sister, Miltonic and morose. He described Wordsworth as the happiest man he'd ever known because he was "surrounded by idolaters in his own house." Strongly criticized by the press for his colonial policy, he regarded himself as a lonely outsider: "The hostility it has been my lot to encounter has always tended to awaken in me a sort of morbid self-esteem." James Stephen often felt "oppressed by myself" as an "unwelcome, familiar and yet unknown visitor." He felt as if he were "two persons in one, and were compelled to hold a discourse in which soliloquy and colloquy mingled oddly and even awfully." Like his granddaughter, he kept a diary asking what he had accomplished, castigating himself, "I might as well have asked the old elms for their annual biography." In his periodic madnesses, he had his wife and sister and daughter to mother his mind and nurse him back to health, to deal with that devilish doppelgänger, his conscience. Even "madness" was a Stephen family art, practiced with the ascetic control of the Clapham Saints.

The doctor whom Sir Leslie Stephen chose to consult about his daughter Virginia was Sir George Savage. Sir Leslie had had his share of problems with madness and must have thought deeply on the subject. After the suicide of his violently mad nephew, J. K. Stephen, in 1892,[7] his brother Fitzjames descended into harmless madness and died in 1894. Within a year Leslie had written a huge biography of his brother, in which the deaths of both father and son were hallowed as history. Stephen brushes aside the fact that Fitzjames had been hounded out of office for prejudicing the jury in the Maybrick case.[8] He also had the madness of his daughter by his first wife, Minny Thackeray, to consider, and to weigh what effect Laura's behavior had on the other children. The deaths of Julia and Stella, the resident nurses in Hyde Park Gate, would naturally disquiet the inmates. Vanessa did not choose to be an artist/nurse but an artist/artist. What was Virginia to do? Playing artist/patient did not bring her mother back. Her breakdowns brought the advice of England's most distinguished "neurologist," Dr. George Savage.

Because of the continuing debate among scholars over the nature of Woolf's madness and Leonard Woolf's responsibility for her treatment, it seems to me that we might clear a little smoke from the battlefield by examining exactly what her doctor thought about mental illness and by trying to imagine what ideas she herself formed in her youth about her body, her mind, and their illnesses. Nothing dates faster than medical knowledge, and it would be unfair to blame Savage for the sins of his age. But one gets a sense of the appalling cruelty and ignorance of the treatment of the insane in late Victorian England by comparing Savage's *Insanity and Allied Neuroses* (1884) with the wise and compassionate work of Woolf's sister-in-law, Karin Stephen, in *Psychoanalysis and Medicine* (1935). What intervened and changed the theory and practice of the treatment of the mentally ill was the work of Freud, published in England by the Woolfs' Hogarth Press. Why, many people have asked, didn't the Woolfs consult a Freudian analyst? The answer, I think, lies in the family's perception of the nature of Virginia's illness and the doctor's perception of it. They had strong evidence to support a belief in hereditary Stephen insanity, and, believing in genetic or physical causes, they also believed in a physical treatment—food, rest, and no mental work. They did not believe that an effort of will or imagination could cure what appeared to be a neurological disposition to madness. There was probably also an unspoken assumption that this disposition was a natural accompaniment of her genius. And if rest and food had "cured" her before, why shouldn't they work again?

Savage's *Insanity and Allied Neuroses: Practical and Clinical* was first published in 1884. It was the standard medical text on the treatment of the mentally ill in Victorian Britain. It was reprinted in 1886, revised in

1890, reprinted in 1893, 1896, 1898, 1901, and 1905, and a new and enlarged edition appeared in 1907. Sir George Savage was one of the leading men in his field, an M.D. and M.R.C.P., superintendent of Bethlem Royal Hospital, a consultant at Guy's, and joint editor of *The Journal of Mental Science*. In his preface to *Ten Post-Graduate Lectures*, which Savage delivered at the Royal College of Medicine, Sir Clifford Allbutt calls him "one of the happiest, wittiest, kindest, and, in his own subject, most experienced members of our profession." He had already, like his colleague Sir William Gull, served the Stephen family well in treatment of the difficult case of J. K. Stephen. He was well versed in all the legal and social aspects of insanity and recommended private rest homes for his well-to-do patients.

"Among special predisposing causes," Savage explains, "heredity stands first in importance . . . The torch of civilization is handed from father to son, and as with idiosyncrasies of mind, so the very body itself exhibits well-defined marks of its parentage."[9] He gives many examples to support his opinion that "insanity by inheritance" is the "most dangerous" kind of mental illness; "perhaps," he ventures, "the suicidal tendency is one which appears to be most directly and distinctly transmitted . . . the same family tendency to self-destruction, the same inability to bear reverses philosophically, the same unrestrained motor impulse to end their troubles has manifested itself."[10] Leslie Stephen does not describe his nephew J. K. Stephen as a suicide, and one cannot be sure that Virginia Woolf knew of the manner of his death in a rest home, but her family knew and must have been made anxious by her symptoms. Savage makes very clear that a doctor ought to be consulted on the advisability of marriage and childbearing in cases of hereditary insanity. Instead of blaming Leonard Woolf for too little originality and self-confidence in his care of Virginia, let us try to imagine the young husband in an interview with the famous neurologist, hearing, perhaps in shocking detail, the description of the case of his wife's first cousin. If the sexual disappointment of the honeymoon caused a second suicide attempt, with what fortitude and fear did Leonard Woolf face a future as a monk and a nurse?

Virginia's first attempt to kill herself came after a long sojourn as nurse at her father's deathbed. Dr. Savage claims that Bethlem was full of women whose grief at the deaths of loved ones they had nursed turned into guilt at their inability to prevent the patients from dying: "Good examples of what is meant by the effect of grief in producing insanity are frequently seen in the wards of Bethlem. . . ." Seldom can one see more clearly the changing position of women in society than in the pages of Savage's text. His wards, he says, are full of grief-stricken women, hundreds of Hecates worn out from watching at the gates of death. And then there were the governesses, confused and collapsed, in a state he clearly defines as resulting from both overwork and the debilitating effects of consciousness of class discrimination.

But most female insanity he describes as hysteria, and all mental illness in women is ascribed to their sexuality. Savage reminds us of the doctor in that classic story by Charlotte Perkins Gilman, "The Yellow Wallpaper." He recommends force-feeding the woman who refuses to eat, and for "neurasthenic" women he orders two hours of massage a day, milk every hour, and electrical stimulation. (This is the origin of the infantilizing milk cure that so upset Virginia.) In the course of his work in asylums, Savage "noticed a marked increase in the number of female general paralytics seen in the middle classes." But, he remarked, "women seem to be more readily cured, and are more liable to recurrences of insanity." "That there is an excess of female lunatics," he declared categorically, "might be expected from the greater nervous instability of women living at any one time in England, to the greater tendency of insanity to recur in women, and to the greater tendency of mothers to transmit insanity to their female children."

With such a spirit of scientific objectivity to guide him, Savage also made social observations and pronouncements that ought to have appealed to the author of *Jude the Obscure:*

> I have constant examples in Bethlem of young men, who, having left the plough for the desk, have found, after years of struggle, that their path was barred by social or other hindrances, and disappointment, worry and the solitude of a great city have produced insanity of an incurable type.

In fact, one of the major concerns of his book is to speak against both the education of working men and the education of women. In her teens, Virginia Stephen had found an extremely effective weapon against depression and anxiety in reading and study. And these were precisely the things forbidden her by the doctors: Books were the cure, not the cause of her anxiety. Indeed, what sensible parent, reading the expert, would have the heart to expose a daughter to such danger?

> A strong, healthy girl of a nervous family is encouraged to read for examinations, and having distinguished herself, is, perhaps, sent to some fashionable forcing house, where useless book learning is crammed into her. She is exposed, like the Strasbourg geese, to stuffing of mental food in over-heated rooms, and disorder of her functions results. Or if a similarly promising girl is allowed to educate herself at home, the danger of solitary work and want of social friction may be seen in conceit developing into insanity. It is in this manner that the results of defective education become often apparent in the case of the weaker sex nowadays.[11]

When Virginia fell ill in 1897, the doctor's advice was to replace her pen with a spade. Books were forbidden, and she was ordered to make a garden.

His remarks on the "imagination as the most attractive side of mania," his pleasure in the patients' punning, rapid verbal associations, and verse-making show another side to his character. He tells the story of a patient who could be a cousin to Rhoda in *The Waves,* or her inventor. There was, Savage says

> a patient who associated all her ideas of moral qualities with colour and was brilliantly imaginative. Everything that was good and pure was white and upright or straight, perfection to her mind being a square of perfect whiteness. Unfortunately she looked on me as a black round.[12]

He was also ahead of his time in insisting, on the basis of his observations and against the opinions of his colleagues, that there was such a thing as male menopause, because he had observed it often among professional men. He was a pioneer in studying the relations of syphilis to insanity. In 1907 he wrote, "The feeling undoubtedly exists that insanity is one of the most transmissable of all diseases, and this has weighed, and still weighs, heavily on the lay mind."[13] Genius, he said, was associated with danger, and he claimed that auditory hallucinations in particular were inherited (Virginia heard the birds speaking Greek and King Edward shouting obscenities in the bushes). Patients who came from "neurotic stock" were more likely to "go out of their senses" periodically, but not necessarily "out of their minds." He associated much mental illness and depression with the aftermath of influenza, and here we may note the particular care Virginia required during and after bouts of the flu. He felt that an inflammation of the nerves occurred during influenza, and that it was a dangerous time for those with a hereditary disposition to insanity. I think that this explains much about Virginia Woolf's perceptions of her illness, as well as those of her family, husband, and friends.

Between 1919 and 1920 George Savage gave a series of postgraduate lectures at the Royal Society of Medicine. Among the cases he discussed was that of a soldier returned from the front who, like Septimus Smith, felt pursued and shunned by everyone. "He told me after," Savage writes, "he heard them coming and threw himself from the window, and though he lived for a few hours, he died."[14] One often thinks of Holmes and Bradshaw in *Mrs. Dalloway* as drawn from Savage and his colleague Sir William Gull. Woolf's fierce attack on psychiatrists as the social police of society would have had a likely source in Savage's own pronouncements on the overeducation of men of the artisan class. And she may well have imagined them in ruthless pursuit of her cousin J. K. Stephen.

The point of this discussion has been to establish a reasonable basis for imagining Virginia Woolf's conception of the illnesses of her body and her mind, to see how she sought out what she called "maternal protection" from women all her life. She chose her "mothers" and her nurses carefully, the one prerequisite for the role being the absolute antithesis of motherhood—chastity.

There were a series of real women who "mothered" Virginia Woolf's mind: Clara Pater, her Latin teacher; Janet Case, her Greek teacher; Violet Dickinson, who read her first essays and got them published; Caroline Emelia Stephen, "Nun," her Quaker aunt, who helped her into the discipline of work and left her a legacy of economic freedom to do it; Margaret Llewelyn Davies, who brought her into the world of the Cooperative Working Women's Guild, to a lifetime commitment to feminism, pacifism, and socialism—these were the formative influences on Virginia Woolf's mind. From them she learned the self-discipline of study, the classical structures that form the architecture of her novels, the value of intellectual work, the use of Quaker visionary experiences and "rational mysticism," and a politics based on a pure, ideal ethics. These are the saints of her sanity and her survival. They stand in her imagination like the "saints in the light" of her Clapham Sect ancestry, haloed by lives of "single blessedness," virgin martyrs to the causes dear to her. Their portraits appear in her work as "conspirators" for the freedom of their sex, as founders of what she called "the women's republic." Clara Pater appears as a music teacher in "Slater's Pins Have No Points," and her pupil Fanny's progress is similar to the narrator's in "An Unwritten Novel." Gossip has made her suspect that Julia Craye was unhappy because she was unmarried. "No, Miss Craye was steadily, blissfully, if only for that moment, a happy woman . . . obstinately adhering, whatever people might say, in choosing her pleasures for herself." Julia blazes, kindles, burns "like a dead white star" and kisses Fanny on the lips.[15] Janet Case is recalled as Lucy Craddock in *The Years,* and Woolf wrote her obituary. Violet Dickinson is celebrated in "Friendships Gallery," and Ellen Hawkes has described her "gift of self" to Virginia in "Woolf's Magical Garden of Women."[16]

Caroline Emelia Stephen was undoubtedly the most important of Woolf's early mother/mentors. She too was the subject of a spoof biography, which has been lost. Virginia wrote her obituary, which attempted to repair the damage done to her aunt's reputation in her father's *Mausoleum Book. A Room of One's Own* takes its title as well as its theme of an aunt's legacy directly from Caroline's life. In 1904 at The Porch, her aunt's Cambridge cottage or "nunnery," Virginia Stephen the professional writer was born. She was recovering from illness and a suicide attempt after her father's death. Between them, the two Quaker spinsters Violet Dickinson and Caroline Stephen wove a professional life of work for the lost young woman. Violet encouraged her to write reviews and got them published through a friend at the *Guardian* (church weekly). Caroline insisted she train and discipline herself as a historian, and together they collaborated with Maitland on the biography of Leslie Stephen. Virginia learned then the value of writing and keeping diaries and letters, that life was "fully lived" if it was written down. As a corrective to the history of great men in her father's *Dictionary of National Biography*, she imagined the life of a feminist historian searching out domestic history, in the story of Rosamond Merridew in "The Journal of Mistress Joan Martyn" (1906).[17] It is not too much to say that Virginia Woolf's "moments of being" were born of her aunt's mystical illuminations in *The Light Arising: Thoughts on the Central Radiance* and that Caroline is that mysterious "lady at a table writing" who appears so often in Woolf's writing.[18]

Margaret Llewelyn Davies first appears as Mary Datchet in *Night and Day,* and later as a source for Eleanor Pargiter in *The Years*.[19] Both characters reflect the "central radiance" in figures of light, lighthouse, and sun.[20] She, like Caroline Stephen, reinforced Virginia's pacifism and encouraged her socialist feminism.

Margaret Llewelyn Davies, Caroline Emelia Stephen, Violet Dickinson, Clara Pater, and Janet Case were the first and formative figures in the mothering of Virginia Woolf's mind. They were the cellists whose sensitive, chaste, and hardworking bows could draw forth the music from Virginia's cello. They could be trusted not to violate her sense of self and to encourage by their example the growth of "the self that took the veil and left the world." Caroline Stephen's Quaker doctrine of silent worship and the search for "inner light" taught her the methods of "rational mysticism," self-reliance, and self-discipline that became the core of her working life as an artist. Her teachers and friends gave her "maternal protection" and praise. We can see them as a "strings section" of talented and happy women in an orchestra of nuns, imposing music, order, and harmony on the life of a youthful writer tormented by guilt, grief, and self-destructive despair. Work, as Mary Datchet says in *Night and Day,* is what saves one.

Virginia's relation to her sister Vanessa was emotionally more primary and less an intellectual process than that to her mother/mentors. And her relation with Leonard Woolf was more complex but not as inspiring or creative. He nursed her and cared for her health with the strict, obsessive discipline of her mother in the sickroom. She needed his praise and approval of her work, his partnership in the daily hard work and decisions of publishing life at the Hogarth Press. His approval relieved her anxiety. His harsh, ascetic, rational behavior was a source of great security, and his moral beauty was impeccable. There was a monk in Monk's House. But he did not, alas, make her feel like a violin being played upon. Woolf was serious when she told Ethel Smyth, "Women alone stir my imagination." She thought that if her father had lived, his life would have entirely ended hers. But did she ever allow herself to think what would have happened if her mother had lived? Neither the writing of books nor the marriage to a Jew would have been possible. The life with her Greek translations, reading, concerts, arguments with Bloomsbury men, would not have been possible. A proper marriage to a proper young man of Julia's choosing . . . ?

As it was, Virginia's choice of Leonard for a husband was as brilliant a move as possible. The only parallel that comes to mind is the marriage of Beatrice Potter to Sydney Webb. The class background of Miss Potter and Miss Stephen was essentially the same. Middle-class marriage, with its servilities, civilities, and humiliations, would have ruined the careers of both. Each woman chose a partner over whom she had the upper hand economically and socially, an outsider, below her in class and status, and passionately in love with her beauty. Beatrice and Virginia made it clear to Sydney and Leonard that they were not attractive physically, and the women's money made it possible for the men to devote themselves full time to Labour politics. Marriage, Beatrice told Virginia, was the "waste pipe" of the emotions, and an old family servant would do as well. Their freedom depended on a spartan life, childlessness, and the continued adoration of their husbands. Both women achieved more than was possible for any more fully "married" woman of their class. The "penniless Jew" and the Cockney intellectual were not only the agents of their wives' freedom. They were able, within such marriages, to do exactly the work they chose to do. These "partnerships" were liberating for both parties. Virginia Woolf had in her marriage a nunnery with a knight in shining armor to guard it. Her suicide notes are not quite like a message to an old family servant. Rather they are like an invalid parent's message to an unmarried daughter who has spent years nursing her. They are a *nunc dimittis* to the faithful nurse, urging him to take his reward of a full and happy life. And certainly it appears that he did. She absolved him of guilt, and of guilt, it appears, he felt none. A happy love affair appears to have followed, and one of the finest autobiographies of modern times.

One thing is pretty certain. The person who mothered Virginia Woolf's body, ordered her daily life, and watched over her illnesses was not eligible for the post of mothering her mind. Leonard was neither inspiration nor ideal audience for her work. If she was a musical instrument, he was a meticulous and expert craftsman, keeping it in order, replacing strings, polishing the wood, keeping it out of the damp and the drafts, applying rosin to the bow. But he did not play. He was a harsh and demanding judge of execution and performance, a jealous guardian of her health—not a role to be minimized in any sense. But the distance is like the distance between Bertram and Sasha in "A Summing Up." He doesn't understand her "soul," that "creature beating its way about her and trying to escape." The soul, she thinks, "is by nature unmated, a widow bird; a bird perched aloof on that tree."[21]

Katherine Mansfield was certainly an important influence on Virginia Woolf. And here again the question of sexuality is crucial. Woolf first recoiled from a woman she felt behaved like an amorous street cat. But as soon as Katherine was dead, she was made an honorary virgin in Woolf's mind, and appears in the diary in a white veil, wreathed in orange blossoms, in bridal purity. Virginia's love for Vita Sackville-West is also a special case, for it was truly sexual, and Vita had real children to mother, a husband to care for, and primary sexual needs herself. She was not the selfless nun who could mother Virginia's mind and minister to her demands with the kind of unconditional love Virginia required. There was, I think, much more of a professional camaraderie than has been suggested, and a real respect for each other's craft. But ultimately Vita did not pass the purity test. Her flirtation with fascism and her list of lovers locked her out of the orchestra, though they did not lock her out of Virginia's heart.[22]

Woolf's relationship with Vita Sackville-West was the only one in which she was willing and able to play mother to another woman's mind and to give the intellectual nourishment she had so often taken from her own mental "mothers." It is significant that her love affair with Vita was also her most fully sexual experience. When Vita reviewed *A Room of One's Own* (*The Listener,* November 1929), she was understandably enamored of the idea of the androgynous mind of the artist, but, she promised the reader, "Mrs. Woolf is too sensible to be a thorough-going feminist." One may imagine that Vita's lessons began with a refutation of that assertion. Though she had a chip on her shoulder at her lack of formal education, Virginia Woolf found that, compared with Vita Sackville-West, she was a learned woman. And, to her credit, she tried to influence Vita as she had been influenced. (We know that Virginia Woolf spent a great deal of time and energy over the years advising young writers and reading endless piles of manuscript as an editor at the Hogarth Press. But little attention has been paid to this mothering role of hers.) In the case of her influence on Vita, it may be seen most clearly in Vita's most explicitly feminist (and Woolfian in structure) novel, *All Passion Spent* (1931).

The novel is the story of Lady Slane's liberation after the death of her husband at ninety-four, as she moves from Mayfair to a cottage in Hampstead. Her first trip on "the tube" is her "voyage in," and her fantasy of freedom is marked by a parenthetical punctuation of the tube stops from Leicester Square to Hampstead. Marriage is mocked, and many passages in the novel suggest Virginia Woolf's speech "Professions for Women," given the same year: "Is it not for this function that they have been formed, dressed, bedizened, educated—if so one-sided an affair may be called education—safeguarded, kept in the dark, hinted at, segregated, repressed, all that at a given moment they may be delivered or may deliver their daughters over, to Minister to a Man?" (*APS*, 154). The novel is both a confession and a fantasy of feminist freedom in old age, when all passion is spent.

We can see in the relationship of Lily Briscoe and Mrs. Ramsay in *To the Lighthouse* that it is not easy for the artist to find a mother/mentor. Lily longs to go back to the womb in the most explicit way, and to merge with the mother. But Mrs. Ramsay does not encourage her art, her work. In fact, she wants her to marry, to minister to men. Mrs. Ramsay is an inspiration to Lily, who adores her, but Lily gets more good out of old Carmichael, who does not lie or flatter, than she does from Mrs. Ramsay. But then, Lily is a painter. She is an "active" artist, as Woolf thought of her sister Vanessa as self-sufficient and independent.

The writer, she thought, plays a more passive role. Romantically, she is an instrument waiting to be played, like Coleridge's Aeolian harp, waiting for the muse, like Keats's negative capability. And this condition demands collaboration—the wind, the world, another person. Its analogue, of course, is illness. In "On Being Ill" Virginia Woolf describes the "astonishing" spiritual change she experiences, "the undiscovered countries" disclosed "when the lights of health go down." Illness is a "voyage in" for the artist, a trip into those silent catacombs where the self withdraws and takes the veil. The experience is so remarkable that "it becomes strange indeed that illness has not taken its place with love and battle and jealousy among the prime themes of literature. . . ."

> Those great wars which the body wages with the mind a slave to it, in the solitude of the bedroom against the assault of fever or the oncome of melancholia, are neglected. . . . To look these things squarely in the face would need the courage of a lion tamer; a robust philosophy; a reason rooted in the bowels of the earth. Short of these, this monster, the body, this miracle, its pain, will soon make us temper into mysticism, or rise, with rapid beats of the wings, into the raptures of transcendentalism.[23]

Only Proust, she feels, deals with the drama of illness. But English lacks the language of physical pain: ". . . let a sufferer try to describe a pain in his head to a doctor and language at once runs dry." As women writers need "a little language unknown to men," so writers on illness need not only a language "more primitive, more sensual, more obscene, but a new hierarchy of the passions; love must be deposed in favour of a temperature of 104; jealousy give place to the pangs of sciatica; sleeplessness play the part of the villain, and the hero become a white liquid with a sweet taste—that mighty Prince with the moth's eyes and the feathered feet, one of whose names is chloral."

Illness, she claims, is a confessional; one may tell the truth and return to childhood. The kind of reading one does in bed is the reading of an outlaw, "with the police off duty." One may be "rash" in reading Shakespeare intuitively. Illness makes one an outsider to rational, busy, daily activity. The sick person, like the artist, is a "deserter" from the battlefield of life.

Illness is an opportunity to strike out for virgin territory: "There is a virgin forest in each; a snowfield where even the print of birds' feet is unknown. Here we go alone, and like it better so." Here she contemplates the indifference of nature and the nonexistence of God. Creativity is clearly a convent, a clean, well-lighted cell of one's own, the perfect white square that Dr. Savage's patient longed for. It is a nunnery like Caroline Stephen's retreat, The Porch, a catacomb in which to cloister the imagination, a snowfield on an inaccessible glacier. If this cloister is to remain unsullied, "maternal protection" is necessary from male aggression, male sexuality.

In *Psychoanalysis and Medicine: A Study of the Wish to Fall Ill,* Karin Stephen, a Freudian, regards illness as a defense mechanism of the psyche, and often an extremely useful one. "Praise for health and blame for illness do not belong here" she says, and "moral indignation is surely out of place in the science of medicine." She urges her students not to deprive the patient of his symptoms. For they were created in order to avert a danger of which the person is terrified. Civilization, she says, echoing Freud, is based on repression. Repression cannot solve conflicts but only shelve them. "The foundation of psychogenic illness always dates from the early conflicts between desire, disappointment and fear in childhood." She does not minimize the suffering involved but claims that "the healthy person is one who has bought stability and freedom from anxiety cheaply enough to outweigh his losses by his gains."[24] Karin Stephen does not go so far as to regard this capacity to fall ill as the work of the artist, but she does say, "A neurosis is, indeed, a very remarkable human achievement which proves the extraordinary capacity for renunciation possessed by mankind, but it is an unnecessary heroism and is based ultimately on groundless fear", and "the renunciation of sex becomes tolerable and possible in so far as it can draw strength from sexuality itself."

Karin Stephen's analysis is useful in understanding Woolf's obsession with chastity and helps to explain her need for "maternal protection" and her open seeking for it, her feeling that life was a heroic struggle and that women like Ethel Smyth in their mothering saved her from "instant dismemberment by wild horses." A "mighty and awful" experience of the incestuous embraces of her half-brothers in adolescence may have been the source of her fears. Rachel Vinrace dies, we sometimes feel, in *The Voyage Out,* because Helen Ambrose denies her complete maternal protection. She does not save her from Mr. Dalloway's kiss, or even reprimand him. She kisses Terence over Rachel's head after they have all tumbled in the grass in that "rape of Persephone" scene, making clear that she will not play the perfect Demeter.

But in the last decade of her life Virginia Woolf had a mother/mentor to match her early teachers, Ethel Smyth. And Ethel helped her to release all her anger at male aggression, which she finally "spat out" in *Three Guineas.* In *Melymbrosia,* the earlier, more political version of *The Voyage Out,* Woolf wrote, "Music is a tiny tin sword which was clasped into their hands to fight the world with, if other weapons failed."[25] Ethel Smyth returned this weapon to Virginia Woolf, and taught her how to fight, as earlier she had literally taught Mrs. Pankhurst and the suffragettes how to throw rocks. She taught Virginia Woolf how to let loose her righteous anger. Dame Ethel could conduct real orchestras as well as tune up the imaginary cellos of Virginia's art. In "The String Quartet," Woolf had described the effect: "Flourish, spring, burgeon, burst! The pear tree on the top of the mountain. Fountains jet; drops descend." With Ethel Smyth on the scene, there was a perpetual pear tree on top of a mountain. Virginia courted Ethel by calling her a pear tree, in an image very like one in Katherine Mansfield and also in a sketch by Pater. It meant memory, virginity, motherhood, music.

Ethel Smyth entered Woolf's life on a wave of praise for *A Room of One's Own.* In Ethel's first surviving letter, she asks to see Virginia (January 28, 1930) for advice on a feminist talk she is about to give for the BBC. She says that her object is to drive home "what women should do if war ever again threatens." She wants to broadcast advice to women, "Stow patriotism and simply say you will strike." This is, of course, the theme of *Three Guineas* (1938), and one might say that Woolf learned to let her anger loose from an expert feminist fighter.[26]

Virginia and Ethel shared their love for their dead mothers. Ethel wrote:

. . . with me and I think many women the root of love is in the imaginative part of one—its violence, its tenderness, its hunger . . . the most violent feeling I am conscious of is . . . [her dots] for my mother. She died thirty-eight years ago and I never can think of her without a stab of real passion; amusement, tenderness, pity, admiration are in it and pain that I can't tell her how I love her (but I think she knows). Now you can imagine how much sexual feeling has to do with an emotion for one's mother![27]

Virginia agreed that both Ethel's mother and her own were "adorable." But the essence of their relationship was a discussion of the career each artist made with the help of a series of mother/mentors, those women who mothered their art. They discussed in detail what it meant to be a "daughter" and an artist. Daughterhood is the universal female condition. It was also a role each artist played with a series of women in order to insure "protection" for that convent of the mind where creativity was centered. Virginia told Ethel that Ethel provided "protection" and saved her psychiatrist's fees, that she could "confess" to her the story of the molestations of her half-brothers as she had earlier confessed to her Greek teacher, Janet Case. Their friendship was a fight from beginning to end over who was to mother the other, over whose daughter-need was the greatest. Virginia could be cruel and ungenerous. Ethel called her "four pence for ninepence," and Virginia withdrew from Ethel's self-pity and fury at the rejection of her music by the establishment, hating what she called her "eldritch shriek." But Virginia wanted to have her cake and eat it too, in posterity. Most of her criticism and mockery of Ethel is in letters to her nephews, Julian and Quentin Bell. And yet she flirted outrageously with Ethel and begged for love.

Ethel had been lucky in her friendships. Her success as a composer was due to the care of women in Leipzig, where she studied—Lisl von Herzongoberg, the wife of her composition teacher; Lily Wach, Mendelssohn's daughter, and Clara Schumann. They urged her not to marry, to encourage her talent, spoiled her and encouraged her, played her music, discussed her technique with Brahms, trained and trusted her, as if she were their own youthful selves, the composer each had longed to be. The list of Dame Ethel's mother/mentors is endless, from Lady Ponsonby to Mrs. Pankhurst, as well as a series of sisters and their husbands who sponsored and supported her. Women had recognized genius in both Woolf and Smyth, and they had given them the teaching, discipline, and love they needed to survive. Virginia's and Ethel's names for each other were "the Snow Queen" and "the Old Buccaneer." It was a battle over who was to play mother and who daughter, when both were needy. They compared notes on the ministrations of their past muses. Virginia gave Ethel the strength to write her last volumes of memoirs and her opera/oratorio *The Prison*. Ethel inspired some of *The Waves* and *The Years*, but most especially the anger of *Three Guineas*.

In one of Virginia's love letters, she describes Dame Ethel as a burning bush in a sexual portrait that strikes one as anticipatory of the plates in Judy Chicago's *The Dinner Party*. Ethel is

> a quickset briar hedge, innumerably intricate and spiky and thorned; in the centre burns a rose. Miraculously, the rose is you; flushed pink, wearing pearls. The thorn hedge is the music; and I have to break my way through violins, flutes, cymbals, voices . . . to this red burning centre . . . I am enthralled that you, the dominant and superb, should have this tremor and vibration of fire round you—violins flickering, flutes purring; (the image is of a winter hedge)—that you should be able to create this world from your centre. . . .[28]

The image of female sexuality, the labrys of roses and music is exquisite, feminist, and, perhaps, frightening. But it is Woolf's clearest expression of her vision into "the heart of the woman's republic."

The last of Virginia Woolf's "mothers" was Dr. Octavia Wilberforce. But Octavia was confused by Virginia and did not understand her needs. She did not know Virginia's history or how she herself stood in a long line of chaste mother/mentors. Still engaged as "daughter" to her own mother/mentor, Elizabeth Robins, she did not see herself as a savior for Virginia. Part of the problem surrounding Virginia Woolf's suicide resides in this misunderstanding.[29] Leonard Woolf's autobiography expresses his relief that Virginia was in Dr. Wilberforce's hands. Virginia told Vita that she loved Octavia, and she was making a "sketch" of her life. But Octavia was busy with war work and her patients. She visited Virginia socially not professionally, as a dutiful response to Elizabeth Robins's request, and told Virginia the story of her life with much discomfort and unease. Though she brought milk and butter, she brought no mothering nor, until the night before Woolf's suicide, was she sought as a doctor. She did not know the history of Virginia's mental instability, nor was she cognizant of her medical history.

There was little Dr. Wilberforce could do under the circumstances. She herself was ill at the time. What had happened was a failure of the support system of mother/mentors Virginia had devised for herself. Octavia Wilberforce did not understand what was expected of her. She wrote Elizabeth Robins in detail on every conversation and consultation she had had with Virginia. And, in the process, she absolved herself of any guilt or blame. Virginia had asked for permission to have lunch with Clive and a publisher. Octavia agreed with Leonard that it would be too much for her. What Virginia had wanted was a motherly voice to permit her to have a treat. When she didn't get it, her "tiny tin sword" was no match for the voices in her head, and she threw herself into the arms of "Mother Water." Virginia Woolf had worn out the possibilities for unconditional love. She had failed to recognize the daughter in Ethel Smyth and to give back some of the mothering she had received. She had failed to recognize that the woman-bonding she called for in *Three Guineas* had been effectively squelched in a patriarchal war. It was no time for music; the instruments were out of tune. She went down to the sound of German bombs and German planes smashing the orchestra of her mother country.

NOTES

Another version of this essay appears in *Virginia Woolf: Centennial Essays*, ed. Elaine Ginsberg, NY: Whitson Press, 1983.

1. See Mary Helen Washington, ed., *I Love Myself When I Am Laughing: A Zora Neale Hurston Reader*, introduction by Alice Walker (Old Westbury, N.Y.: Feminist Press, 1980).

2. Virginia Woolf, *The Moment and Other Essays* (New York: Harcourt Brace, 1948), p. 179.

3. Louise A. De Salvo, "1897: The First Fully Lived Year of My Life," in *Virginia Woolf: A Feminist Slant*, ed. Jane Marcus (Lincoln: University of Nebraska Press, 1983).

4. Julia Stephen, *Notes from Sick Rooms* has been reprinted by Constance Hunting (Orono, Maine: Puckerbrush Press, 1980).

5. Virginia Woolf, *The Moment and Other Essays*, p. 9.

6. See Caroline Emelia Stephen's edition of her father's letters, *Sir James Stephen, K.C.B., L.L.D., Letters with Biographical Notes by His Daughter, Caroline Emelia Stephen*, printed for private circulation (Gloucester, England: John Bellows, 1906). All quotations in the next paragraph are from this source. See also my "The Niece of a Nun: Virginia Woolf, Caroline Stephen and the Cloistered Imagination," in Marcus, *Virginia Woolf: A Feminist Slant*.

7. J. K. Stephen (1859–1892) left behind him after suicide by self-starvation two volumes of poetic parody, often pathologically misogynist, *Lapsus Calami* and *Quo Musa Tendis?* Plaques at Eton and Cambridge testify that he was adored by his friends. Called the bard of Eton and of boyhood, he celebrated "the bright boy faces" of his old school. He was the favorite pupil of Oscar Browning and left with him for several months on the continent when the Eton master was dismissed in scandal. Browning took a fellowship at King's, and Stephen came up as an undergraduate and joined the Apostles, like his old tutor. His career promised to be brilliant, though he annoyed Browning by winning the post of tutor to the Duke of Clarence, which Browning had wanted for himself. His dissertation on international law was published, and he wrote a

defense of the compulsory study of Greek at Cambridge. A failure at law, he worked prodigiously at higher journalism and produced a weekly journal, *The Reflector* (1888), which also failed. J. K. Stephen's ghost has been revived recently by a series of books that suggest him as a likely candidate for Jack the Ripper. Information on J. K. Stephen may be found in Leslie Stephen's *Life of Sir James Fitzjames Stephen* (New York: Putnam's, 1895), Oscar Browning's memoir (*Bookman*, March 1892), Desmond MacCarthy's *Portraits* (New York: Macmillan, 1932), E. F. Benson's *As We Were* (London: Longmans, Green, 1930), Michael Harrison's *Clarence* (London: W. H. Allen, 1972), and Donald Rumbelow's *The Complete Jack the Ripper*, Introduction by Colin Wilson (Boston: New York Graphic Society, 1975).

8. For details on Fitzjames Stephen and the Maybrick case, see Mary S. Hartman, *Victorian Murderesses* (New York: Schocken, 1977).

9. George H. Savage, *Insanity and Allied Neuroses: Practical and Clinical* (Philadelphia: Henry C. Lea's Son, 1884), p. 37. Virginia explained to Ethel Smyth the exact nature of the relationship of influenza and heredity to her madness in February 1930: ". . . This influenza has a special poison for what is called the nervous system; and mine being a second hand one, used by my father and his father to dictate dispatches and write books with—how I wish they had hunted and fished instead! . . . To think that my father's philosophy and The Dictionary of National Biography cost me this!" *The Letters of Virginia Woolf*, ed. Nigel Nicolson and Joanne Trautman, 6 vols. (London: Hogarth Press, 1978), IV, letter 2148.

10. Savage, *Insanity and Allied Neuroses*, p. 39.

11. Ibid., p. 24.

12. Ibid., p. 108.

13. G. H. Savage, *The Increase of Insanity*, Lumleian Lectures, Royal College of Physicians (London: Cassell, 1907), p. 63. Lumley was commemorated in these lectures, and it may or may not be a coincidence that it is outside Lumley's shop in *The Years* that Rose is terrified by the sight of a man exposing himself.

14. G. H. Savage, *Ten Post Graduate Lectures*, Royal Society of Medicine 1919–1920 (London: William Wood, 1922), p. 5. Since this essay was written, Stephen Trombley's *All that Summer She Was Mad* has appeared, and also treats Dr. Savage.

15. "Slater's Pins Have No Points," *A Haunted House and Other Stories* (New York: Harcourt, Brace & Co., 1944), pp. 110–11.

16. See Ellen Hawkes's edition of "Friendships Gallery," *Twentieth Century Literature* 25 (Fall/Winter 1979), 3–4, and her "Woolf's Magical Garden of Women," in *New Feminist Essays on Virginia Woolf*, ed. Jane Marcus (London: Macmillan; Lincoln: University of Nebraska Press, 1981). Also in this volume is my essay "Thinking Back through Our Mothers," which discusses some of the issues raised here and reprints Woolf's obituary of Caroline Emelia Stephen.

17. See the edition of this story by Susan M. Squier and Louise A. De Salvo in *Twentieth Century Literature* 25, and an analysis of the story by Louise De Salvo, "Shakespeare's Other Sister" in Marcus, *New Feminist Essays on Virginia Woolf*.

18. See Jane Marcus, "The Niece of a Nun: Caroline Stephen, Virginia Woolf and the Cloistered Imagination," in *Virginia Woolf: A Feminist Slant*.

19. For a discussion of the women who influenced *The Years*, see Jane Marcus "*The Years* as Greek Drama, Domestic Novel and Götterdämmerung," *Bulle-*

tin *of the New York Public Library,* Winter 1977, and "Pargetting *The Pargiters,*" ibid., Spring 1977.

20. For a discussion of Margaret Llewelyn Davies's political influence on Woolf, see my "No More Horses: Virginia Woolf on Art and Propaganda," *Women's Studies* 4 (1977), 264–90.

21. *Virginia Woolf, A Haunted House,* p. 148. See De Salvo's "Lighting the Cave," *Signs,* Winter 1982, and her essay in Susan Squiers, ed., *Cities of Sisterhood,* (Knoxville: University of Tennessee Press, 1983).

22. I am grateful to Louise De Salvo for discussions about Woolf and Vita Sackville-West and for reading her essay "Tinder and Flint," part of a longer study of the two writers. Vita Sackville-West, *All Passion Spent* (New York: Doubleday, Doran 1931).

23. Virginia Woolf, "On Being Ill" in *The Moment and Other Essays,* p. 10.

24. Karin Stephen, *Psychoanalysis and Medicine: A Study of the Wish to Fall Ill* (Cambridge: Cambridge University Press, 1935.)

25. See Virginia Woolf, *Melymbrosia,* ed. Louise De Salvo (New York: New York Public Library and Reader Books, 1982).

26. Letter from Ethel Smyth to Virginia Woolf (in possession of Lawrence Graham Middleton Lewis, London), quoted by permission of Letcher and Sons for the Smyth Estate.

27. Letter from Ethel Smyth to Virginia Woolf, The Berg Collection, The New York Public Library, Astor, Lennox and Tilden Foundation. For further discussion of Ethel Smyth and Virginia Woolf, see Jane Marcus, "Thinking Back through Our Mothers" in *New Feminist Essays on Virginia Woolf,* pp. 1–30. My edition of Dame Ethel's letters to Virginia Woolf, *One's Own Trumpet,* is in progress.

28. *The Letters of Virginia Woolf,* IV, letter 2183.

29. This information on Dr. Octavia Wilberforce is taken from her letters to Elizabeth Robins in the Fales Collection, New York University and Sussex University Library, with the permission of her estate. It is part of a more detailed study called "A Drop of Common Blood."

Friends as Family and Family as Friends

Swinburne (seated)
and Watts-Dunton at
the Pines. Courtesy of
Chatto and Windus
and Mrs. Hilda Mason

Closer than a Brother
SWINBURNE AND WATTS-DUNTON

John O. Jordan

Algernon Charles
Swinburne. Courtesy
of the National Por-
trait Gallery, London

*⤳Algernon Charles Swinburne was born in London in 1837. He at-
tended Balliol College, Oxford, where he met William Morris, Dante Gabriel Rossetti,
and Edward Burne-Jones, Pre-Raphaelites with whom he remained associated. His
classic verse tragedy* Atalanta in Calydon, *published in 1865, made him famous, but in
the following year his* Poems and Ballads *was fiercely denounced by the critics as inde-
cent and blasphemous. In addition to his fame as a poet, Swinburne also played an
important role among the Victorians as an early advocate of Blake, Baudelaire, Hugo,
Mallarmé, and Whitman.*

*Swinburne's ill health, worsened by years of dissipation, almost caused his death in
1879. With the help of his friend Walter Theodore Watts (later Watts-Dunton) (1832–
1914), he recovered his health and resumed an active career of writing and publication.
Watts, a London lawyer and literary reviewer, took over the management of Swinburne's
domestic life and financial affairs. From 1879 until Swinburne's death in 1909, the two
men lived together at No. 2 The Pines in the quiet London suburb of Putney.*

⁓ Swinburne and Watts-Dunton are the Victorian odd couple—aging poet and stolid solicitor, two old codgers walled in behind their books and settled snugly for thirty years in the middle-class London suburb of Putney.[1] Something about their household arrangements invites comic description, calls forth the tone of gentle disparagement and whimsical condescension that marks Max Beerbohm's famous essay, "No. 2 The Pines," and lingers in Mollie Panter-Downes's more recent telling of the story, itself an act of homage to the Beerbohm classic. Perhaps, as Beerbohm suggests, the very idea of Swinburne's getting old strikes us as incongruous. The poet of *Atalanta in Calydon,* of "Dolores," "Félise," and "Anactoria," is a young man brashly in revolt against all the pieties of mid-nineteenth-century England. We resist the thought of him embracing respectability and smile sadly over the compromises that middle life makes to necessity. Watts-Dunton (or Watts, as he remained until adding his mother's name in 1896) is a more obvious target for ridicule. Prudent, managerial, cultivator of friendships with men whose literary talent far surpassed his own, he hovers protectively about his more volatile companion like a moral nursemaid, screening the outside world and administering a solitary bottle of ale to Algernon at every meal. Visitors like Beerbohm remember him as shaggy and a little plump, with walrus mustache and crumpled frock coat, always eager to discuss the latest literary gossip from town, while Swinburne, oblivious to the modern world and living in the library of ancient volumes and obscure first editions, shows flashes of his former self, cooing and warbling like some strange, rare species of bird.

Beerbohm's unforgettable narrative weaves together fact and fancy into a story that has powerfully influenced subsequent imaginings of the Swinburne–Watts relationship. Equally influential if somewhat more malicious has been the version of the story recounted by Swinburne's friend and official biographer, Edmund Gosse. Jealous of the ascendancy that Watts acquired, Gosse presents him as a benign domestic tyrant who, while he may have saved Swinburne from an alcoholic breakdown, kept him in virtual captivity thereafter and stifled his creative spirit. Biographers like Lafourcade and Nicolson, who follow Gosse and rely on his account, have taken a similarly dim view of Watts's character, suggesting that the quality of Swinburne's poetry deteriorated as a result of bland admonishments from his less imaginative friend. Watts's staunchest defender is his widow, Clara Watts-Dunton, who in 1922 published *The Home Life of Swinburne* partly as a rebuttal to Gosse and partly as a celebration of her beloved Walter. Although it covers only the final period of Swinburne's residence at The Pines (from shortly before her marriage in 1905 until Swinburne's death in 1909), Clara's memoir contains some of the most detailed descriptions that we have of the two men's daily routine. Its sentimental bias, however, keeps the book from being an entirely reliable portrait. Without endorsing Clara's uncritical perspective in its entirety, recent biographers of Swinburne have tried to give a more balanced picture of Watts and of Swinburne's Putney years, but in so doing they sacrifice the sharpness of focus that Beerbohm and Gosse, whatever else their limitations, successfully achieve. Among recent investigators, only Panter-Downes manages to evoke the felt quality of a living friendship, and she succeeds because she dares to dream her way back into the house and down among its inhabitants. However dull or commonplace it may first appear, the Putney household does not easily yield its secrets to the outside world.

When the two men first met in 1872, Swinburne, then thirty-five, was already a well-known poet, the author of *Atalanta, Poems and Ballads,* and *Songs before Sunrise.* Watts, five years older, was an obscure solicitor from St. Ives who had recently settled in London, seeking to combine a literary vocation with his legal career. Introduced to Swinburne by the painter Ford Madox Brown, Watts soon made himself useful by settling a delicate legal matter involving Swinburne's publisher, Hotten. From then on the two men began to dine together and soon became good friends (though not until much later did they adopt the intimacy of calling each other by first names). At first glance, they make an unlikely pair—the excitable, aristocratic poet, educated at Eton and Oxford; and the steady, conservative lawyer, solidly middle class, not a university man and not (initially, at least) a member of the select literary and artistic circle among whom Swinburne found his friends. But Watts had literary ambitions of his own, as well as a shrewd head for business, and these qualities, together with a large capacity for admiration, enabled him to win the confidence of men like Dante Gabriel Rossetti, who along with Swinburne relied increasingly on Watts for practical advice. By the mid-1870s Watts was acting in effect as Swinburne's literary agent while at the same time establishing himself as a reviewer and critic for the *Examiner* and the *Athenaeum.* In the meantime, he began work on a romance of gypsy life, a subject of passionate interest to him that he had picked up from the writer George Borrow. Progress on the novel was painfully slow, however, and *Alwyn,* as it was called, did not appear until 1898 (though set up in page proofs as early as 1885). Watts's timidity about publication and his habit of procrastination contrast sharply with his confident manner as a social creature.

During the 1870s Swinburne kept up a regular flow of publication, including two verse dramas, *Bothwell* (1874) and *Erechtheus* (1876), and a major volume of poetry, *Poems and Ballads,* Second Series (1878). This steady output is deceptive, however, and does not reflect the extent of personal difficulty that he was undergoing at this time in his life. As is well known, the late 1870s were for Swinburne a time of deepening personal crisis. The death of his father in 1877 and his mother's decision to sell the family estate of Holmwood marked two serious ruptures with the familiar past. Poor health, bouts of alcoholism, loneliness, and depression brought worried inquiries from friends and family and led finally to an exchange of telegrams between Lady Jane Swinburne, the poet's mother, and her son's trusted adviser. Between them a plan to "rescue" Algernon developed. The plan was executed by Watts, who (according to the story told by Gosse) arrived at Swinburne's rooms one morning in the summer of 1879 and carried him off by force in a four-wheeler to the house of Watts's married sister, Mrs. Mason, at Ivy Lodge, Putney. When it became apparent that the poet's desperate condition required an extended cure, Watts, always consulting closely with Lady Jane, arranged to lease one of the large, newly constructed villas near his sister's house in Putney. There, toward the end of September, he and Swinburne installed themselves at No. 2 The Pines. Though he could hardly have suspected so at the time, it was to remain Swinburne's residence for the rest of his life.

Although Watts held the lease, money for the new establishment came from Swinburne, or rather from the sale of his father's library, out of which Lady Jane agreed to grant her son £1,000, conditional upon his giving up lodgings in London and moving in with his friend. In addition, she arranged to pay Watts £200 a year for Algernon's maintenance, out of the proceeds of the Holmwood sale. Thereafter, Watts took charge of all business matters, relieving Swinburne of his worries over money and serving as financial counselor to Lady Jane where Algernon was concerned. Watts also took upon himself the task of regulating Swinburne's moral character, and it is here that the most remarkable transformations seem to have occurred. Whereas in June Swinburne had been too ill to care for himself, by the fall of 1879 he appears to have recovered his robust good health and to have adopted the routine of daily rest and exercise, combined with regular periods of work, that he was to maintain for the next thirty years. Moreover, at Watts's insistence, he gave up drinking, except for a bottle of ale with meals and another bottle at midday, taken at the Rose and Crown on his morning walk across Wimbledon Common. Watts brought about this miracle of temperance, so we are told, by a subterfuge so transparent as surely to have failed, had it met with any determined resistance. Reminding Swinburne that Tennyson drank only port, Watts persuaded his friend to abandon

brandy and to adopt the poet laureate's regime. Having won this important first concession, Watts then gradually weaned the poet to French
wines (the drink of Dumas), and finally to Shakespeare's own good English ale. If the story as a whole sounds improbable, there is likely a grain
of truth in Watts's holding up the Tennysonian example as a model.
Swinburne's vanity thrived on such comparisons. "Here I am, like Mr.
Tennyson at Farringford,

> Close to the edge of a noble down,"

he wrote to Lord Houghton on November 21, 1879, describing his new
residence.[2] If it took flattery to keep Algernon content in the suburbs
(and only some strong potion could persuade him that Wimbledon Common was a "noble down"), then Watts was ready with an ample store,
seeing to it, for example, that the other residents of Putney referred to
Swinburne as "the Bard."

Whatever the reasons for Swinburne's sudden reform, the change
in his habits proved enduring and brought great comfort to Lady Jane.
In October 1880 she wrote Watts to express her pleasure at seeing
Algernon "so well and happy" and to state her gratitude for "your care
of him."[3]

As one reflects on the familiar story of Swinburne's rescue by Watts
and on their subsequent co-residence of thirty years, several points deserve particular attention. First, there is the question of Swinburne's own
role in the process of his spiritual and physical recovery. Biographers,
whether hostile or kindly disposed toward Watts, have agreed in portraying Swinburne as the helpless recipient of his friend's well-meaning
intervention. Not only during the crisis of 1879, but during the entire
Putney period, Swinburne is depicted as a childlike innocent, incapable
of handling his own affairs and dependent on Watts for direction and
support. Clara Watts-Dunton, for example, reports her husband as saying of Swinburne, "'It is because of his helplessness that I love him so
much.'"[4] To some degree, this report deserves credence. Swinburne's
physical condition during 1878 and 1879 was by all accounts desperate,
and he obviously needed help in averting a self-destructive course. But
to place Watts in the role of rescuer and Swinburne in the position of
helpless victim is to deny the poet's own agency in resolving his
difficulties. As I have argued elsewhere,[5] the crisis of 1879 must be
understood in part as a crisis in Swinburne's imaginative life. He was
facing the prospect of creative as well as personal stagnation and needed
to decide whether to live or die as a poet. The temptation to throw
himself (figuratively) from a cliff in imitation of his beloved Sappho was
strong, but he chose instead to follow her in the role of poet and to echo
her sweet, triumphant song of anguish in his own poem, "On the Cliffs,"

written shortly after his arrival at Putney and published in *Songs of the Springtides* (1880). Understood in this context, Swinburne's rapid return to good health and his ready compliance with the plan to moderate his drinking correspond to the poet's conscious rededication to a life of the imagination. Watts, in the emphasis I would give, may have served as a minister of Apollo, but it is the god of poetry himself, and Swinburne's profound indentification with him, who brought about the recovery so gratifying to Lady Jane.

If I am correct to insist on the willed quality of Swinburne's initial reformation at Putney, then it makes sense to think of his long friendship and joint tenancy with Watts as also having a greater element of self-direction than is generally considered to be the case. Biographers have exaggerated the extent of Watts's control over his friend, or rather, have confused the delegation of various practical responsibilities, including management of the house and the handling of all business matters, with an attitude of passivity and emotional dependence on Swinburne's part. His letters from The Pines betray no sense of loss or feeling that his world was in any way restricted by the move to Putney. On the contrary, his correspondence recovers much of the feisty spirit and playfulness that it had shown during the 1860s. Sadean humor (of which Watts could hardly have approved) reappears as frequently as ever in the letters to his intimate friends, and he does not hesitate to fire off indignant letters to the editors of various journals or to spar in print with persons from whom he imagined some injury or offense. The letters to his publisher, Andrew Chatto, are full of brusque, peremptory command and bristle at the discovery of each printer's error. Their tone is that of the professional writer taking care of business in the one area of practical concern that he judged to be important. The letters to Watts when the two men are apart (usually on the occasions of Swinburne's visits to his family) issue confident instructions for the dispatch of this manuscript, that volume from the library, or the latest issues of the London literary journals. They show few signs of "helplessness" other than a reliance on Watts to keep him supplied with clean linen, handkerchiefs, and socks.

The usual explanation for this independent, sometimes even headstrong tone in Swinburne's letters is to say that Watts exercised his guardianship with such subtlety and tact that Swinburne remained unaware of its existence and went about the business of being a famous poet, oblivious to the structured environment that Watts so carefully prepared. Perhaps this is the case, or perhaps it may be more correct to say that Swinburne allowed Watts to structure the environment so that he as poet could concentrate his energies on the work that most required attention: his writing. To view the friendship in this way is to accord

Swinburne more power in its creation and to regard Watts as playing a role that Swinburne in some degree imagined for him. A similarity thus exists, in one respect at least, between the Swinburne–Watts relationship and the Swinburne–Mary Gordon love affair of the 1860s, which most critics now take as the biographical source for the unhappy love poetry of *Poems and Ballads,* First Series (1866). Jerome McGann, however, has pointed out that some of the love poems antedate the events on which they are supposedly based. McGann argues that Swinburne incorporated Mary into a private myth of romantic love, one that already existed in his imagination and that derives ultimately from literary models.[6] In somewhat the same way, I believe, Swinburne drew Watts into his life and established a relationship with him that fostered and sustained creative work. As with Mary Gordon, the relationship with Watts also had a literary antecedent. Writing to his mother in June 1880, Swinburne describes his new project for a "book (in prose) of studies in English Poetry." After summarizing its contents, he continues: "Watts praises both the design and (thus far) the performance to the skies—in terms which I will not quote lest you should be reminded of the glowing praises recorded by Mrs. Gamp as having so 'frequent' been bestowed on her by Mrs. Harris."[7] Joking references to Mrs. Gamp abound in Swinburne's correspondence, as any reader of *The Swinburne Letters* knows, but here the joke illuminates something important that Swinburne sensed intuitively about his friend. The role that Watts would play in his life, like that of Mrs. Harris to her friend, was to reflect and validate the author's sense of self by confirming all opinion and supplying measureless quantities of uncritical admiration. Moreover, like the fictitious companion invented for this purpose by Mrs. Gamp, Watts was himself a creation of the author's mind.

To claim that Watts was an imaginary friend made up by Swinburne to serve as an embellishing mirror is of course to overstate the facts. Watts did exist, and he did provide real emotional support for his friend, especially in times of difficulty such as when the poet's brother Edward died in 1891. No one could doubt the sincerity of Swinburne's appeal to Watts for comfort during the final hours of Edward's illness. "Please send me a line as soon as you get this," he writes. "Not that I need any assurance of your sympathy, but that the sight of a written word from you would be the next best thing to the sight of your face or the touch of your hand."[8] The letter to Watts written immediately following Edward's death contains one of Swinburne's most direct personal tributes: "I feel very thankful to you when I think I have one who is more to me and nearer than a brother."[9] If we ask what family connection is "nearer than a brother," the answer must be the one suggested by Clara Watts-Dunton: "On Walter's side, the love for his friend seemed to be largely composed of what, for want of a better word, I must call the mothering instinct."[10] Clara's sentimental comment actually points to an essential quality in the friendship. The previous relationship in Swinburne's life which most closely resembles the one with Watts is that between Algernon and Lady Jane. Watts's role in Swinburne's life was, in effect, to be a second mother to the poet. As we have already seen, he acted closely in consort with Lady Swinburne during the crisis of 1879. Other aspects of his caretaking role, such as his "weaning" Swinburne away from brandy, have a distinctly maternal cast. Although relatively little is known about the details of Swinburne's early life, the intimacy between him and his mother is a well-established fact. Their closeness continued until her death in 1896 at the age of eighty-seven. The strong bond between mother and child is a major theme in Swinburne's work, notably in *Atalanta in Calydon,* and much of his poetry is devoted to that "great sweet mother," the sea. The mothers about whom Swinburne writes are usually overpowering figures toward whom considerable ambivalence is felt. In their more sinister and erotic incarnations, they sometimes prove dangerously destructive to the poet-lover, like the fictitious "Dolores" and "Félise" of his poetry, or like the Amazons of St. John's Wood, to whom Swinburne went in real life and paid to have himself beaten.

The mother whom he found—or created—in Watts was of a very different order. Watts's role was to soothe and calm, not to overstimulate. He helped provide a secure, orderly environment in which Swinburne could commune with the poetic voices of the past and reecho them in his own work. He lent his steadiness to the poet and reflected a stable self-image whenever Swinburne felt threatened with disintegration, as he surely did in 1879 or again at the time of his brother's death. As a stabilizing and supportive maternal figure, Watts effectively counterbalanced the overwhelming mothers of Swinburne's erotic fantasies. His presence served as a defense against the dangerous and potentially destructive mother-muse. For this reason, perhaps, Watts himself never played the part of muse. He seldom figures directly in Swinburne's work other than in formal poems of dedication. His was an enabling function, not an inspirational one. The muses of Swinburne's poetry are absent— the lost mother of infancy or the lost love of adolescence, Mary Gordon—whereas Watts was always there, steady and reliable. He gave encouragement, but never became himself the lost object of desire.[11]

There are two poems that help to define more precisely the enabling maternal function Watts performed in Swinburne's imaginative life. The first is the sonnet written to accompany Swinburne's dedication of *Tristram of Lyonesse* to his friend.

Spring speaks again, and all our woods are stirred,
And all our wide glad wastes aflower around,
That twice have heard keen April's clarion sound
Since here we first together saw and heard
Spring's light reverberate and reiterate word
Shine forth and speak in season. Life stands crowned
Here with the best one thing it ever found,
As of my soul's best birthdays dawns the third.

There is a friend that as the wise man saith
Cleaves closer than a brother: nor to me
Hath time not shown, through days like waves at strife,
This truth more sure than all things else but death,
This pearl most perfect found in all the sea
That washes toward your feet these waifs of life.[12]

Composed at The Pines in the poet's birth month of April 1882, the poem is a celebration of the third return of spring witnessed by the two friends since their move to Putney. The proverbial phrase "closer than a brother" and the pervasive imagery of rebirth suggest a maternal dimension to the friendship. The poet sees himself and his poetry ("Spring's light reverberate and reiterate word") as literally having been reborn through the agency of his friend. Twice the friend is referred to as a precious object "found," implying that he is a replacement for some lost object, presumably the original mother. The poet's verses are compared to orphans, "waifs of life," now washed up from the sea at the friend's feet and thus united with their foster mother. Time is now marked from the date of the poet's relocation, "As of my soul's best birthdays dawns the third," suggesting, as Panter-Downes points out, that Swinburne may at times have imagined himself a small child in Watts's protective care.

The second and more important poem for locating the place of Watts in Swinburne's life is the long mythic narrative "Thalassius," written in 1879–1880, soon after the move to Putney, and published in *Songs of the Springtides* (1880). This poem, often discussed by Swinburne's critics as a spiritual autobiography, tells the story of the young poet Thalassius, a son of Apollo and the sea nymph Cymothoe. The central action of the poem involves a crisis in which the poet, having pursued the deadly muse Erigone, undergoes a spiritual conversion as a result of the return, after a long absence, of his mother. The poem presents a generalized myth of the imagination, but it also contains a relatively faithful account of Swinburne's 1879 crisis. The return of Cymothoe corresponds to the intervention of Watts—in other words, to the presence of a soothing maternal figure who provides release from the frenzied eroticism of devotion to Erigone. Reunited with his mother, the poet undergoes a process of controlled regression:

And his eyes gat grace of sleep to see
The deep divine dark dayshine of the sea,
Dense water-walls and clear dusk water-ways,
Broad-based, or branching as a sea flower sprays
That side or this dividing.[13]

Just as Watts did for Swinburne at Putney, so Cymothoe calms her charge until "he communed with his own heart, and had rest."[14] As in the dedicatory sonnet to *Tristram*, rebirth imagery is prominent. Reunion with the mother, however, does not complete the process of the poet's recovery. The full realization of his powers requires the "father's fire made mortal in his son,"[15] and the poem concludes with a coming together of Apollo and Thalassius and with the issuance of a paternal benediction. Like Watts, Cymothoe helps to regulate the poet's environment and to establish rhythms of continuity that support creative work. True inspiration, however, comes only when the poet moves beyond the attitude of passive dependence and achieves a positive and active identification with the god of poetry himself.

Although written early in the friendship, "Thalassius" is prescient in its anticipation of the mothering role that Watts would continue to play in Swinburne's life for the next three decades. It is a role that he must have enjoyed greatly, for he performed it with no trace of bitterness or resentment that we can see. If ever he felt that his own writing suffered from the time and attention devoted to Swinburne's care, no comment to this effect has been recorded. So protective was he toward the friendship that he refused to let his biographer, a young Irishman named Douglas, say anything about it.[16] After Swinburne's death, Watts (by then Watts-Dunton) steadfastly declined all suggestions that he should write his friend's biography. The few poems that he writes about the friendship are in the same idealizing vein as Swinburne's dedicatory sonnet. Although of little literary interest, they do indicate that Watts persisted in attributing childlike qualities to his friend. For example, in a sonnet from 1882 describing "a morning swim off Guernsey with a friend," he addresses Swinburne in the following terms:

In your eyes, dear friend,
Rare pictures shine, like fairy flags unfurled,
Of child-land, where the roofs of rainbows bend
Over the magic wonders of the world.[17]

The poem is appropriately entitled "Nature's Fountain of Youth."

The idea that Swinburne had drunk from the fountain of perpetual youth and that he remained in some way forever a child has appealed to other writers besides Watts. In "No. 2 The Pines," Beerbohm concludes the factual account of his visits to Putney with the description of an imaginary encounter in Elysium between himself and the two friends. Watts, in Beerbohm's fantasy, is still old and shaggy, still dressed in the same frock coat as ever, but Swinburne, he insists,

> will be quite, quite young, with a full mane of flaming auburn locks, and no clothes to hinder him from plunging back at any moment into the shining Elysian waters from which he will have just emerged. I see him skim lightly away into that element.[18]

Watts starts to caution the poet about catching his death of cold, but breaks off suddenly, remembering that "here in Elysium, where no ills are, good advice is not needed." The point of Beerbohm's parable is clear: The poet's immortal soul is strong and has no need of caretakers. Beerbohm is correct to insist on the poet's enduring vitality; it would be a mistake, however, to imagine Swinburne as abandoning his friend and leaving him behind on the shore, even in Elysium. In Watts, Swinburne created a companion who was essential to the maintenance of his imaginative powers. After surviving the personal and imaginative crisis of 1879, he continued to plunge into the element of poetry, but he always returned, not to the "great sweet mother" of his early verse, but to the second mother whom he had created in the person of his friend.

NOTES

1. A basic bibliography of the Swinburne–Watts relationship should include the following: Max Beerbohm, "No. 2 The Pines," in *And Even Now* (London: Heinemann, 1920); Edmund Gosse, *The Life of Algernon Charles Swinburne* (London: Macmillan, 1917); Clara Watts-Dunton, *The Home Life of Swinburne* (London: Philpot, 1922); Harold Nicolson, *Swinburne* (London: Macmillan, 1926); Georges Lafourcade, *Swinburne: A Literary Biography* (London: G. Bell, 1932); Mollie Panter-Downes, *At The Pines* (Boston: Gambit, 1971); Philip Henderson, *Swinburne: The Portrait of a Poet* (London: Routledge and Kegan Paul, 1974); Donald Thomas, *Swinburne: The Poet in His World* (London: Weidenfeld and Nicolson, 1979). Essential as a primary source is Cecil Y. Lang, ed., *The Swinburne Letters*, 6 vols. (New Haven: Yale University Press, 1959–1962).

2. *The Swinburne Letters* IV, 111.

3. Ibid. IV, 166.

4. Clara Watts-Dunton, *The Home Life of Swinburne*, p. 75.

5. John O. Jordan, "Swinburne on Culver Cliff: The Origin of a Poetic Myth," *Biography* 5 (1982), 143–60.

6. Jerome McGann, *Swinburne: An Experiment in Criticism* (Chicago: University of Chicago Press, 1972), pp. 213–18.

7. *The Swinburne Letters* IV, 151.

8. Ibid. VI, 12.

9. Ibid. VI, 13.

10. Watts-Dunton, *The Home Life of Swinburne*, p. 71.

11. One lost object of desire who did become a muse in Swinburne's later poetry is Watts's young nephew, Bertie Mason, whose absence while on holiday Swinburne lamented in a group of poems entitled *A Dark Month*, written in the summer of 1881. Bertie was then seven years old. Swinburne's delight in babies and young children probably reflects, through a process of projection and identification, his own need for mothering. For a fuller account of Bertie Mason's friendship with the poet, see Henderson, *Portrait*, pp. 238–41.

12. *The Poems of Algernon Charles Swinburne* (London: Chatto and Windus, 1904) IV, 3.

13. Ibid. III, 308.

14. Ibid.

15. Ibid., p. 309.

16. James Douglas, *Theodore Watts-Dunton: Poet, Novelist, Critic* (London: Hodder and Stoughton, 1904), pp. 267ff. More informative is Thomas Hake and Arthur Compton-Rickett, *The Life and Letters of Theodore Watts-Dunton*, 2 vols. (London: T.C. and E.C. Jack, 1916).

17. Quoted in Douglas, *Theodore Watts-Dunton*, p. 268.

18. Beerbohm, *And Even Now*, p. 87.

Ralph Waldo Emerson
in lecture garb, at ap-
proximately fifty years
old. Courtesy of the
Ralph Waldo Emerson
Memorial Association
and the Houghton
Library

Emerson and the
Angel of Midnight

THE LEGACY OF
MARY MOODY EMERSON

Evelyn Barish

This silhouette of Mary Moody Emerson, the only known representation of her, probably dates from her youth. Courtesy of the Concord Free Public Library, the Ralph Waldo Emerson Association, and the Houghton Library

*⌒◦R*alph *Waldo Emerson (1803–1882), the descendant of many generations of New England ministers, was nineteenth-century America's major representative of Protestant thinking as it wrestled with its loss of orthodox faith, and one of its finest poets. Out of that struggle came his role, still both important and problematical, as a shaper of America's sense of identity. His lectures and books told audiences of the absolute necessity of choosing to live now, not later, and at almost any risk, setting aside as a false guide the "sucked eggshell" of Calvinism with its fear of death and conformity to a dead past, and insisting instead on the growth of individual consciousness. His essay on "Self-Reliance" eventually became a perennial high school text in spite of its fervent protest against conformity and its institutions. Like those of all great philosophers, his ideas have entered the public domain and are a part of public wisdom.*

Many of the underlying intellectual and religious assumptions leading to his unconventional positions had first been mediated by his aunt, Mary Moody Emerson (1775–1863), in her stance as a passionately believing nay-sayer—one "of the Sect of the Seekers," as her nephew said of them both. Raised as a virtual orphan in rural isolation and poverty and entirely self-educated, she was nevertheless brilliantly endowed with intellectual and religious gifts and widely read. Deliberately unconventional, she never married, but devoted herself to the life of the mind in a long career as both an anti-Calvinist and anti-Liberal thinker. Described by her nephew as having been the best writer of her day in New England, she wrote voluminously, although her letters and journals, elliptical and often obscure in style, have remained largely unpublished.

All your letters are valuable to me; those most so I think which you esteem the least. I grow more avaricious of this kind of property like other misers with age, and like expecting heirs would be glad to put my fingers into the chest of "old almanacks" before they are a legacy.

—Emerson, age twenty-four,
to his aunt

For most of his life, Ralph Waldo Emerson had a passion for the ideas and language of his aunt, Mary Moody Emerson. His admiration for her, though sometimes ambivalent, was remarkable; even as a mature man he regarded her in her prime as the best writer in Massachusetts, and named her as the deepest early influence on his own religious voice and language.[1]

Numerous aunts in literary history have influenced their talented younger relatives. What makes Waldo Emerson's nephewhood different is the intellectual quality of the sister of his dead father, the intellectual intimacy between them, and the complexities and ambivalence of their interaction. During Emerson's formative years he probably had no other literary contact who so shaped his mind or who posed so useful a challenge against which to test his own continuing growth. For her part, Mary Moody Emerson, regarded as eccentric as well as brilliant even by those who loved her, never found elsewhere so generous, subtle, or appreciative an audience. To him, as he wrote a friend, she was "alone among women"; she was his "muse" and the mediator of an intensely individualistic, romantic stance, which he was, with modifications, to make his own. To her he was from his adolescence at once "genius," "deer play Mate," a fellow student, and finally, a doctrinal opponent.[2]

Little, however, is known today about these dynamics, for the two or three commentators who have been interested in Mary have largely focused their interpretations as Emerson himself did in his late essay, which is reverential and entertaining, but does not express the nature of their interaction.[3] His conclusion, that her meaning was essentially expressed as "Faith alone, Faith alone," is considerably less than half the story, for a subject so intimately involved with his own development almost half a century earlier was inevitably elusive. Their relationship is contained largely in two insufficiently explored sources: Waldo's letters to his aunt, letters which appeared partly in the early *Journals* but which were omitted in part from Rusk's later *Letters* and in toto from the newer *Journals and Miscellaneous Notebooks;* and Mary's own letters, still almost entirely unpublished.[4] These sources, together with "Uilsa" itself, provide a double picture of a brilliant if uncertain young writer, intent on shaping a unique self, significant elements of which he had first glimpsed through the mediatory vision of the aunt he justly named his muse, who was herself a seeker, knower, and perhaps artist as well.

One of the literary practices he absorbed from her was the keeping of a voluminous journal. He began his when he was sixteen, naming it "Wide World," and liking to exchange it for her own productions, called "almanacks." It was against this background in 1822 that she wrote him when he was nineteen, telling him tartly that she had shared one of his writings, "the sorry tale of the old hag," with a young woman who "was so glad to read something new" that it had "amused her." "I promised something better," Mary noted, and then entreated further installments of the journals from which this "sorry tale" had been taken: "Send the wide or narrow *world* . . . be sure to send many pages to one who ever loves you."[5] The mixture of reproof and love in Mary's tone seems understandable—even restrained—when we realize that the "old hag" of the "sorry tale," known in the family as "Uilsa," contained central elements of a portrait of Mary herself, recognizable within the family if not beyond it.[6] It says something about the forty-eight-year-old aunt's sense of humor and detachment about her peculiarities that she could thus publicize this early example of Waldo's fictions. ("My taste was formed in romance," she once wrote, "and I knew I was not destined to please.")[7]

We may share Mary's interest, however begrudging, for "Uilsa," though a youthful tale of gothic terror rather than a work of filial piety, represents a significant new stage in Emerson's development both as a writer and in relation to his aunt. He began it just after graduating from Harvard at age eighteen, when questions of personal and vocational identity were beginning to press hard upon him, and he worked on it in four separate stages between August 1821 and February 1822. Still embedded in the journals and never printed together as a separate unit, each of the four sections halts so abruptly that I have called these breaks stammers, a characteristic which may give the impression that "Uilsa" is fragmentary. On the contrary, however, the narrative structure and language are complete, coherent, and often powerful.[8] The manuscript contains few corrections and seems to have flowed easily from Emerson's pen.

Part I begins without preamble:

Her habits were very singular; she would come to the neighbouring village and while a family were warmly seated about their evening fire they encountered her bright eye and frightful face at the window, where she would remain motionless a moment and suddenly start away and reenter the wood. If pursued she would be found perhaps squatted on the heath near her hut twisting a string out of the dead grass and muttering to herself." [*JMN* I, 266–67]

Uilsa has lived there about thirty years when the narrator arrives at the town and inevitably hears of her from the "peasants." After secretly watching her, he finally seeks her, sitting down near a pile of leaves, and is soon "shocked—to see a bare arm outstretched" and to hear her "screaming to the woods and the sky"—evidently out of the leaf pile. Her words reveal her magnificent sense both of self and of great loss:

"Fall, fall, scarlet leaves! The trees are my servants to cover me with a royal crimson mantle. And am not I a queen of the woods? I scared the wild eagle at the dawn, for the eye of my mother's daughter was fiercer than his. And who is he," she said, turning suddenly upon me, "who comes to the Cave of the Grey Queen? Is the spoon or the doublet . . . or the gold stolen . . . or is the magistrate come up that they have hunted out Uilsa again?"

When he asks if she can offer guidance for his life, Uilsa replies that although she is despised by the crowd as a "decrepit worm" and has "lived in a land which is hateful [,] I did not come from the vulgar dust— Uilsa is highly and proudly descended from an hundred weird women [,] fatal and feared daughters of Odin" (*JMN* I, 268). The youth mentally acknowledges her claim of having "supernatural light" as the sibyl, looking north "as if expecting a sign in the firmament . . . stood up between two blasted oaks [,] glaring on me." There suddenly the narrative breaks off.

It will resume in midsentence later, but the next entry, a variant opening, also begins in the middle of things: "By the time Wilfred had reached the heath the north wind which had before been resounding faintly in the glens began to flow fiercely and [,] while it rapidly separated the clouds [,] gave indication of a cold night. The sun had set and the stars shone with increased brilliancy through the purified atmosphere." He stops to listen to the wind, but as the gale dies, he hears "an articulate sound which no ear could mistake for the breeze" (*JMN* I, 273–74). And here, once again, the piece breaks off.

In this haunting passage of chilly beauty, an isolated figure without patronym or earthly tie moves through the empty terrain of the frozen North, avoiding the coal pits "which were supposed to make a nocturnal path dangerous." In these negations, as in their broken landscapes and even the sounds of their names, Wilfred and Uilsa are cognate figures; Emerson probably realized this, for he quickly returned to the main story, in which Uilsa's "fiery eyes and perturbed countenance" seize the narrator's attention until "I forgot the world I had left and saw nothing but the Spirit of Prophecy" (*JMN* I, 284). She speaks, Uilsa says, as "a voice from the sepulchres and caves [,] a voice from the wrinkled rottenness which the earth spurns from her bosom." In earlier years, she relates, she had borne a son who was seized from her by a "gold caravan with galloping horses and tasseled elephants from Birmah." In reply to her screams, "Odin knew me and thundered." Her violent language emphasizes the capacity for tearing and eating alive possessed by Odin's wolves, who defend her and in some sense are identified with her:

> A thousand wolves ran down by the mountain scared by the hideous lightning and baring the tooth to kill; they rushed after the cumbrous host. I saw when the pale faces glared back in terror as the black wolf pounced on his victim. I saw them as he dashed his tooth into the Indian's throat and mangled his bones in the sand. They died, and the wild thunder crashed the wolves but one escaped with mine infant son to the cave of the forest, and nourished him from her dugs. I made my bed in the cavern, my feast with the whelp of a wolf. . . .

The distinction between Uilsa herself and the wolves who both defend and betray her has faded: a wolf suckles Uilsa's son while Uilsa feasts with a wolf whelp in a cavern. The sadistic, almost cannibalistic elements of the tale expand further, as the boy grows up to reject and hate her:

> My son commanded the snows of the pole. Who is he now but Vahn, the Master of Magicians? But the proud magician forgot the mother that bore him, and the circle of enchantments which he drew was a ring of fiend-dogs to bay at me,—to scare me over the snow-drift in the cold starless night. [*JMN* I, 285]

This is the only reference in the story to Vahn (Vain? Wan?), who is clearly meant to be the magician of the title, but never actually appears. Uilsa herself does not speak again until the very end; the focus on her seems to shift, as she becomes larger, more mythic, and more strange. The narrator, from a more distant point of view, now calls her a "barbarian," and her animality in sex and eating (two linked taboos for Emerson)[9] associates her with wild, dangerous terrain. That setting is to become metaphoric of her moral extremity: To be as Uilsa (Else?) is to be Other, not human.

The tale now moves vaguely forward in time, with the speaker no longer a youth, but a rather protective gentleman. He shows a literary attitude toward nature and self-consciously appreciates it—unlike Uilsa, who lives in a cave, erupts out of a leaf pile, and seems almost a part of nature, auctocthynous. He seeks her out among "those fine shades which never failed to elevate the imagination" (*JMN* I, 286), but she is not there. Instead, his attention is caught by a strange young boy, who calls him to follow to "dangerous places . . . in the midst of the coal mines" where sudden abysses open to unfathomable depths.

But the narrative breaks off for a third time. When Emerson resumes it four months later, the seeker moves on, now accompanied not by a child but by a villager who wants to warn Uilsa that a large "ottar-snake" lies among the rocks. They pursue her, though she outruns them until they suddenly see the "immense folds" of a serpent coiled on the edge of a chasm. The now speechless narrator sees every detail of the scene as Uilsa with "majestic gait" advances consciously toward the monster, looking north toward dark clouds:

> She came within a few yards of the snake, and stopping abruptly, raising both arms to the sky, stood like a giantess and cried aloud, "Art thou come, Minister!" The next moment that terrible animal was wound around her, tightening his terrific folds while his victim seemed struggling with superhuman strength and her hand grappled with the head of her destroyer. Suddenly they sunk and I rushed to the mouth of the abyss and listened, as there murmured up from its depths a loud cry to Odin from the suffocating gripe of the Serpent. THE END. [*JMN* I, 302–303.]

It is a terrifying dénouement, for we must now see into the abyss that had earlier threatened Wilfred. There are hints here also of the primal scene, as it is perceived ambiguously on the one hand by an adult and his companion—who in a previous metamorphosis had been an oddly knowledgeable child—and on the other by two uncomprehending persons who are childlike beside the giant Uilsa.

Inherent in the structure of the tale is a criticism of moral extremity and violent emotion. Uilsa never articulates an answer to the young man's question about how to guide his steps in life; her flow of language describing her violent personal history is followed only by silence and then a dreadful metamorphosis. But her real message is clear through the transparent paradox of her silence, for she acts out a terrifying animalism that in fact "guides his steps" literally to the brink of destruction. The narrator holds back from the abyss, but he has learned that the way she points is one he cannot take.

There are parallels between Mary Moody Emerson and this gothic portrait. She was the daughter of a minister who went off to the Revolution as a chaplain but inexplicably first removed his child from his wife's care and gave her to his mother and sister to be raised. Mary grew up on the farm of these relatives, taught by poverty to shift for herself and others, out of contact with her mother, siblings, and almost all society. Not until she was around twenty did she gain some freedom and begin to see more of her relatives. Despite her unusual intellectual gifts, she was almost entirely self-educated. Emerson tellingly reported that one of her few early books was a volume of poetry she found on the farm without cover or title page, which she learned intimately; only in later years did she learn that the author was Milton, the poem *Paradise Lost.*[10]

After the death of Waldo's father in 1811, Mary—who had refused a respectable offer of marriage and now had a small income of her own—helped Ruth Emerson to bring up the five boys by running a series of boarding houses. Mary's interests, however, were not domestic. With a passionate interest in religion and an equally passionate attachment to solitude, nature, and writing, she oscillated between life in Boston with her relatives and retreats to her country farm, where she read, wrote her journals, and meditated. Sometimes she had visionary experiences. Brilliant, difficult, a self-acknowledged "scourge" with a sharp wit, she could be deliberately cruel and had difficulties in dealing with other people. Nevertheless, she sought out gifted persons and took a great interest in certain young people, particularly her nephews, who could respond to her eccentric magnetism and to whom her appearance was a "holiday."[11]

The points of similarity between her and Uilsa are numerous. Both women have been in the neighborhood for about thirty years when they come into the lives of their observers, and both live, by preference, in a condition marginal to society, deep in the woods. Uilsa inhabits a cave or a leaf pile, while Mary, harbinger to Waldo of the romantic, preferred to dwell on a remote farm deep in the woods of central Maine, from which she preached the spiritual benefits of communion with nature. But although both women choose to live outside society, they also insist that they are a kind of royalty. Uilsa is the "Grey Queen," while Mary, in a family given to jocular grandiloquence, was typically referred to by her nephews as "Your proud ladyship," "Abbess," and even "Dr. Moody."[12] Uilsa is directly descended from Odin, greatest of the Norse gods. Mary, for her part, never ceased to remind her nephews that they came from six generations of New England's aristocracy, God's ministers on earth. "The kind Aunt whose cares instructed my youth," Emerson wrote a few years later, "told me oft the virtues of her and mine ancestors." He added significantly that "the dead sleep in their moonless night; my business is with the living" (*JMN* I, 316). Uilsa is also an outlaw, the mother of an illegitimate child, who is hunted down by her son and the magistrate alike. Mary Moody Emerson traveled from town to town in New England in search of enlightenment, health cures, and, most probably, new experience, but she frequently quarreled with her fellow boarders, her hosts, and the ministers she sought out. On two occasions she borrowed men's horses. Though these acts were more joyrides than thefts, the antisocial quality preserved them in her relatives' memories.[13]

Both figures speak darkly, like sibyls—a term Waldo applies to both. Thus Uilsa's language is said to be "severe and abrupt and always mingled with unintelligible terms" (*JMN* I, 267), while Mary's language is often so difficult to construe (one reason that she remains unstudied) that she demands closer reading than anyone but her nephew has been willing to grant. Uilsa and Mary, moreover, are equally associated with death, and specifically with worms. Uilsa seeks her own death in the embrace of a "worm," while Mary was literally obsessed by death. She rode around in public draped in her shroud, until it wore out and had to be replaced—several times. She also had her bed made in the shape of a coffin.[14] Her letters emphasized her longing for death, and one of her oddities was her well-known fascination with snakes, worms, and reptiles, which stood, supposedly, for that yearning. "There are many," she wrote Waldo, "who are forced to creep thro' the entrails of reptiles . . . to find an infinite Designer. Never dislike their little lobes and [livers]" (*JMN* I, 380). And he might end a letter to her by saying, "Your imagination is fond of recurring to the poor reptiles and I give you joy of the worm!"[15]

One of the most interesting verbal parallels between the two is Waldo's use of the term "weird women" for both of them. Uilsa claims that she is "proudly descended from an hundred weird women, feared and fatal daughters of Odin."[16] In his journals some months before composing his tale, he described Mary as "the Weird-woman of her religion" (*JMN* I, 49). "Weird," of course, means gifted with second sight, and he was then thinking of religious vision, but in the context of "Uilsa" and the poem by Thomas Gray to which he alludes, a weird woman is also one who is capable of almost any kind of perversity and destruction. It may have been these resonances, in addition to the unwelcome compliment of the tale itself, which led Mary, weary of the joke, to write four years later to Charles, Waldo's younger brother: "Pardon the whim, if such it be, to ask you not to compare me to any weird woman. I who lived so as to try never to offend by one singular word, whose whole time is devoted to one and the same object, pray you spare my age and vocation."[17]

No characteristic shared by Uilsa and Mary is more important than their supernatural powers and capacity for prophecy, for with these they name their followers and endow them with their identity and genius. In the tale the narrator asks the Grey Queen "how to guide his steps in life" because she is the "Spirit of Prophecy" and has supernatural powers, and she relates how she has passed these on to her son Vahn, "the Master of Magicians" (*JMN* I, 268, 285). Mary apparently purported at some indefinite time to have something like second sight, and her letters reveal her in the posture of the Watcher, straining after ethereal revelation. At times she prophesies—though refusing coyly to do so—for her nephews, while at others she urges the boys to develop their own visionary powers: "I won't prophesy half the good things I know." Waldo called her "Cassandra" and wanted to share her knowledge,[18] undoubtedly encouraged by the fact that from his early teens she had named him as one with magical powers; he was the "Magician maker" and the "magician of nature and art."[19] Most striking is the letter she wrote to him in some excitement when he went off to Harvard at fourteen:

> What dull Prosaic Muse [herself] would venture from the humble dell of an unlettered District to address a son of Harvard? Son . . . of poetry of genius—ah were it so and I destined to stand in near consanguinity to this magical possessor. Age itself would throw off its gravity for a moment and dream that there is a vestige of fame to attach it to earth—that a name so dear was one day to leave some memorial. Vain wish . . . A name on this flying planet . . . is not matter of sin when viewed by the celestial light of faith. . . . In that great assembly, where human nature is purified from its native dross and ignorance, may the name of my dear Waldo be inrolled.[20]

Did Emerson, by age seventeen, feel a need like Vahn's to keep such a sibyl at some distance? Whether they are tangible or "such stuff as dreams are made on," great gifts, like identity and "genius," mean great debts for the recipient. Despite the depth of Emerson's obligation, it is important to distinguish between the significance and meaning of "Uilsa" and the ongoing relationship of Waldo and Mary Moody Emerson. Obviously the structure of the story expresses distrust of its protagonist's mode of life, ending as it does on a note of gothic terror and seeming defeat. But if Emerson were rejecting the psychic presence of an overwhelming parent, or parent surrogate, as Vahn does, we should expect Emerson's contact with this aunt to have diminished over the next five years. Such distancing, after all, would only have been normal for a young person in his early twenties. In reality, however, the opposite was true. Between his graduation from Harvard in 1821 and his being licensed to preach in 1826, he turned to her above all other correspondents.

It was a period in his life when Emerson had little helpful family contact. When he graduated in 1821, Charles was only thirteen, and Edward at sixteen was already chronically ill with the tubercular symptoms that required three extended absences by 1825.[21] Emerson was on a more equal footing with William, with whom he jointly kept a school, but this older brother left to study in Germany late in 1823 and stayed almost two years.[22] Waldo's brothers were either too young or too far away to discuss ideas with. His classmates had scattered, and he was left to himself, burning with ambition but trapped in schoolteaching and poverty. He reached out to two or three contemporary correspondents for intellectual contact, but the letters of one left him, as he complained, "hungering and thirsting"; like Mary, who wished to receive only "treatise[s]," he wanted real thought, not gossip or news.[23] His well-known contact with Dr. Channing was actually, as he told Oliver Wendell Holmes, comparatively superficial. It did not begin until 1823, and consisted of Dr. Channing's giving Waldo a reading list but refusing to "undertake the direction" of his studies. They talked "from time to time," but their temperaments were equally remote, and although Emerson revered the older man's sermons, the two "never really came together."[24]

More significantly, almost immediately after entering Harvard Divinity School in early 1825, Waldo lost the use of his eyes for reading and retired to work on a country farm, thus entering an even more lonely period. Undoubtedly this and subsequent episodes of disease, which culminated in the breakdown of his health in 1826–1827, were related to Waldo's sense of personal and intellectual stress.[25] Since he had no other guide or mentor during the difficult years when he was forging his vocational and personal sense of self, his contacts with Mary were central.

The literary nature of this interaction must be stressed, for they saw little of each other. "*We* can only commune by pen," Mary once wrote him after a tiff, exaggerating perhaps only a little.[26] Their relationship in some ways is less a personal one than that between two texts, hers having a privileged status won by her style and her long concentration on and insight into her "sole object," while his writings from an early stage received from her flattering respect and serious criticism.

His intellectual and personal isolation encouraged, though it could not have produced, the intense interest Waldo felt in his aunt's ideas, style, and, above all, her visionary stance. He gave direct testimony to this fascination frequently, both to her and to others. Emerson read widely and continually throughout this period, and even without Mary he would have become acquainted with the religious controversies and the romantic, visionary stance she made her own. But he felt that he could not unravel these controversies alone. "I ramble among doubts," he wrote her, imploring her answer to puzzles prompted by skeptical philosophy. "My reason offers no solution. Books are old and dull and unsatisfactory; the pen of a living witness and faithful lover of these mysteries of Providence is worth all the volumes of all the centuries." That pen worth "all the volumes" of "all . . . centuries" was hers not only because of her faith but because of her interest in "the connexions existing between this world and the next." He valued in her precisely that capacity which he was to develop highly in himself: the ability to draw analogies between the real world and the transcendent world of moral order and to see "the marvellous moral phenomena" which Providence daily exhibited.[27]

He valued equally her example as a writer, with a true writer's obsessive commitment to her task. In later years he reflected that there could be "no strong performance without a little fanaticism in the performers"; only that could account for the "fervid work in M.M.E.'s journals . . . the vehement religion which would not let her sleep nor sit, but write, night and day, year after year."[28] Interestingly, Emerson by then had long since become a writer whose practices, as the seemingly endless journals and notebooks show, were very similar.

He also testified that she had provided the model for his use of religious language. "Religion was her occupation," he noted, and he said that he had learned as a youth the very nature and sound of religious language from repeating hers. When he later came to write sermons, "I could not find any examples or treasuries of piety so high-toned, so profound, or promising such rich influence as my remembrances of her conversations and letters" (*JMN* I, 323–24). Sometimes he might be jocular on the subject of his aunt and her prophetic stance, as when he wrote a contemporary that by comparison with his aunt, "of whom . . . you have heard before and who is alone among women," he felt like a "coarse, thrifty cit [who] profanes the grove [of Nature] by his presence." In her view, he went on, Nature was a temple ". . . where the fiery soul can begin a premature communication with other worlds."[29] But while he might joke, he shared that yearning to know the unknowable, desiring, in passages that parallel this essay's epigraph, to "know what living wit . . . has . . . concluded upon the dark sayings and sphinx riddles of philosophy and life; I do beseech your charity not to withhold your pen," and requesting "the legacy of all your recorded thought."[30]

The language Emerson desired so avidly has proved difficult for other readers, as he finally acknowledged.[31] She wrote all her life either for no reader or for only one; this lack of audience undoubtedly increased the densely allusive tendencies of her language. Hurried and elliptical, she often carelessly dropped words or whole phrases. She also liked to experiment with style, pushing meaning into wild, baroque structures. For all its difficulties, however, her writing, as Emerson said, is always spontaneous, unexpected, and sometimes brilliant.

Her fundamental theme, which later was to become in some degree Emerson's, was to see in nature, as eighteenth-century divines had done, a perpetual allegory of God's provenance. Her interest in nature was less theological than literary and aesthetic; where eighteenth-century philosophers had used metaphors drawn from the material world heuristically to strengthen the argument from design, Mary's practice was to dwell on her experience of the natural world, like a brooding poet, until it led her almost ecstatically with baroque syntactic twists to the visionary stance she sought. "Do we love poetry. . . ," she asked rhetorically one evening after a night walk, "as we do the flowers of the field—because they supply not the necessaries, but the luxuries of life and give presentiments to the soul so rich, of an existence where all cares and labours cease."[32] She watched a cloud, then thought about "éclat of name—of fame" and the relation of these to the movement of the cloud "as it . . . climbs the sides of the mountain over bog and brake and tree and suddenly disappears at the instant of arriving at its summit." Just as "shadows add to the beauty of fleeting scenes," so does "the aspirant of other mounts to the interest of life." She did not have to add that the "éclat of name" was of course to be Waldo's, and his future was to mount—fleeting, like clouds and all human wishes—the peaks of human renown and disappear perhaps in some apotheosis. "This richly laden season," she went on that September day, "when every leaf begins its own mystic story, which soothes the soul and dwells upon the soul and blends itself into the soul, derives a zest . . . from prophecy of those who are rising into honor."[33] She embroiders on the idea that "there does appear a soul in nature. And when we clothe it in a human form, its head is lost amongst clouds—we behold—we live only in her skirts. . . ."[34] The subject, the soul of nature, may have been suggested by Waldo, but the figure of nature as a giant, its head in the upper atmosphere, its feet on the ground, dwarfing tiny humanity, may well be a source of Emerson's later use of this trope.

Waldo could learn not only from the emphasis Mary as a romantic gave to natural theology, but from her emotional posture as well. As one who cultivated religious enthusiasm, rather than a "frigid" rational faith, she was identified in the Emerson family with the term "sentiment," which became her byword and a family joke. When her nephew asked her for some "facts or news," she replied in a phrase he later adopted in "History": "What indeed are *facts* to me?"[35] To one who understood intuitively, facts *per se* were irrelevant, except for their analogical meaning. Alluding probably to Jonathan Edwards and the treatise he wrote at the age of twelve on spiders, she went on to say that some might study spiders or the petals of a flower, "and say they are finding the way to a designing Cause." Similarly, a friend has shown her the "peculiar dandelion . . . in each petal or blade hung a perfect flower itself. The little children will soon amuse themselves with seeing its downy leaves fly away. Now my dear Waldo," she commented, archly denying her role, "if your imagination wanders into regions of *sentiment,* don't blame me. I will keep to fact."[36]

Mary could tease him the more freely because Waldo was known to be her disciple in this, advocating to his brothers the "sentimental" or even the "flashy sentimental" style as a way of looking at nature, shaking off depression, and finding food for thought. He asked how the ten-year-old Edward could "read a letter of Aunt Mary's, an enthusiast in rural pleasures, and yet want a subject?" Ten years later, now encouraging Charles, Waldo used several of Mary's figures of speech: "Is it not a better inquiry than hunting new minerals or dissecting spiders or counting lobes and petals of flowers to explore observe the obscure birth of sentiment at the frugal board perhaps of a poor wise man and see how slowly it struggles into fame."[37] The dissection of spiders, the counting of "lobes," insects, and petals of flowers, the slow growth of "sentiment" into "fame" and glory—these figures were not only identified with Mary, but were her very language and thought itself. If she had provided his "treasuries" of religious language, as he wrote in 1837, Waldo became at times her moral treasurer, coining that gold and issuing it.

In addition to Mary's sharply observant eye for natural details, her imagination loved to soar from them to cosmic and supernal imagery: Angels, stars, and the light night skies are favorite tropes for the crescendo passages of her letters. As stylists and eventually doctrinal opponents, she and Waldo often interchanged imagery. When Waldo after his return from the South wrote in late 1827 that he had determined not to be guided by any mysticism or sentiment that his reason condemned, he added that he would not "surrender to the casual and morbid exercise of the sentiment of a midnight hour the steady light of all my days, my most vigorous and approved thoughts [and] barter the sun for the waning moon."[38] This new departure stung Mary to extend and elevate the metaphor, dramatizing it almost into a scenario: "The lover of beauty," she replied, "will not desire to analyse the mystic mistress of his heart . . . its source is God. . . . If the Angel of 'midnight' who is commissioned to turn the starry mirror of reflection has oftener visited him—it may be that truth is more clearly discerned then [than] in the sunny influence of vigorous thoughts and business."[39] The image of the angel of midnight (who in some sense must be Mary herself) turning the mirror of reflection so that Emerson might see into his soul is effective, equal to the offhand scorn she feels for his "approved thoughts" and sunny, businesslike days.

A lover of poetry who was almost as eager for her nephew to be a poet as a preacher, she was certain these great gifts could not be practiced within society's purview. She, more than any other influence, undoubtedly taught Emerson the necessity of solitude for the growth of individual talent. Emerson tended "to talk with the most apparent simplicity of the sympahties of society—they are needed, it is true, to form the 'common mind' to principles of action"—but not minds, clearly, such as their own. She would prefer that poetry, "my young favorite," as Mary called her, much as she might a protegée-niece, "would wander wild among the flowers and lairs of nature—would scale the 'tempel where the Genius of the Universe resides' [and] view herself in the rays of distant stars, while you are getting her a home more permanent."[40] In later years Emerson had a wonderful dream in which "I floated at will in the great ether, and I saw this world floating also not far off, but diminished to the size of an apple. Then an angel took it in his hand and brought it to me and said, 'This thou must eat'—and I ate the world," he wrote (*JMN* VII, 525). To see the world "in the light of distant stars" or "to get beyond the precincts of this earth" was a shared urge, but such a vision could not be pursued in society.

Emerson asked his aunt the difficult religious questions, especially about the afterlife. When her ideas of "the posthumous" were requested, Mary was at first coy, questioning the advantage of parting with such ideas, "that portion of one's soul." Then she responded by conjuring up the shade of the intellectual, religious, and yet worldly Madame de Staël, a contemporary and a heroine of Mary's, evoking that lady's performing a similar sacrifice: "Think of a De Staël . . . treasuring up sentiments and ideas for a Son—abandoning her own publick existence that he might be 'decked with unfading honors!'" Madame de Staël in fact had had no son, but this was irrelevant; since she had *not* so renounced public glory, "*Never,* oh no not one leaf of amaranthine will deck the brow of mere genius like hers. The humblest example of meekness will shine in light when the meteors are gone . . . Good night. Oh for that 'long and moonless night' to shadow my dust, tho' I have nothing to leave but my carcase to fatten the earth—it is for my own sake I long to go."[41] That "humblest example of meekness" is again clearly Mary herself in this grotesquerie.

Emerson's own early writings often link death with magical prophecy, as "Uilsa" does.[42] These themes are also often linked in his aunt's letters: "Before I ever knew you, I did not ask even a dirge. I invoked nature with rapture to sweep over my grave with her roughest elements: for there would be the voice of a strange spirit, and there might be a strange light to guide the icy worm to his riot." Once he asked her to play Cassandra for him. "Were I a seer," she rejoined, the failure of certain of his writings on drama would "bode good. . . . I do ask the favour to be remembered rather as a dead Cassandra, not prophesying but praying for thy welfare."[43] In her fantasy, death and salvation meant translation to a more romantic realm, where, lit by "strange light," she, the "icy worm," would yet pulse with consuming and immortal energy. Similarly, in portraying herself as a dead but prayerful Cassandra, Mary improved on the Greek model, Christianizing the pagan seer and transmuting classical power into protestant witness. Implicit in her rebuff of Emerson's critical writings was the idea that, like Mary, he ought to turn from the pagan to the Christian world, from drama to theology. Using her gift for rapid, dense, and allusive language, she never lost an opportunity to evoke models of spiritual progress, even in this wayward example of what one might call *imitatio rinascimento.*

But for all her pursuit of the visionary gleam and her willingness to involve Waldo in it, Mary Emerson was sharp and hardheaded in sniffing not heresy but the kind of ambivalence that could lead to half-hearted professions and subsequent disappointment. When her nephew had publicly joined his congregation, an ancient custom requisite for a budding minister, she inquired sharply, *"What mean you by this rite?"* hinting at a suspicion that it might be "the *key* to a profession."[44] Her criticism was as consistent as her admiration. Emerson had complained that his muse had become " 'faint and mean.' " "Ah well she may," Mary replied, "and better oh far better leave you . . . [if he were to be] one whose destiny tends to lead him to sensation rather than sentiment, whose intervals of mentality seem to be rather spent in collecting facts than energising itself. . . . Oh would the Muse forever leave you, till you had prepared for her a celestial abode. . . . You are not inspired in heart, with a gift for immortality, because you are the Nursling of surrounding circumstances—you become yourself a part of the events which make up ordinary life." She wanted him, in short, to be as self-reliant as she was. But she went on to prophesy more happily the "approaching period I dread worse than this sweet stagnation—when your Muse shall be dragged into éclat—tho' like Cicero['s] perhaps, your poetry will not be valued because your prose is so much better." Emerson later wrote on the bottom of this page, "this letter is a most beautiful monument of kindness and highminded but partial affection. Would I were worthy of it."[45]

Emerson went through a period of skepticism and especially took an interest in the writings of David Hume, but only to Mary did Waldo dare voice speculations deriving from Hume's ideas in any significant way. She, however, secure in her faith, was scornful of the philosopher whom she called "that bloated old scotsman" and whose influence she alone—and accurately—saw as pervading her nephew's thought and style. Hume's arguments against intuitive knowledge left her unmoved, for to her even "walking and riding before breakfast . . . so cloudy, so exquisitely cloudy," made her sure that "we are more certain of this beauty than if it were real." "Old Hume," she snorted, "was a morbid hermit in the nest of being" and his impoverished mind could have drawn no such inferences. But as late as 1828, while praising writing by Waldo, she commented, "Your reading Hume when young has rendered you, I cannot but think, so imbued with his manner of thinking, that you cannot shake him off. There seems or I am stupid, so much of his *manner,* tho' better, in this letter that I feel as I do when reading him. But to *my old* frame his arguments, if such they can be called, make no more impression than the spray of a child's squirt."[46] To Emerson the problems of skepticism could not be erased so easily, and he and Mary began to draw apart in later years over his gradual resolution of these issues. That separation, however, was intellectual rather than personal; Mary lived more consistently, although not permanently, in Concord after he moved there in the 1830s, and their mutual respect continued.

Given the multiple and dense connections and parallels between the thinking of the two Emersons, any reduction of this relationship or of Mary to the plot or protagonist of "Uilsa" would be uninteresting. Mary was rueful about the story of "Uilsa" because in her own mind she had played the part of a Madame de Staël, not of an "old hag," to the only person whose "mind" had met hers "in sympathy."[47] Emerson, for his part, knew Mary to be no destructive witch, but a "seeker," like himself—though one who knew answers, as well as asked questions.[48] Mary was not Uilsa, but she provided Waldo with a model of the pilgrim, the self-reliant seeker in whom romantic individualism was uneasily yoked with a neo-Calvinist desire to subsume earthly to spiritual glory. Uilsa is intensely an invention of the romantic literary tradition, especially that of Scott, but she is also a figure in search of transcendent experience, which when it comes has spiritual as well as demonic and sexual connotations. The young Emerson liked to attribute to his aunt quasi-magical powers desired by but denied to himself, because he imagined that they enabled one to stand romantically and heroically outside society and grapple with dangerous knowledge. For several years after writing this tale he prepared himself for that role by a variety of means, not least of which was coming to grips with Mary herself in their protracted and frequently argumentative correspondence. He moved from but did not need to struggle to throw off her influence; on the contrary, even in childhood he seems to have known instinctively the right distance from which to maintain the good humor of their game. Rather he made it his task to internalize Mary's voice, her daring, her faith, and her sense of the grandeur of her pursuit, while establishing for himself a more stable relation to society than hers. More than a decade later he began in Concord to carve out for himself a position that was deliberately marginal to the established church and Boston's intellectual life, a place from which he exercised the privileges of the critic's stance during his productive years. He managed to live there, in a sense, on the edge of the abyss, a "stink in the nostrils" of the Brahmin class, to quote his friend Clough, without moving over its edge into the virtually complete isolation of his aunt.[49] It was to be years before he could establish that balance, however, and the writing of "Uilsa" may have been to some extent a first project toward that end, a stage in the process of inventing himself and shaping the space he needed around him in which to evolve myths of human beings engaged in far more nurturant relations with nature than he had once been able to dream. Mary is not Uilsa, but without the model of his aunt's peculiar combination of literary and personal daring and reserve, he could never have invented the great myths with which he conjured a young nation to imagine itself free of history and able to cross the abyss of nonentity, as he called it, into personhood. "Uilsa" as a juvenile fiction has been justifiably forgotten, but Mary Moody Emerson deserves recognition for her own contribution toward those strange dreams.

NOTES

1. Franklin Benjamin Sanborn, "A Concord Note-book: Sixth Paper: The Women of Concord—I," *The Critic* 48 (February 1906), 157; Ralph Waldo Emerson, *The Journals and Miscellaneous Note-books of Ralph Waldo Emerson*, ed. Merton M. Sealts, Jr. (Cambridge: Harvard University Press, 1965), V, 324. Further references to this text will be abbreviated *JMN* and included in the text.

2. Ralph L. Rusk, ed. *The Letters of Ralph Waldo Emerson* (New York: Columbia University Press, 1939) I, 133 (cited hereafter as *L*); Emerson MSS., Houghton Library, Harvard University, bMS Am 1280 226.18 [?], 1820. All quotations from the Emerson family manuscripts come from this source, which will be abbreviated as H. MS. and distinguished by year. For clarity, I have regularized the punctuation but kept Mary's idiosyncratic spelling and capitalization; I render the ampersand used by her and her nephew as "and." All other emendations are indicated by square brackets and ellipses.

3. Van Wyck Brooks, "The Cassandra of New England," *Scribner's Magazine* 81 (February 1927), 125–29; Rosalie Feltenstein, "Mary Moody Emerson: The Gadfly of Concord," *American Quarterly* 5, No. 3 (Fall 1953), 231–46; Ralph Waldo Emerson, "Mary Moody Emerson," in *The Complete Works of Ralph Waldo Emerson*, ed. Edward W. Emerson (Cambridge, Mass.: Riverside Press, 1904), X, 433 (cited hereafter as *Works*). The privately printed monograph by George Tolman, *Mary Moody Emerson*, ed. Edward Emerson Forbes (Cambridge, Mass., 1929), was not widely circulated. See also my earlier studies: Evelyn Barish

Greenberger, "Emersonian Gothic: The Misprision of an Aunt," Bunting Institute Working Paper, Radcliffe College (Cambridge, Mass., 1979); and Evelyn Barish, "Emerson and 'The Magician': An Early Prose Fantasy," *American Transcendental Quarterly,* No. 31, pt. 1 (Summer 1976), 13–18, parts of which have been incorporated in the present paper. Phyllis Cole's "The Advantage of Loneliness: Mary Moody Emerson's Almanacks," in Joel Porte, ed., *Emerson: Prospect and Retrospect,* (Cambridge: Harvard University Press, 1982), pp. 1–32, came to my attention only after the present paper had been prepared for publication.

4. *Journals of Ralph Waldo Emerson: 1820–1876,* Edward Waldo Emerson and W. E. Forbes, eds., 10 vols. (Cambridge, Mass.: Riverside Press, 1909–1914); cited hereafter as *J.* See *JMN* I, xxxviii. The omission of Emerson's draft letters from *JMN* tends to obscure the relationship, as the large majority of these were to Mary, and many of the final versions are not available elsewhere, since the *Journals,* which printed excerpts, is out of print. The revised edition of the *Letters* being prepared by Professor Eleanor Tilton should remedy this problem.

5. H. MS. 1822.

6. My first discussion of this previously unknown tale in 1976 (see note 3 above) referred to it as "The Magician," but later research suggests that it was known in the family as "Uilsa" (Charles Chauncy Emerson, letter to his brother, H. MS. 1827).

7. *Works* X, 404.

8. *JMN* I, 266–68, 273–74, 284–86, 302–303.

9. Evelyn Barish Greenberger, "The Phoenix on the Wall: Consciousness in Emerson's Early and Late Journals," *American Transcendental Quarterly,* No. 21, Pt. 1 (Winter 1974), 45–46.

10. *Works* X, 411.

11. *Works* X, 403, 402.

12. H. MS. 1824; *L* I, 22.

13. Edward Waldo Emerson, *Emerson in Concord: A Memoir* (Boston: Houghton Mifflin, 1889), pp. 52–53.

14. *Works* X, 428–29.

15. *L* I, 105.

16. The allusion here is not primarily to Shakespeare, but to Thomas Gray, who wrote two so-called "Norse poems," one named "The Weird Sisters" (an alternative title for "The Fatal Sisters"), and the other entitled "The Descent of Odin" (A. L. Poole, ed., *The Poetical Works of Gray and Collins,* 2nd rev. ed. [London: Oxford University Press, 1926], pp. 65–79). In these grisly works, the hundred weird women are valkyrie-like creatures of evil who clank and flit over battlefields after a war, gathering up the dismembered parts of slain warriors to use in their horrible tapestries. We know that Emerson alludes to Gray for two reasons, the first being that he makes Uilsa the daughter of these children of Odin, who are Gray's invention. Second, Emerson twice mentions Gray's companion poem, in which Odin visits the underworld to coax his estranged wife, Hela, to do his bidding, although her only reply is "Now my weary lips I close,/ Leave me, leave me, to repose." Emerson teased Mary when he was trying to get her to answer his letters by telling her she was like "those weird women" who uttered this line; he echoed it also in "Uilsa" when he remarked, "At one time, her only answer to all who approached her was Avoid, avoid" (*L* I, 197).

17. H. MS. 1826.

18. *L* I, 104–105.

19. H. MS. 1827, 1828, 1823.

20. H. MS. 1817 [?].

21. H. MS. 1820, 1822, 1825.

22. *L*, p. 141n.; Ralph L. Rusk, *The Life of Ralph Waldo Emerson* (New York: Columbia University Press, 1949), pp. 113, 518n.

23. *L* I, 132; H. MS. 1823; *L* I, 171.

24. Oliver Wendell Holmes, *Ralph Waldo Emerson* (Boston: Houghton Mifflin, 1885), p. 102.

25. Evelyn Barish, "The Moonless Night: Emerson's Crisis of Health, 1825–27," in Joel Meyerson, ed., *Emerson Centenary Essays* (Carbondale: Southern Illinois University Press, 1982), pp. 1–16.

26. H. MS. 1826.

27. H. MS. 1823; *L* I, 137.

28. E. W. Emerson, *Emerson in Concord*, p. 95.

29. *L* I, 133.

30. *J* I, 357.

31. *Works* X, 601n.

32. H. MS. 1821.

33. H. MS. 1824.

34. H. MS. 1821.

35. *Works* II, 32–33; H. MS. 1822 [?].

36. H. MS. 1821.

37. *L* I, 66, 62, 246.

38. *J* II, 222–23.

39. H. MS. 1828.

40. H. MS. 1821.

41. H. MS. 1821.

42. Barish, "The Birth of Merlin: Emerson, Magic, and Death," in Saul N. Brody and Harold Schecter, eds., *CUNY English Studies 1979* (New York: AMS Press, forthcoming).

43. H. MS. 1821.

44. H. MS. 1822.

45. H. MS. 1822.

46. H. MS. 1827, 1828.

47. H. MS. [1825].

48. *L* I, 208, 205.

49. Frederick L. Mulhauser, ed., *The Correspondence of Arthur Hugh Clough* (Oxford: Clarendon Press, 1957), II, 340.

William Wordsworth, drawn in charcoal and white chalk on mauve paper by Francis William Wilkin in 1831. Dorothy Wordsworth wrote: "I value it much as a likeness of . . . William in company, and something of that restraint with chearfulness [sic], which is natural to him in mixed societies." Courtesy of the Museum of Fine Arts, Boston

"A Spirit, Yet a Woman Too!"

DOROTHY AND WILLIAM WORDSWORTH

Thomas A. Vogler

The only known portrait of Dorothy Wordsworth, 1833, by Samuel Crossthwaite. "A Creature not too bright or good / For human nature's daily food" (William Wordsworth, "She Was a Phantom of Delight"). Courtesy of BBC Hulton Picture Library

William Wordsworth was born in 1770, in the remote area of Cocker-mouth in Cumberland. Dorothy was born a year and a half later. The deaths of their mother (1778) and father (1783) caused the early separation of the pair into different households, and gave rise to a shared dream of living together and reconstituting the intimacy that was broken in early childhood. After Wordsworth's trip to France in 1791–1792, where he had a liaison with Annette Vallon (their illegitimate daughter, Anne Caroline, was born after his return to England), he committed himself to a career as a writer and to the goal of living with Dorothy. They moved together to Racedown in 1795, traveled together to Germany in 1798–1799, and settled at Dove Cottage, Grasmere, in 1799, never to be separated for more than brief intervals until Wordsworth's death in 1850.

Wordsworth frequently credited Dorothy as the source of his psychological and artistic well-being, referring to her as "She who dwells with me, whom I have loved/ With such communion that no place on earth/ Can ever be a solitude to me." His acknowledged period of greatest poetic productivity corresponds with his period of most intense intimacy with Dorothy. After he married their childhood friend, Mary Hutchinson (1802), Dorothy continued to live with the growing family as a maiden aunt, never marrying, and devoting her full energies to the service of Wordsworth's career and family. In 1829 she suffered the first of a series of severe illnesses, which reduced her, by 1835, to a wheel-chair-bound existence, with only intermittent periods of lucidity. She continued in a strange half-world of consciousness and physical restriction for twenty years, surviving her brother by five years, to die in 1855.

Poetry is the orphan of silence. Maternal silence. That in you which belongs to the Universe. The mother's voice calls its name at dusk over the roofs of the world. Whoever hears it, turns towards his ancestral home.

—Charles Simic

⌒My title for this essay is taken from Wordsworth's characterization of his sister Dorothy in "She was a Phantom of Delight"—a poem which reflects the double role that Dorothy played for William to match his double roles of man and poet:

> She was a phantom of delight
> When first she gleamed upon my sight;
> A lovely Apparition, sent
> To be a moment's ornament;
> Her eyes as stars of Twilight fair;
> Like Twilight's, too, her dusky hair;
> But all things else about her drawn
> From May-time and the cheerful Dawn;
> A dancing Shape, an Image gay,
> To haunt, to startle, and way-lay.
>
> I saw her upon nearer view,
> A Spirit, yet a Woman too!
> Her household motions light and free,
> And steps of virgin-liberty;
> A countenance in which did meet
> Sweet records, promises as sweet;
> A Creature not too bright or good
> For human nature's daily food;
> For transient sorrows, simple wiles,
> Praise, blame, love, kisses, tears, and smiles.
>
> And now I see with eye serene
> The very pulse of the machine;
> A Being breathing thoughtful breath,
> A Traveller between life and death;
> The reason firm, the temperate will,
> Endurance, foresight, strength and skill;
> A perfect Woman, nobly planned,
> To warn, to comfort, and command;
> And yet a Spirit still, and bright
> With something of angelic light.[1]

With Wordsworth, perhaps even more than with any other Romantic poet, this "and" connecting "poet" and "man" is unnecessary. But with Dorothy the conjunction "yet" connecting the two modes of presence she had for Wordsworth is crucial and little observed; most of the attention has been to Dorothy as woman. The first movement of Wordsworth's poem is from the apparitional aspect of Dorothy as a "shape" or "image" to her embodiment "upon nearer view" in the form of one "not too bright or good / For human nature's daily food." The union of the idealized form with its material embodiment, though it risks a descent into the mundane, is nevertheless accomplished without losing the spiritual form and the delight associated with it, which was the basis of the attraction in the first place. Even after prolonged intimacy and material suffering, Dorothy remained for William "A perfect woman . . . And yet a Spirit still." In what follows I shall attempt to show that the full development of Wordsworth's relationship with Dorothy is reflected in the movement of this poem, and that Dorothy's spiritual presence for Wordsworth emerged as a constantly available, "real" embodiment of the idealized and lost mother in his past.

The presence of Dorothy for Wordsworth as "woman" has been traced and commented on frequently, and is revealed most poignantly in the surviving journals that she wrote, first at Alfoxden (January–May, 1798) and then at Grasmere (May 1800–January 1803). We see her there from day to day, cooking innumerable pies, baking bread, copying poems, reading to William, comforting him and worrying about his health; recording the state of his digestion, his head, his psyche, and his piles, her own headaches and toothaches; waiting for him during the absences that seem like eternities to her, taking him bread and butter when he is indisposed, and making a pillow of her body for him in those quiet hours of silent intimacy that seem for both to have epitomized the best dimension of their relationship. We see vividly the impact of his presence on her in the sudden transformations from gloom to gladness when he returns, and to empty melancholy when he leaves:

> *Wednesday 6th August.* A rainy morning. . . . William came home from Keswick at 11 o'clock. A very fine night. *Thursday 7th August.* . . . A very fine day. . . . A very fine sunset. *Friday Morning [8th].* Very fine gooseberries. . . . A most enchanting walk . . . a heavenly scene.

> *May 14 1800* [Wednesday]. My heart was so full that I could hardly speak to W. when I gave him a farewell kiss . . . after a flood of tears my heart was easier. The lake looked to me I knew not why dull and melancholy, and the weltering on the shores seemed a heavy sound.

The journals themselves are fascinating documents, unusually intimate and revealing in some ways, yet strangely silent in others. They were certainly not written for our eyes, nor entirely for Dorothy's own private purposes. They were written *for* William, "because I shall give Wm Pleasure by it when he comes home again." The journals have been frequently and thoroughly mined for connections with William's poetry, and it seems clear that they were useful to him for his writing. More important than the actual "borrowings" from the journals on a verbal level, however, is the way they helped William to intensify the initial experience itself "for future restoration" in memory and in poems whose modality is "recollection in tranquility." Much that was recorded in the journals was observed by both brother and sister at the same time, and the added intensity of knowing that another pair of eyes and another mind were rapt on the same scene must have enhanced the original mental inscription of the experience even before the journal notations were written down and shared.

> Nor wilt thou then forget
> That after many wanderings, many years
> Of absence, these steep woods and lofty cliffs,
> And this green pastoral landscape, were to me
> More dear, both for themselves, and for thy sake.[2]

Also significant in the journals, though seldom observed, are the patterns of erasures and changes that show Dorothy carefully correcting the dates of entries, as if the date itself were an important part of the experience. William's need for a sequential or narrative context in which to locate experiences that would otherwise be random and incoherent suggests another function that the journals may have filled.

> The seasons came,
> And every season to my notice brought
> A store of transitory qualities
> Which, but for this most watchful power of love
> Had been neglected, left a register
> Of permanent relations, else unknown. [*Prelude* II, 307–12.]

A complete record of the ministry of Dorothy's "watchful power of love" would be endless, and would eventually include everything a woman can physically be for a man except his actual mother or sexual partner.

What is less obvious, yet far more important, is that apparitional "shape" or idealized form for which Dorothy was the constantly available embodiment. To discover what this shape was, and its significance for Wordsworth, we must look at his poetry, and especially at the poetry written between 1798 and 1805. It was not by accident that this period was both the period of Wordsworth's greatest poetic achievement and the period of his most intense and intimate involvement with Dorothy.

The period begins with "Tintern Abbey," the final poem of the *Lyrical Ballads,* and the signal of the transition from the poetry of the earlier period to the regressive and self-analytical poetry that is Wordsworth's greatest achievement. In "Tintern Abbey" we see Wordsworth, in the company of Dorothy, returning "again" to the banks of the Wye after five years' absence; the process of "return" and recapitulation enables him to sketch out a brief narrative form of his life story, and it marks the beginning of a much larger process of return and recapitulation that will be reflected both in *The Prelude* and its companion poem, *Home at Grasmere.* During this period Wordsworth had both a "project" and a constant companion, without whom he could neither have undertaken it nor carried it forward.

The project may be characterized briefly as a form of prolonged self-analysis, during which most of his poetry constituted a subjective autobiography, a writing in which he sought to discover or create an idealized version of the integrated self which was also the narrative of his own life story, an active writing that was not merely about, but was in itself "the foundation and the building up / Of a Human Spirit." Coleridge's imagery, in these lines from his poem "To William Wordsworth," echoes the most frequent image for writing in Wordsworth's poetry, that of laying foundations and building up structures. The dynamic aspect is apt, for Wordsworth is not merely recording events but is also building a narrative out of the raw materials of his life, a narrative that will be the structure or plot of his life, from the "fair seed time" to the "appointed close. . . . All gratulant if rightly understood." The "close" in this project was not to be the close of life by death, but the culmination of the process of the growth of a poet's mind in the achievement of a poetic identity. The Wordsworthian activity of writing during this period combines the textual goals of a completion of form with the psychological goal of achieving a coherent identity. Like a psychoanalytic case history, where the analytical reconstruction takes place in a historical process whose lack of completion provides a constant pressure both on the activity of writing and the continuing life of the subject, this pressure on the continuing "now" of living and writing fueled the nostalgic and retrospective desire to reinterpret and recreate the past as an idealized form of growth toward completion.

The enabling basis for the project, both as writing and as living, was the reconstruction of a psychic foundation for his entire life in the recovery of a primal relationship with an idealized maternal "nature," which, once experienced in a prelinguistic state, should always be available for restoration in an affective form as a source both for living and for writing. In one sense, this was a projected return to and recovery of something that was *there,* with the recovered feeling its own confirmation. ". . . the soul, / Remembering how she felt, but what she felt / Remembering not, retains an obscure sense / Of possible sublimity," (II, 334–37). But in another and more active sense, the recovery was a form of creation or re-creation spurred by a sense of loss:

> I was left alone,
> Seeking the visible world, nor knowing why.
> The props of my affections were remov'd,
> And yet the building stood, as if sustain'd
> By its own spirit! [II, 292–96.]

In this precise imagery, the "building" is the form itself, the "shape" or "image" for which the "prop" is the physical manifestation of the form in a concrete embodiment. The loss of the parental props for the building, and for the process of "building up" a life, leads to the need for alternative props in the form of a real nature or a real woman (Dorothy) available for a re-creation of the form of bonding implied by the "affections." Nature and Dorothy are both props in making the otherwise apparitional form available to experience, and each is a different version of

> The anchor of my purest thoughts, the nurse,
> The guide, the guardian of my heart, and soul
> Of all my mortal being.[3]

Thus the whole theoretical *basis* for Wordsworth's project, to be confirmed both in the life and the poetry, can be found in the brief summary of the normative life in Book II of *The Prelude:*

> Bless'd the infant Babe,
> (For with my best conjectures I would trace
> The progress of our being) blest the Babe,
> Nurs'd in his Mother's arms, the Babe who sleeps
> Upon his Mother's breast, who, when his soul
> Claims manifest kindred with an earthly soul,
> Doth gather passion from his Mother's eye!
> Such feelings pass into his torpid life
> Like an awakening breeze, and hence his mind
> Even in the first trial of its powers
> Is prompt and watchful, eager to combine
> In one appearance, all the elements
> And parts of the same object, else detach'd
> And loth to coalesce. Thus, day by day,
> Subjected to the discipline of love,
> His organs and recipient faculties
> Are quicken'd, are more vigorous, his mind spreads,
> Tenacious of the forms which it receives.
> In one beloved presence, nay and more,

In that most apprehensive habitude
And those sensations which have been deriv'd
From this beloved Presence, there exists
A virtue which irradiates and exalts
All objects through all intercourse of sense.
No outcast he, bewilder'd and depress'd;
Along his infant veins are interfus'd
The gravitation and the filial bond
Of nature, that connect him with the world.
Emphatically such a Being lives,
An inmate of this *active* universe;
From nature largely he receives; nor so
Is satisfied, but largely gives again,
For feeling has to him imparted strength,
And powerful in all sentiments of grief,
Of exultation, fear, and joy, his mind,
Even as an agent of the one great mind,
Creates, creator and receiver both,
Working but in alliance with the works
Which it beholds.—Such, verily, is the first
Poetic spirit of our human life;
By uniform control of after years
In most abated or suppress'd, in some,
Through every change of growth or of decay,
Pre-eminent till death. [II, 238–80.]

Wordsworth's imaginary journey back in time takes him beyond the reach of memory to a state so primal that it "Hath no beginning," a state of relatedness to a maternal Presence that determines all future development "Through every change of growth or of decay, / Pre-eminent till death." The existence of such a Presence cannot be proven, so must be asserted ("Emphatically . . . verily . . .") in a rhetoric that reflects the psychic affirmation that both sustains (or "props") and is sustained by the ideal model.

Wordsworth's emphasis on the "Presence" of the mother as the enabling basis of a feeling of coherence, without which the "parts of the same object" are "detached / And loth to coalesce," corresponds strikingly to Melanie Klein's view of the primacy of the mother's body as the focus for the child's quest for knowledge and the primal source for the development of the psyche. For Klein, the child's libidinal drives threaten the inner space of the mother's body and its fantasy attacks on her lead to fantasies of a fragmented body which through projective identification becomes the basis of a fragmented image of the child's own body and ego. All processes of symbolization are marked by this primal scene of conflict, and driven by the desire to make reparation through the construction of an idealized portrait of the mother. When the process works, it is a continuous circular fantasy of oneness, in which the fantasy of an unfragmented self provides the basis for constructing the idealized mother, whose fantasy existence is mirrored by the unfragmented self-image of the child or adult. In his "infant Babe" evocation of this idealized "infant sensibility" Wordsworth catches the circular and mirroring quality of this construct ("creator and receiver both") and asserts the possibility of its endless continuation throughout life.

Although she concentrates primarily on the fantasy life of the child in her research and writing, Klein is well aware that "the desire to rediscover the mother of the early days, whom one has lost actually or in one's feelings, is . . . of the greatest importance in creative art. . . ."[4] She is also aware that "the manifold gifts of nature are equated with whatever we have received in the early days from our mother," and that "the relation to nature which arouses such strong feelings of love, appreciation, admiration and devotion, has much in common with the relation to one's mother, as has long been recognized by poets."[5] It is the child's faith in the mother's constant availability and adequacy to fulfill its needs that establishes the individual's lifelong trust or *lack* of trust in the world. It is only as Wordsworth has such a faith that he will be able to "create" an idealized maternal nature from whom he is the "receiver" of all that makes him what he is.

One of the basic paradigms of the West, on the mythical level, is a three-part narrative that always begins with the evocation of an original unity, which is now lost, dispersed, into a fragmented existence in time and language, but can be regained at some point of future return to unity, which will make the loss (or time) a form of narrative detour. It is no accident, given the universality of this basic narrative code, that the Christian myth of redemption emphasizes Mary as a redeemed Eve or primal mother, the "physical" source of the Logos and the necessary mediatrix of the saving message of the Word made flesh. This "New Testament" maternal poetics can only exist over against the "Old Testament" paternal poetics that denies either the existence or the possible recovery of a primal maternal relationship—a discourse which asserts that the man is father of the child, rather than the child the father of the man. Thus Wordsworth's intuitive narrative plan, seeking to be informed at every stage by the continued availability of the primal maternal object-relationship, must exist over against the paternal narrative that follows a different path, *away* from the mother, who is permanently subsumed as the taboo object by the Freudian narrative of the family romance.

In this context, Wordsworth's emphasis on the prelinguistic foundation of his narrative project is crucial. He must be able, while "musing in solitude," to revive "fair trains of imagery . . . affecting thoughts . . . And dear remembrances."

—To these emotions, whencesoe'er they come,
Whether from breath of outward circumstance,
Or from the Soul—an impulse to herself—
I would give utterance in numerous verse ["Prospectus," 3–13.]

In such a state, the moment of the "awakening breeze" which we have
seen associated with the mother in the "infant Babe" passage is felt as the
recurrence of the original "breath of life," which made man "a living
soul" (*Genesis* 2:7), the animating breath of the mother. Whether the
principle of animation is felt as an internal impulse or an external
breath, or whether they fuse into the feeling of being "creator and
receiver both," the state is represented as both preceding and making
possible the "utterance" of inspired verse. Return to the primal moment
is necessary as the only escape from the "shades of the prison house" that
"close / Upon the growing Boy" in the "Intimations Ode." These are the
"shades" of the prison house of language, with its potential for preempt-
ing inspired poetry with the "dialogues of business, love, or strife" to
which the growing Boy "frames his song" and "fit[s] his tongue."

For Wordsworth the moment and mood of recovery are always
silently preverbal, based on seeing and feeling ("with gentle hand /
Touch—for there is a spirit in the woods"), but as poetry they must be
expressed and described in the words of a language which, *if* it evokes
the moment, must simultaneously mark its termination and transformation. Perhaps nowhere is this fact so clear as in the text of *Home at
Grasmere,* Wordsworth's most prolonged attempt to recapture and express his relationship with Dorothy as an instance of the recovered moment of symbiotic relationship, in which inner expectations, wishes, and
desires are perfectly congruent with what the external world has to
offer.

The unappropriated bliss hath found
An owner, and that owner I am he.
    . . . What wonder if I speak
With fervour, am exalted with the thought
Of my possessions, of my genuine wealth
Inward and outward. . . .
For proof behold this Valley and behold
Yon Cottage, where with me my Emma dwells.
    Aye, think on that, my Heart, and cease to stir;
Pause upon that, and let the breathing frame
No longer breathe, but all be satisfied.
Oh, if such silence be not thanks to God
For what hath been bestowed, then where, where then
Shall gratitude find rest? . . .
What Being, therefore, since the birth of Man
Had ever more abundant cause to speak
Thanks. . . . [85–119.]

The movement here, from speaking to silence and then to speaking again, is a move toward and then away from Dorothy. The move toward is expressed in the lip-closing murmuring sound of his poetic name for her ("with *me* *my* Em*ma*") which is followed by the even more silent evocation of her name in the word-play on the name of "Dorothy" in its etymological sense as a "gift of God." The tension between the recovered "rest" of "silence" and the "abundant cause to speak" which it provides continues through the next stages of the poem until the tentative resolution in the third-person presentation of the poet's "prelusive songs."

> It loves us now, this Vale so beautiful
> Begins to love us! By a sullen stor*m*,
> Two *m*onths unwearied of severest stor*m*,
> It put the te*m*per of our *m*inds to proof,
> And found us faithful through the gloo*m*, and heard
> The Poet *m*utter his prelusive songs
> With chearful heart, an unknown voice of joy
> A*m*ong the silence of the woods and hills,
> Silent to any gladso*m*eness of sound
> With all their Shepherds. [268–77, emphasis added.]

"Mutter" is a singularly apt word here (as are "murmuring," and "musing" in other contexts), as we hear the poet *mutter*ing to Em*ma* in (and about) Gras*mère*. Its onomatopoeic emphasis on speaking with nearly closed lips achieves the "*m*ute dialogues with *m*y mother's heart" (*Prelude* II, 283), and the etymological relation of "mutter" to "mute" may remind us that Wordsworth never speaks Dorothy's name directly in his poetry, preferring "Lucy," or the "gift of God" pun, or "Emma" as a diminutive of "Emmeline." "Emma" is itself a "muttering" word, both framed and emphasized by Wordsworth's phonemic patterning.[6] He locates the origin of his poetry in prelusive, muttering songs, and equates his condition at Grasmere conspicuously with that of Adam in the garden, reflecting his theory that speech and poetry begin in the scene of maternal bonding, which can be and has been recovered.

Home at Grasmere is the central text of Wordsworth's maternal poetics and of the secret of his relationship with Dorothy, a poem begun almost immediately after William and Dorothy moved to Grasmere in fulfillment of the dream they had shared for many years. Their journey together to Grasmere may be seen as a journey forward through time and place—from Racedown to Alfoxden to Germany to Grasmere—but it was also a journey back in time through the regressive movement of Wordsworth's self-analysis. Wordsworth makes much of the curative influence of Dorothy in the process, especially in *Prelude* X, and it would be informative to trace the formulation of his project in the earlier stages of the project itself—for example, in the emphasis of the *Lyrical Ballads* on "tracing the maternal passion through many of its more subtle windings, as in the poems of the IDIOT BOY and the MAD MOTHER,"[7] or in the prelusive third-person attempts at idealized autobiography in the creation of the figure of the Pedlar in *The Ruined Cottage*.

With the curative presence of both Dorothy and nature, experienced in the timely return to the banks of the Wye, Wordsworth was able to experience the sensation of blossoming again and to make the final poem of the volume both more backward-looking and more forward-looking than it otherwise would have been. Technically, the effect of Dorothy's presence on Wordsworth may be seen as a form of transference, comparable to that in the psychoanalytic setting, which provides the ability to recover and work through repressed experience as if it were present, rather than dealing with it through the mediation of memory, as though it belonged permanently to the past.

> Very often, as development proceeds, a sister or a cousin takes the mother's place in the boy's sexual phantasies and feelings of love. It is obvious that an attitude based on such feelings will differ from that of a man who seeks mainly maternal traits in a woman; although a man whose choice is influenced by his feelings for a sister may also seek some traits of a maternal kind in his love-partner. . . . Of course, in considering the bearing early relationships have upon the later choice, we must not forget that it is the impression of the loved person that the child had at the time, and the phantasies he connected with her then, which he wishes to rediscover in his later love relationship.[8]

If I am right in my assertion that the logic of Wordsworth's narration requires a return to the mother, and that the return requires a state of separation, then it should not be surprising that the plot of his narrative as an ordering of sequence and succession requires the same movement away from and back to the mother surrogates: Dorothy and nature. The complete pattern is one of successive states of relationship to Dorothy, who punctuates the whole life by her presence *(da!)* and her absence *(fort!)*. These terms come, of course, from Freud's analysis of the child's game in *Beyond the Pleasure Principle,* where the disappearance and reappearance of the mother are controlled by the child's manipulation of the reel. In Wordsworth's narrative the dynamics remain the same, but the *fort* movement is his own movement away from home to France, which includes both his involvement with the Revolution and with Annette Vallon. The return, in the poem as in his life, is to the mother country, the mother tongue, and Dorothy. A complete reading of the relationship between the life and the poem would show how the move to France starts as a "growing up" move for Wordsworth, in which he attempts to live the Freudian or Oedipal script, including a symbolic parricide in his involvement with the Revolution. This movement leads to a crisis and a breakdown, but continuing and changing the narrative enables these events to be inscribed as *detours,* thus bringing both the life and the narrative back under control and to acceptable form.

The narrative detour is brought under control in Book X by being inscribed as an indulgence in "juvenile errors," or "errors into which I was betray'd / By present objects . . . turn'd aside / From nature by external accidents." When this perspective is gained, and his own primal innocence reaffirmed, the poet can rediscover the redemptive presence of Dorothy, who turns out always to have been there:

>   and *then* it was
> That the beloved Woman in whose sight
> Those days were pass'd, *now* speaking in a voice
> Of sudden admonition, like a brook
> That does but cross a lonely road, and *now*
> Seen, heard and felt, and caught at every turn,
> Companion never lost through many a league,
> Maintain'd for me a saving intercourse
> With my true self; for, though impair'd and changed
> Much, as it seem'd, I was no further changed
> Than as a clouded, not a waning moon:
> She, in the midst of all, preserv'd me still. . . .
> And lastly, Nature's self, by human love
> Assisted, through the weary labyrinth
> Conducted me again to open day,
> Revived the feelings of my earlier life,
> Gave me that strength and knowledge full of peace,
> Enlarged, and never more to be disturb'd,
> Which . . . [X, 907–27, italics added.]

There is a conflation of the *then* and the *now* of Dorothy's presence in Wordsworth's narrative as it appears toward the end of Book X that suggests how her presence *now* in the time of writing is inscribed in the retrospective narrative as both an enabling starting point for the narrative project and a goal toward which the narrative constantly moves in its recovery of the fusion between beginnings and all points along the narrative.

In the writing of Book XI, Wordsworth is finally ready to "discover" the famous "spots of time" which, by being out of time, are the firm base of his narrative. Before moving to a consideration of these spots that Wordsworth calls the "hiding-places" of his "power" (XI, 336), it should be noted that the repetitive doubling of Dorothy's presence (then and now) is emphasized in the spots of time with particular force. Wordsworth remembers her having been present at a previous return to the place of the first spot of time, and he does so twice, first in Book VI

(208–32) and again in Book XI (316–23). In both memories there is a move from melancholy to the "spirit of pleasure and youth's golden gleam," and this phrase itself is used in connection with both passages (VI, 245; XI, 323). But both "memories" are of an event that *did not happen* during the summer of 1789, as can clearly be demonstrated and is perhaps also confirmed by Wordsworth's removing both references to Dorothy's presence in the 1850 version of *The Prelude*. It is thus a case of what he acknowledges, vis-à-vis Coleridge, as a "strong / Confusion":

> . . . and I seem to plant thee there.
> Far art Thou wander'd now in search of health,
> And milder breezes, melancholy lot!
> But Thou art with us, with us in the past,
> The present, with us in the times to come. [VI, 247–52.]

Even though Dorothy was not literally *there* in his remembered return to the scene of the spot-of-time experience, he wants her there narratively as she is present in the now of his writing. His need for her presence is so crucial that he misremembers her having been there on a previous return,

> My sister and myself, when having climb'd
> In danger through some window's open space,
> We look'd abroad . . . [VI, 228–30.]

Just as it is significant that the initial experience recalled in the spots of time was solitary, it seems equally significant that Wordsworth's return to the scene either in memory or in fact must be felt as being with or in the presence of Dorothy. At an equally important moment in "Nutting," after telling of having dragged the tree down with "merciless ravage," Wordsworth experiences a comparable ambiguity.

> *Then* up I rose,
> And dragged to earth both branch and bough . . .
> . . . and unless I *now*
> Confound my *present* feelings with the *past*,
> Ere from the mutilated bower I turned . . .
> I felt a sense of pain . . .
> *Then*, Dearest Maiden, move along these shades
> In gentleness of heart; with gentle hand
> Touch—for there is a spirit in the woods. [43–56, italics added.]

Dorothy's physical presence was a prop both for the regressive movements in memory and for the certainty that there is (was) a "spirit in the woods." There is something about the intensity of such moments, as sources and hiding places of "power" (XI, 325, 336), that leads Wordsworth to associate the presence of Dorothy both with the moments and with the repetition of the moment in the act of return.

Even after many readings of *The Prelude,* it can be a surprise to return to the "visionary dreariness" of these two spots of time in Book XI, which Wordsworth identified so intensely with "youth's golden gleam." How can the memory of being lost and stumbling onto the scene of execution of a murderer be "fructifying" or "vivifying" or "renovating"? Or how can the memory of the death of his father during a Christmas vacation have the same effect? If we follow Wordsworth's narrative through the French period in the way I have suggested, as a revelation of Wordsworth's recovery of the infantile fantasies of a crime against the father, and of how close he came in his twin involvement with Annette and the Revolution to a symbolic acting out of that crime, this "spot of time" makes more sense. What is restorative about the spots of time is that they too can be gone into and returned from without perishing; they represent the return to the scene of a crime Wordsworth *did not commit,* and therefore establish his innocence. Being innocent, he can "Long afterwards" roam about "In daily presence of this very scene," in daily presence also of "those two dear ones," Dorothy and Mary, who together combine the maternal and wifely functions so crucial to the plot of the narrative. But it is not merely that he *can* return with them, it is their presence—and especially Dorothy's—that enables him to return to and from the scene. For Wordsworth, to be in the presence of Dorothy-as-mother *without guilt,* and to return in her presence to the scene of a crime that was not his, that he avoided, is to be able to write a narrative return to the psychic Garden of Eden and to avoid the Freudian script.

Wordsworth's narrative of "growth" begins and ends with the archetypal forms of the spots of time, as his life narrative leads up to the magical maternal spot of Grasmere, where he recovers what turns out not to have been lost. The two main texts for what life was like at Grasmere are Wordsworth's *Home at Grasmere* and Dorothy's *Grasmere Journals.* Both texts are private, not written to be sent out into the world but rather written of home for home. They circle around and occasionally express a sense of the quiet mystery of a sacred place, a "home / Within a home" and a "love within a love," a spot with a secret:

> Something that makes this individual Spot,
> This small abiding-place of many men,
> A termination and a last retreat,
> A Centre, come from wheresoe'er you will,
> A While without dependence or defect,
> Made for itself and happy in itself,
> Perfect Contentment, Unity entire. [164–170.]

Wordsworth's sense that the home at Grasmere was a recapitulation of the original home shared with Dorothy is explicit, as is his sense that being at Grasmere is itself confirmation of the success of the project.

> Our home was sweet;
> Could it be less? If we were forced to change,
> Our home again was sweet . . . [179–81.]

> Nor have we been deceived; thus far the effect
> Falls not below the loftiest of our hopes . . . [216–17.]

The narrative of life at Grasmere flows on, through Dorothy's journals and Wordsworth's poems, until Wordsworth discovers the next stage of his narrative, the addition of a wife in the form of Mary Hutchinson, their longtime companion and friend. The narrative stages of this new development are carefully prepared for, and can be traced through various entries in Dorothy's journals, from the time when the plan seems to have been agreed upon, through the trip to Calais and the marriage itself, until the three travelers finally return to "the spot." Part of Wordsworth's preparation can be seen in the poem Dorothy calls "his poem on Going for Mary." Titled in manuscript "Our Departure," and published as "A Farewell," the poem is very emphatically structured as a departure in the spring anticipating a return in the fall.

> We go for One to whom ye will be dear;
> And she will prize this Bower, this Indian shed,
> Our own contrivance, Building without peer!
> —A gentle Maid. . . .
> Will come to you; to you herself will wed;
> And love the blessed life that we lead here.[9]

The departure of two is part of a move that will result in the return of three, the third being she whose "presence" was already sanctioned by memory in the return to the first "spot of time" in *The Prelude*. The implicitly sexual nature of the move and the addition of a wife is mitigated by the metaphor of marriage of Mary to the bower, to the "Dear Spot!" rather than to the man. And the actual hints of sex are dislocated from the bower in the narrative leap from spring to fall in the two-month move outward and back.

> Two burning months let summer overleap,
> And, coming back with Her who will be ours,
> Into thy bosom we again shall creep.

Rather than his leaving the spot, the bower, the Vale and Dorothy, they go out together *to* the bride, who will be brought back into the common "bosom" shared by all three actors in the narrative. As if this preparation were not enough, Wordsworth's plans for the two months also included a trip to Calais, a repeat of the original trip out to Annette and a repeat of the *return*. This time, however, the trip will be taken with Dorothy, and the return with her will be to the proper wife, wedded in Dorothy's company and accompanied by her and William on the journey back to the bower. Along the way, as carefully recorded in the journals, the various stages of the original journey to Grasmere are ritually observed to confirm *this* trip to Grasmere as a repetition of the original trip.

> When we passed thro' the village of Wensley my heart was melted away with dear recollections, the Bridge, the little water-spout the steep hill the Church. They are among the most vivid of my own inner visions, for they were the first objects that I saw after we were left to ourselves, and had turned our whole hearts to Grasmere as a home in which we were to rest.... [157–58.] The afternoon was not chearful but it did not rain till we came to Windermere. I am always glad to see Stavely it is a place I dearly love to think of—the first mountain village that I came to with Wm when we first began our pilgrimage together. [160.]

The marriage itself is performed with a ring Dorothy wore all the night before, and except for the actual ceremony, during which she lies in a trance on her bed, she is as completely involved in the events as is possible. Clearly her "presence" is as prominent for this matrimonial stage of Wordsworth's life narrative as it was for the recovery stage. In *The Prelude* IX, Wordsworth tells the lengthy tale of two lovers, Vaudracour and Julia, which is in significant ways similar to his own involvement with Annette Vallon. The tale leads to a melancholy scene, in which the two lovers, who cannot marry, huddle together with their illegitimate infant. Vaudracour is described

> Propping a pale and melancholy face
> Upon the Mother's breast, resting thus
> His head upon one breast, while from the other
> The babe was drawing in its quiet food. [IX, 811–14.]

This melancholy scene, which reflects the frustrations of having only one woman, who cannot be either his wife or his mother, gives way in Wordsworth's life to a situation where one male, Wordsworth, has two women totally devoted to him and neatly and harmoniously fulfilling all his needs:

> On Monday 4th October 1802, my Brother William was married to Mary Hutchinson. I slept a good deal of the night and rose fresh and well in the

morning. At a little after 8 o'clock I saw them go down the avenue towards the Church. William had parted from me upstairs. *I gave him the wedding ring—with how deep a blessing! I took it from my forefinger where I had worn it the whole of the night before—he slipped it again onto my finger and blessed me fervently.* When they were absent my dear little Sara prepared the breakfast. I kept myself as quiet as I could, but when I saw the two men running up the walk, coming to tell us it was over, I could stand it no longer and threw myself on the bed where I lay in stillness, neither hearing or seeing any thing, till Sara came upstairs to me and said "They are coming." This forced me from the bed where I lay and I moved I knew not how straight forward, faster than my strength could carry me till I met my beloved William and fell upon his bosom. . . . Wm fell asleep, lying upon my breast and I upon Mary. I lay motionless for a long time, but I was at last obliged to move. [pp. 154, 158; Italicized section is erased in the ms.]

Although Wordsworth's narrative of recovery ends happily with his return to Dorothy and Grasmere, supplemented by the carefully arranged marriage to Mary, his life did not stop but continued on for another forty-five years, producing little poetry comparable to that written between 1798 and 1805. It is thus easy, and thoroughly conventional, to take Wordsworth's great seven-year period as only a stage in a larger narrative that belied its promise, and to agree with William Minto's narrative of Wordsworth's life that saw *Home at Grasmere* as written "in the first heat and confidence of the enterprise, before the mirage that lured him on had faded, and glad anticipations had given place to despondency and a cheerless sense of impotence."[10] Minto's formulation is even more powerful for being an echo of the life narrative Wordsworth felt he was living at the time he wrote "Resolution and Independence":

> We Poets in our youth begin in gladness;
> But thereof come in the end despondency and madness . . .

I would like to end my narrative of Wordsworth's career and its relationship to Dorothy on a speculatively different note, one that tries to rescue Wordsworth's project from the failure of having been only a prelude to decline, or the recovery of a home that was lost again, never to be recovered.

For my purposes, I suggest that Wordsworth's poem "Michael" is a model both for the status of his project and for our reading of it. Michael's project, the building of the sheepfold, is comparable to Wordsworth's project of building up a work that would endure—both were begun in hope and seem defeated by fate and time. In the case of Michael's project, all that remains is "a straggling heap of unhewn stones! / And to that simple object appertains / A story." In the case of

Wordsworth's project, all that remains is a straggling heap of poems and manuscripts as traces of the activity that went into their making.

Wordsworth's constant alteration of almost all his poems, even after they were published, is notorious. "I am for the most part uncertain about my success in altering poems," he wrote to Mary, at a period in which we can see from Dorothy's journals he was constantly engaged in altering his poems. If we see these poems as evidence of a scene of writing, rather than as finished products, we can sense how Wordsworth had to keep altering the poems in order to keep the activity of writing going. The endless process of alteration was a way of avoiding a closure of identity in a fixed text, of becoming one who had written rather than one who was writing. This is of course a positive way to construe a writing project that can never reach a final state, given its self-definition as a project; a project that must continually inscribe itself as something ever more about to be in order to avoid being a copy of something that already was.

Long after Wordsworth had left the home within a home at Grasmere, for the home away from home at Rydal Mount, he could still return to the manuscripts of his poems as a scene of writing, and through an active engagement with his text he could return to the spring of 1800, which he shared at Grasmere with Dorothy. The project in this sense did not end or fail, but entered a new phase in which, although life went on, it included the possibility of a return to the scene of writing, even if, as was often the case, he simply reinstated lines that he had previously deleted. To keep that primal scene of writing with, to, and about Dorothy, and to keep it as fresh as the spring in which the first few hundred lines were written (these were in fact the lines most altered by Wordsworth during the next fifty years), was perhaps the only way to continue to "return" even though the stream of life was carrying him forward, trying to inscribe his life in that prescripted plot which Minto claimed led to a "cheerless sense of impotence."

Michael, in the poem that bears his name, had a child in his old age as evidence of his "forward-looking thoughts." When that child is grown, and Michael is eighty-four, he has Luke begin the sheepfold by laying the cornerstone, and bids him to think of "this moment" of beginnings as what will get him through the trials of life and enable him eventually to return.

> When thou return'st, thou in this place wilt see
> A work which is not here: a covenant
> 'Twill be between us.

Luke, like the period of Wordsworth's youth, of course does not return. But even after Michael hears the "heavy news" of Luke's "ignominy and

shame" and permanent departure, he himself can still return to the
sheepfold:

> Tis not forgotten yet
> The pity which was then in every heart
> For the old Man—and 'tis believed by all
> That many and many a day he thither went,
> And never lifted up a single stone. . . .
> The length of full seven years, from time to time,
> He at the building of this Sheep-fold wrought,
> And left the work unfinished when he died.
> . . . and the remains
> Of the unfinished Sheep-fold may be seen
> Beside the boisterous brook of Greenhead Ghyll.

Perhaps on some of those returns—or even only one—Michael did pick
up one of those stones and place it on the wall, with a return of the spirit
of the moment in which the project was begun in hope. What severe
realist can with complete certainty deny the possibility that William in
the woods, altering his poems, was at times "willingly deceived," so that
for a moment at least "the building stood as if sustained by its own spirit"
with the feeling of being present again with Dorothy at that primal scene
of writing?

NOTES

1. Unles otherwise noted, all quotations from the shorter poems are from
the de Selincourt revision of the Hutchinson edition of *The Poetical Works of
Wordsworth* (London: Oxford University Press, 1959). Quotations from *The Prelude* will be from the 1805 version, edited by Jonathan Wordsworth, M. H.
Abrams, and Stephen Gill (New York: Norton, 1979). They are cited by book
number (Roman numerals) and lines. Quotations from *Home at Grasmere* are
from the Beth Darlington edition (Ithaca: Cornell University Press, 1977), MS.B.
Quotations from Dorothy's journals are from Mary Moorman, ed., *Journals of
Dorothy Wordsworth*, 2nd ed. (London: Oxford University Press, 1978).

2. "Lines Composed a Few Miles Above Tintern Abbey, on Revisiting the
Banks of the Wye During a Tour, July 13, 1798," ll. 155–59.

3. Ibid., ll. 109–11.

4. Melanie Klein, *Love, Guilt and Reparation & Other Works, 1921–1945*
(New York: Dell, 1977), p. 334.

5. Ibid., p. 336.

6. Roman Jakobson has observed that in almost all languages some varia-

tion of "Mama" or its reversal, as in "Emma," is the familiar term for "mother" (cf. "Why 'Mama' and 'Papa,'" in *Selected Writings* I [The Hague: Mouton, 1962], 538–45). Julia Kristeva has made some pertinent observations in this context on what she calls "the semiotic," a phase of rhythmic babble that precedes the acquisition of speech and marks the period in which the child is still bound up with the presence of the mother's body (cf. "From One Identity to Another," in *Desire in Language* [New York: Columbia University Press, 1980]). One can hear the "gift" pun explicitly in contexts such as *The Prelude* VI, 216–18 ("Now, after separation desolate / Restor'd to me, such absence that she seem'd / A gift then first bestow'd."); it more subtly signals the silent presence of Dorothy in lines such as *The Prelude* I, 21–24 (". . . it is shaken off, / As by miraculous gift 'tis shaken off, / That burthen of my own unnatural self, / The heavy weight of many a weary day"), which record his joyous anticipation of settling with Dorothy at Racedown in 1795.

7. *Preface* of 1800, in H. Littledale, ed., *Lyrical Ballads* (London: Oxford University Press, 1959), p. 229.

8. Melanie Klein, *Love, Guilt and Reparation*, p. 324.

9. *Journals of Dorothy Wordsworth*, Appendix I, p. 217.

10. William Minto, "Wordsworth's Great Failure," *Nineteenth Century* 26 (September, 1889), 441. F. W. Bateson summarizes the standard view: "The rest should have been silence. *The Prelude* was completed in May 1805 and from this point a gradual deterioration in the quality of Wordsworth's poetry becomes noticeable" (*Wordsworth: A Re-interpretation* [New York: Longman, Green, 1956], p. 169).

About the Contributors

Evelyn Barish, professor of English at the College of Staten Island (CUNY), is currently completing a book titled *Emerson and the Roots of Prophecy,* focusing on his early life and writing. She is also the author of *Arthur Hugh Clough: Growth of a Poet's Mind* (as Evelyn Barish Greenberger) and various articles and reviews on Emerson and Clough. Her work has been supported by research grants from the NEH, American Philosophical Society, and other sources. Research for the present article was done while she was a Fellow of the Radcliffe Institute.

Martine Watson Brownley, an associate professor of English at Emory University, works with seventeenth- and eighteenth-century literary historiography and has published essays on Gibbon and on Clarendon in *Daedalus,* the *Journal of the History of Ideas, Studies on Voltaire and the Eighteenth Century,* and other journals. In the field of women's studies she has published on Aphra Behn, Christina Rossetti, and Hester Thrale Piozzi.

W. B. Carnochan is professor of English at Stanford University. He is author of *Lemuel Gulliver's Mirror for Man* and *Confinement and Flight: an Essay on English Literature of the Eighteenth Century.* From 1975 to 1980 he was dean of graduate studies and vice-provost at Stanford.

John O. Jordan is associate professor of Literature at Kresge College on the Santa Cruz campus of the University of California, where he teaches courses on the Victorian period. His recent publications include essays on Swinburne, Dickens, and Picasso. He is currently completing a study of the theme of paternity in Picasso's work.

U. C. Knoepflmacher is a professor of English at Princeton University. He has written a study of George Eliot's early novels and has coedited, with George Levine, a collection of essays on Mary Shelley's *Frankenstein.* The author of two other books on Victorian fiction and coeditor, with G. B. Tennyson, of *Nature and the Victorian Imagination,* he is currently engaged in a book-length study of Victorian fantasies written for children.

Jane Lilienfeld holds degrees from the University of Maryland, the University of Chicago, and Brandeis University. Teaching in the English department at Assumption College in Worcester, Massachusetts, she has spoken nationally and in Britain on feminist theory and Virginia Woolf. Her first book is due to appear from Routledge and Kegan Paul in 1985: *The Possibility of Sisterhood: Women Writers, Their Mothers, and Their Texts.*

Jane Marcus, associate professor of English at the University of Texas at Austin, has published widely as a feminist critic. *The Young Rebecca: Writings of Rebecca West 1911–1917* was published by Viking in 1982. She has also published two volumes of new feminist essays on Virginia Woolf at the University of Nebraska Press, and is editing a third. She is currently finishing *One's Own Trumpet,* a study of the friendship between Dame Ethel Smyth and Virginia Woolf.

Dorothy Mermin is an associate professor of English at Cornell University, where she teaches courses in Victorian literature and in poetry by women. She has published articles in scholarly journals on the poetry of Elizabeth Barrett Browning, Robert Browning, and other Victorian poets. Her new book is *The Audience in the Poem,* a study of works by Tennyson, Browning, Arnold, Clough, and Meredith (New Brunswick: Rutgers University Press, 1983).

Sheryl R. O'Donnell teaches English at the University of North Dakota and has published articles on Locke, domestic fiction by American women, and feminist education. Coeditor of *Menopause: An Interdisciplinary Perspective* (Austin: University of Texas Press, 1982), she is currently editing a women's research issue of the *North Dakota Quarterly.*

Ruth Perry, director of Women's Studies at MIT, writes and teaches about eighteenth-century English life and letters. She is the author of *Women, Letters, and the Novel* (New York: AMS Press, 1981), the modern editor of George Ballard's *Memoirs of Several Ladies of Great Britain* (1752), and most recently has completed a biography of Mary Astell, an early eighteenth-century feminist.

Catharine R. Stimpson is a professor of English and director of the Institute for Research on Women at Rutgers University. The founding editor of *Signs: Journal of Women in Culture and Society,* she now edits a book series for the University of Chicago Press. The author of fiction and nonfiction, she published a novel, *Class Notes,* in 1979. She lives in New York City.

Thomas A. Vogler is professor of English and Comparative Literature at the University of California, Santa Cruz, and author of *Preludes to Vision: The Epic Venture in Blake, Wordsworth, Keats and Hart Crane* (Berkeley: University of California Press, 1971). The essay on William and Dorothy is part of a larger work-in-progress on Wordsworth. He is currently editing a volume of essays on "Blake and Criticism," and working on a book on Blake's *Songs of Innocence and of Experience.*

Mary Helen Washington teaches Afro-American Literature at the University of Massachusetts in Boston. She has edited two anthologies of black women's fiction *(Black-Eyed Susans: Classic Stories By and About Black Women* and *Midnight Birds: Contemporary Stories of Black Women)* and has written the introductions for the Feminist Press editions of the Zora Neale Hurston reader and Paule Marshall's *Brown Girl, Brownstone.* Her articles on black women writers have appeared in *Signs, The Massachusetts Review, Black World,* and *Black American Literature Forum.*